The Prestige

Cambridge 1

Paul Carter

© 2004 Venture Publications Ltd

ISBN 1 898432 43 0

Cover: The red buses of Eastern Counties first served Cambridge in 1931, when the company was set up to amalgamate the local Ortona Motor Company and three other large East Anglian operators. Following Ortona's example, Eastern Counties was originally a keen Leyland user, as shown by **A176** (**NG 1911**), numerically the first of ten Leyland TD1 Titans delivered in 1932. The bus is seen with its crew on the busy town service 101 from Chesterton to the Railway Station, which had been Ortona's first route when operations began in 1907. *(John Banks Collection)*

Rear cover: The first Eastern Counties timetable also included fare tables and covered all the company's services. The 1932 book had 464 pages and included details of local railway services. The company later published separate timetables for its Western Area (which included Cambridge) and Eastern Area.

Title page: The first three-axle bus in Cambridge and definitely the only one of its kind, Tilling Stevens **XB 8389** began life as a normal TS3 double-decker with Thomas Tilling in London. Purchased by Chivers in 1927, it was transformed into this huge, 89-seat double-decker and was used for transporting workers to the company's Histon factory. It lasted in this form until it fell foul of the 1930 Road Traffic Act, after which it was rebuilt as a tanker. The provision of a radiator with the name "CHIVERS" cast into it was not unusual for a Tilling Stevens, but was perhaps an expensive option for a staff-bus operator. *(Cambridgeshire Collection)*

TABLE OF CONTENTS

Introduction and Acknowledgements

Cambridge is a small city, famous for its ancient University, although it has always been an important local centre and market town. More recently it has also become famous as a centre for high-technology industries, which have led to the rapid growth of the city itself and the nearby villages.

The remoteness of the railway station from the centre, together with the loss of agricultural jobs in the surrounding area, led to a need for transport within and into Cambridge. Horse trams were introduced in 1880 and horse buses ran alongside them for a short while. Motor buses first appeared in 1905, although they did not enjoy any real success until two years later. They finally replaced the trams in 1914 and have been part of the local scene ever since.

I was born in 1950 (the year in which this history ends) in a very different Cambridge, which at that time was still regarded as just a town. Despite my initial terror of buses (which then seemed to be rather large), I became increasingly fond of them. The vehicles, the routes they operated and the people who made it all possible fascinated me then as much as they do now. Although there have been many changes since 1950, buses continue to be part of everyday life. In contrast to many towns and cities, Cambridge now has more frequent city services than it has ever had and passenger numbers continue to increase. Although many well-known names and faces have disappeared, some aspects of the local bus scene remain the same. The bus station is still in Drummer Street, despite its shortcomings. The Lee family still own Whippet Coaches, as they have since 1919. The roads to the Railway Station still have the most frequent buses and the country network is largely intact, with a few routes still retaining their 1931 service numbers in 2003.

I hope that this history will capture some of the atmosphere of the early years of bus and coach operations in what is now a rapidly changing area. This book would not have been possible without the help, hospitality and encouragement given by many people. In particular I would like to thank Maurice Doggett, who several years ago passed on the research papers of the late Terry Harley of March, which form the basis of much of the early part of the story. Also greatly appreciated is the help given by The PSV Circle (especially David Gray and Bill Byers) for providing vehicle details; The Omnibus Society (especially Roger Warwick and Alan Mills); Chris Jakes and the staff of the Cambridgeshire Collection. I am also very grateful to Mr and Mrs E A Lainson, Frank Matthews, John Matthews, Mrs Elizabeth Green (née Drayton), Arthur Gill and Cyril Kenzie (who have all been involved with running buses and coaches) as well as Derek Carter, Dennis Greenhill, Philip Holland, Gladys Hughes, and Reg Roope (who shared their memories of their long careers "on the road"). Several of these people have now sadly passed away, making their reminiscences all the more valuable. I would also like to thank Alan Charter, Richard Covill, Terry Dendy, Geoff Mills, Jim Neale, Jack Panter, Mike Petty, Frank Simpson and my mother Brenda Carter. There is no doubt that the book would have been the poorer without the research of the late Terry Harley. Finally, this book would definitely not have appeared without Annette, her IT skills and her endless patience.

The book is dedicated to the busmen and women of Cambridge.

Paul Carter
Wadhurst
December 2003

1. Horse Power 1880 to 1914

CAMBRIDGE

Most people think of Cambridge as a University city, but early settlers made their homes beside the River Cam long before a centre of learning was established. The Romans set up a camp in AD43, referred to as Camborico or Durolipons (meaning 'fortified place with a bridge'). It was easy to defend and was conveniently close to Ermine Street, the main road to the north. A small town developed, which became derelict after the Romans left, although it was soon rebuilt and became an important trading centre. The Saxons, Danes and Vikings all attacked it and in 1069 William the Conqueror built a castle (long since demolished) to remind everybody who was now in charge.

Growth continued and by the 13th century Cambridge was an important market town. Several religious houses were founded and, possibly attracted by these, a group of academics arrived after escaping from rioting mobs in Oxford. Thus was founded a University - a group of teachers with the power to award degrees. The scholars were originally referred to as 'clerkes' and later on as 'undergraduates', abbreviated by the townspeople to 'undergrads' or just 'grads'. The word 'student' was not widely used until much later. From 1284 they lived in self-contained groups known as colleges. These were not popular, for instead of buying supplies from local traders the scholars brought them in from elsewhere, the boats unloading at the colleges' own wharves along what are now known as 'The Backs'. Cambridge slowly declined as a port, although the river trade continued well into the 20th century. As the University became larger, so did its ability to control local affairs, often with Royal approval. More colleges were built, and the demolition of a quarter of the town in 1441 to build King's College and its famous Chapel did nothing to improve relations with the locals. Disputes with the townspeople continued to flare up at regular intervals, and a deep sense of mistrust prevailed for many years. The ancient college buildings remain a dominant feature of Cambridge, along with the mediaeval street pattern, which still causes serious traffic congestion.

THE RAILWAY ARRIVES

Until the 19th century Cambridge was a small place, which had yet to overwhelm the surrounding villages of Cherry Hinton, Chesterton and Trumpington. From 1655 there were coaches between London and Cambridge for wealthy long-distance travellers and in 1700 the journey time was recorded as fifteen hours, although this was halved by 1800. By then there were ten daily coaches to a range of destinations, including two to Oxford. The arrival of the railway in 1845 led to a boom in employment and house building, and the town began to grow rapidly. The railway companies employed large numbers of workers, while other industrial activities expanded rapidly, including brick, cement and tile manufacturing, malting and milling. These were soon followed by engineering and science-based industries. The University was (and remains) an important employer, while farming also continued to play an important part in the local economy.

It was on 30th July 1845 that the Eastern Counties Railway (later the Great Eastern) opened its through route from London (Liverpool Street) to Norwich via Cambridge. As railway building continued it became possible to travel by train to St Ives and Godmanchester in 1847, Ipswich via Newmarket in 1851, Bedford in 1860, Sudbury via Haverhill in 1865 and Mildenhall in 1885. The Great Northern line from London (King's Cross) reached Shepreth in 1851, and during The Great Exhibition horse drawn double-deck buses connected with the trains. The line was extended to Cambridge in April 1852, but it was not until 1866 that through trains were provided. Traffic on the railways increased rapidly, although stagecoaches continued to operate for a while, the coach to Bedford continuing until 1894.

Above: Ready for the road. Cambridge Street Tramways car No. **2**, in its original form as a 24-seat single-decker, was built by Starbuck for the opening of the lines in 1880, and was used on the trial run on 13th October, when it derailed at Great St Mary's Church. *(Cambridgeshire Collection)*

Below: As passenger loadings on the trams increased, No. **2** was rebuilt (along with similar car No. 3) as a double-decker and worked the route from the Post Office to the Railway Station. *(Cambridgeshire Collection)*

TRANSPORT FOR A GROWING TOWN

The impressive Railway Station was built some distance from the town centre, partly because the University authorities insisted that no railway line should pass within a mile of its buildings but also because a large amount of suitable land was needed. Four competing railway companies each had their own freight sidings, although they all shared the passenger station. The rapidly growing town soon reached the station, which by 1878 was being used by 2,000 passengers every day. Some of the grander hotels ran horse buses to and from the station, but only for their own guests. Hansom cabs were available for hire, while the fortunate few owned a carriage of their own. Bicycles (which later became such a feature of the town) had yet to appear, so that for many people the only way to reach the station was to walk. There was clearly a need for internal transport in the town. The first horse-drawn trams had been introduced in 1860 in Birkenhead and had since appeared in many other towns and cities. By November 1878 two concerns, both known as the Cambridge Tramways Company, were proposing to introduce horse trams in Cambridge. One company proposed 3ft 6in inch gauge lines from the Railway Station through the Town Centre to Huntingdon Road, with another line from Hyde Park Corner along East Road to Newmarket Road. At a later date it was hoped to join the Newmarket Road to the Huntingdon Road line by way of Maid's Causeway and Jesus Lane. The second company proposed a smaller system on the standard railway gauge of 4ft 8½in, with one line from the Railway Station to the Town Centre only, and an additional line from Hyde Park Corner along Lensfield Road and Trumpington Street to the Senate House. Public reaction to the plans was generally favourable, although some concern was expressed about the use of the standard railway gauge, in view of the narrowness of some of the streets.

THE CAMBRIDGE STREET TRAMWAYS COMPANY

After much discussion and debate, the proposals of the second company (to be known as The Cambridge Street Tramways Company) were decided upon, but with a narrow gauge. While the original Bill was going through Parliament, additional proposals were submitted to include lines along Trinity Street and St John's Street. The Cambridge Street Tramways Act received Royal assent on 21st July 1879, and on 7th August the promoters of the successful company held a celebration dinner at the Lion Hotel in Petty Cury. It was soon decided to apply for powers to construct additional lines. These were to be from Hyde Park Corner along Gonville Place and East Road to Newmarket Road; from Newmarket Road along Maid's Causeway, Emmanuel Road and Emmanuel Street to St Andrew's Street and from the Senate House to St Mary's Street. These were authorised under the Cambridge Street Tramways (Extension) Order of 1880, although the line along East Road was only built as far as The Turnstile public house, just beyond the depot at the junction with Fitzroy Street. The line from Newmarket Road via Emmanuel Street was never built following objections from the Master and Fellows of Emmanuel College. The very short extension into St Mary's Street was in response to concerns that trams would add to congestion which was already being caused at the Senate House by carts, cabs and animals being driven to market.

Shares in the Tramway Company went on sale at £10 each from 13th December, and on 8th July 1880 work began on laying the tracks. Although a gauge of 3ft 6in had been planned, the actual gauge used was 4ft 0in. The first cars were delivered from Starbuck's of Birkenhead on 9th October. Car 1 was a double-decker with seats for 41 passengers (18 inside), while car 2 was a 24-seat single-decker. A trial run using car 2 was made on 13th October 1880, when it unfortunately derailed at Great St Mary's Church. This apparently happened because the gauge of the track (which at that stage was not permanently laid) was incorrect. This was rectified and a second, successful trial took place, although the sharp curve at this point caused concern throughout the life of the tramway. The line from the Railway Station to the Town Centre was completed by 25th October and, following an official inspection by the Board of Trade

Above: Single-deck cars 5 and 6 worked the line from East Road to Market Hill. Car No. **6** poses for the photographer in Trumpington Street, apparently on a cold day judging by the thick overcoats worn by the crew. *(Cambridgeshire Collection)*

Below: One of the double-deck cars, possibly No. **7** purchased in 1894, is seen at the Post Office terminus in St Andrew's Street, with a noticeable lack of other traffic. Most of the buildings in the picture are still recognisable. *(Cambridgeshire Collection)*

was officially opened three days later. On the first day there was one car in service, running at 30-minute intervals from the old Post Office (opposite Christ's College) to the entrance to the Railway Station yard, and 636 passengers were carried. The fare was 2d all the way, 1d as far as Hyde Park Corner. [1 new penny (1p) is equivalent to 2.4 old pennies (2.4d)]. Books of tickets could be bought for a small discount and season tickets were also available. On the following day passengers numbered 801, while on 30th October two cars ran at 15-minute intervals until 10pm, carrying 1,750 passengers between them. The number of cars increased as more were delivered. Cars 3, 5 and 6 were 18-seat single-deckers, car 4 was a double-decker with 40 seats (18 inside). Cars 2 and 3 were later rebuilt as double-deckers. The cars were painted red and cream with gold shaded 'CAMBRIDGE STREET TRAMWAYS' fleetnames. They also carried prominent advertisement boards.

At the beginning of November 1880 the line from Hyde Park Corner to St Mary's Street was opened, restricted to single-deck cars 5 and 6. The East Road route opened soon afterwards and the tramway had now reached its maximum, with a total of 2.67 miles of track. At this stage the depot had not been completed and the cars and horses were kept overnight in the Great Northern Railway goods yard. The depot eventually opened in March 1881, with a large car shed and stables for up to 30 horses, together with stores and a blacksmith's forge. The company's registered office was at 184 East Road. The trams were obviously intended to become a permanent feature of the town, as the following extract from the 1881 edition of Spalding's Directory of Cambridge shows:

THE CAMBRIDGE STREET TRAMWAYS COMPANY

This company is incorporated by special Act of Parliament and is empowered to lay down, maintain and work a complete and efficient system of Tramways, over three miles in length, running from the Cambridge stations of the Great Eastern, Great Northern, Midland and London & North-Western Railways, to the Post Office and Market Hill, with a branch along Parker's Piece and the East Road, which is thus brought into direct communication with the principal streets.

Although the public generally favoured the introduction of the trams, there were a number of objectors. These included several very conservative and eccentric members of the University, who were opposed to change of any kind. No tram driver ever dared to challenge the awesome and autocratic Professor Newton, who demonstrated his dislike of progress by walking in between the tram lines near Great St Mary's Church. On the other hand, a special early morning car for college cleaners (known as 'bedders') was greeted with great enthusiasm. The company prospered, although the cars were slow, rattled rather a lot to begin with and were frequently overloaded. The fact that they were pulled by a single horse also led to regular accusations of cruelty, although an investigation by the RSPCA concluded that the complaints were exaggerated. The horses were well fed. No horse ever worked for more than eighteen hours a week and never for more than two hours at a stretch. Many years later a retired tram driver, Ben Sharp, recalled that "they were all looked after as though they were thoroughbreds - no horses were better treated." The stables were extended in 1883.

Most of the track was single, although there was double track along part of Hills Road. Loops were provided only at Regent Street and St Andrew's Street, leading to regular delays to cars coming from the station. On the Trumpington Street route there was only one loop, at the old Addenbrooke's Hospital. In spite of these shortcomings passenger loadings and profits increased steadily until 1887, when an unprofitable winter led to various economies being suggested. These included the removal of conductors from the cars (saving £150 a year), the adoption of a flat fare of 1d and the replacement of the horses by a more modern form of power. The first successful electric tramway had been running in Blackpool since 1885 and electric trams were being introduced in many towns and cities. There were also plans for a steam tramway from Histon to Cambridge (although this was never built) and bus operation to Chesterton was another possibility being

Above: An early competitor. From April 1896 the horse buses of the Cambridge Omnibus Company covered the same roads as the trams, as well as serving other parts of the town. This one is seen in Chesterton. *(Cambridgeshire Collection)*

Below: To meet the challenge, the Tramway Company purchased four horse buses of its own. Known as 'bathing machines', they were one man operated with a flat fare of one old penny, and the fare box can be seen beside the driver. They actually entered service before the Omnibus Company began operations and ran along Chesterton Road, Mill Road and Huntingdon Road. The side indicator board reads 'Castle End'. *(Cambridgeshire Collection)*

considered. Concern was also being expressed about the condition of the track. As well as maintaining this, the company was also obliged (under the Tramways Act of 1870) to maintain the road surface between the rails and on either side of them, adding to the financial burden. A new water cart was purchased in 1890 to clean the lines, lay the dust, reduce noise and ease the running of the trams, particularly on the curve into St Mary's Street. Argument between the company and the Town Council continued for several years until 1892, when Cambridge Corporation took over the liability for the upkeep of the roads, for which the company paid the council £325 each year. The Tramway Company continued to be responsible for the sleepers and the rails and for making good any disturbances caused by track works.

THE CAMBRIDGE OMNIBUS COMPANY

In November 1892 the Cambridge Electricity Supply Company opened its power station in Thompson's Lane, not far from the quayside on the River Cam. Alarmed at this latest example of modernity, the authorities of Magdalene College on the opposite bank objected unsuccessfully. Before long many premises (and several colleges) had been connected and the generating capacity of the power station had to be increased. Cambridge thus moved a step nearer to electric trams. The tramway company purchased two cottages in Dover Street, with a view to possible future expansion, and an additional tram was purchased from Starbuck's in 1894, car number 7 being a double-decker similar to car 1. On 3rd May 1895, ambitious plans were announced for a new line along Bateman Street and Trumpington Road, continuing across the water meadows to Newnham on a new viaduct. (The direct road to Newnham known as The Fen Causeway was not constructed until 1926.) This route never materialised (nor did the viaduct) and no further extensions to the tramway seemed likely for a while. On the other hand, Cambridge was expanding. Its population had risen to 38,000 by 1900, and some parts of the town were unserved by the trams. Competition arrived in 1896, when one William Henry Hockey applied on behalf of

the Cambridge Omnibus Company to operate eight two-horse double-deck omnibuses in the town and suburbs of Cambridge. The fare was to be 1d from the Railway Station to the town centre, and an additional 1d to points further afield. Alarmed by this threat, the Tramway Company immediately ordered four new single-deck buses of its own. Two of these entered service on 1st February, serving Chesterton Road, Huntingdon Road and Mill Road. Known as 'bathing machines' they also charged a fare of 1d and operated without conductors. They were kept in a shed in John Street, next to the tram depot.

The Omnibus Company's services began on 29th April, running from a depot in Chesterton Road. It soon became clear that there were not enough passengers to keep both companies going, a situation to be repeated many years later following bus deregulation in 1986. The Tramway Company began a difficult period and, as income fell sharply, more complaints were received about the deteriorating state of the track. This was not helped by road subsidence, caused by the installation of another innovation, sewers. An outbreak of horse influenza made matters worse and for a while it seemed that both companies might disappear from the scene. Eventually, in October 1900, mutual agreement was reached. The Omnibus Company agreed to withdraw from the tram routes and acquired the buses and John Street premises from the Tramway Company. The two then worked side by side but only until September 1902, when the Omnibus Company ceased trading. The buses and horses were sold, and its Chesterton Road depot later became a garage.

ELECTRIFICATION PLANS

In 1898 the Cambridge Street Tramways Company employed fourteen drivers, fourteen conductors and three horse-keepers. There were 28 horses for the seven trams, which ran on the two routes from 8am to 9pm. It was in that year that the British Electric Traction Company purchased shares in the CSTC and the Founder of the BET, Emile Garcke, joined the board. The BET soon announced proposals for new lines along Silver Street and The Backs, to Chesterton to Romsey Town and to

Above: Motor buses appeared on the streets of Cambridge on 9th April 1905, when The Cambridge University & Town Motor Omnibus Company introduced this Straker-Squire, which carried a pale blue livery. It is seen here at Market Hill waiting to depart for the Railway Station. The operation was unsuccessful, lasting only 6 months. *(Cambridgeshire Collection)*

Below: The two dark blue Thornycrofts of The Cambridge Motor Omnibus Company also challenged the trams from April 1905. Several other routes were planned, but the company lost its licence in December after several complaints about its operations. *(Cambridgeshire Collection)*

the Rock Hotel on Cherry Hinton Road. Not surprisingly there was considerable opposition to the plans. There had already been objections to the installation of telephone cables, and the need to erect further overhead wiring for the trams caused an outcry. Professor Darwin of Trinity College led a vigorous campaign against the Silver Street plans. There were also objections from the Fire Brigade, who claimed that the overhead would interfere with the work of the fire engine, while some traders believed that traction poles outside their premises would be bad for business.

Discussions continued for several years, but although the proposals were amended several times, no agreement could be reached and the possibility of electric trams in the town gradually faded. The Corporation lost interest in taking over, Mr Garcke left the board of the Tramway Company in 1902 and soon afterwards the BET shares were sold to the Cambridge Electric Tramways Syndicate. This was associated with the Cambridge Electricity Supply Company and it existed until 1913, although no further progress was made and electric trams were destined never to operate in Cambridge. However, motor buses had now appeared in several towns, and the introduction of these seemed far more likely. Contemporary newspaper reports suggest that as early as July 1901 there were plans to operate a motor bus service from Market Hill to the Railway Station, following recent improvements to the road surface. The proposed service would require six buses with two spares, except on Saturdays when all eight would be running. 'Express' buses in a special livery would serve only one intermediate stop (at Hyde Park Corner) and would connect with all principal trains. The proposals aroused a lot of interest and comment, but nothing came of them.

THE BRITISH ELECTRIC TRACTION COMPANY LTD

Having recognised the potential of electric tramways, Emile Garcke founded the BET in 1895 and three years later he joined the board of the Cambridge Street Tramways Company. By then the BET had started buying shares in established tramway companies with a view to extending and electrifying services. The BET was a vigorous opponent of the Tramways Act of 1870, under which local authorities could take over tramway companies after they had been operating for 21 years. This could have happened in Cambridge in 1901, and the council was already considering the compulsory purchase, extension and electrification of the local system. As the possibility of electric trams in Cambridge became increasingly unlikely, the BET shares in the Cambridge Street Tramway Company were sold in 1904, two years after Mr Garcke's departure.

The BET was more successful in Peterborough, and in 1902 it set up the Peterborough Electric Traction Co Ltd. This started running electric trams on 24th January 1903 and eventually owned 14 cars. By then motor buses had appeared in several towns, and it was quickly realised by the BET directors that buses also had a part to play, both as feeders to tramway routes and also in their own right. Peterborough Electric Traction began motor bus operation in March 1913. The trams continued to operate until August 1930.

MOTOR BUSES APPEAR

By January 1905 the registered office of the Tramway Company had moved to 5 Alexandra Street in the town centre. The trams had reigned supreme for over two years since the Omnibus Company had ceased trading and receipts began to rise again. A dividend of 4% had been paid in 1901 and 1902. The cars ran every 10 minutes for most of the day on the Railway Station route, with a 7-minute frequency during the evening peak and all day on Saturdays, while the East Road to Great St Mary's route had a 20-minute service. Applications were made for further passing loops to make the services more efficient, but a new threat became a reality on 9th April 1905 when the town's first motor bus took to the streets. The Cambridge University and Town Motor Omnibus Company Ltd introduced a pale blue Straker-Squire 25hp double-decker (registered CE 299) which competed with the trams between the station and the town centre. On its first day of operation it carried 1,705 passengers between 4.30pm and 9.30pm, the

Above: The green buses of Mr Walford's Ortona Motor Company took to the streets of Cambridge in August 1907, providing further competition for the trams on the Railway Station route. The intitial fleet included three Scott Stirling single-deckers, purchased from Lancashire United of Atherton. Two of these are shown in their original form in this very early view. The bus on the left appears to have the registration number **BN 276**. *(Cambridgeshire Collection)*

Below: Ortona's reputation for reliability and safety made its services much more popular than those of its predecessors. In 1908 the buses were converted to double-deckers and the route (now known as service 1) was extended to Chesterton, where this one was photographed with a few brave passengers on the upper deck. *(Cambridgeshire Collection)*

fare being 1d. This lasted only until October, for as well as operating losses the company was also faced with litigation costs after an accident in which a conductor was killed.

The Cambridge Motor Omnibus Company Ltd started operations on the same route on 15th April 1905, initially with two Thornycroft double-deckers (CE 308 and CE 336) in a dark blue livery. The CMOC may have been an offshoot of the manufacturers, J I Thornycroft of Chiswick, London, which had previously written to the Town Council offering to provide two motor buses for demonstration. The Thornycrofts were later joined by an Arrol-Johnson (XS 93). The company had ambitious plans to provide services to Chesterton, Mill Road and Newnham, but complaints were soon being made by (almost inevitably) the college authorities and also by local shopkeepers. As well as being unreliable, the Thornycrofts were also involved in several minor accidents, in which shop awnings, kerbstones and street lamps were damaged. The company was also fined £2 for allowing a bus to produce excess smoke. By December 1906 the Council had withdrawn its licence and the Thornycrofts were sold to the London & Westminster Omnibus Company Ltd. The trams received a welcome boost and the opportunity was taken to refurbish them and the depot buildings. Once again the cars had the roads to themselves, but only until the following August, when a more serious challenger appeared on the scene.

THE ORTONA MOTOR COMPANY LTD

James Berry Walford was a motor-cycle dealer and owned a small but prosperous engineering business in Egham, Surrey. He had also gained some experience in operating small Daimler motor buses between Egham and Staines. Encouraged by the success of this venture, he bought the assets of the Cambridge Motor Omnibus Company in August 1907 (the CMOC went into voluntary liquidation on 25th January 1908) and re-launched it as The Ortona Motor Company. This title was apparently chosen after Mr Walford saw the ship 'SS Ortona' while he was on a cruise. He liked the name and adopted it for his new venture. Ortona is also the name of an Italian

seaside town. On 19th August, he introduced buses onto the Railway Station route, again competing directly with the trams. The single-deck buses wore a green and white livery, although allover green (referred to as 'Ortona green') was used thereafter on most vehicles until the late 1920s. The buses themselves comprised three second-hand Scott-Stirling 14hp vehicles from the Lancashire United fleet (BN 139, BN 276, M 1558) and a Coventry-built Maudslay (DU 524). Scott-Stirling was associated with the London Power Omnibus Company, which was based in Twickenham and used the fleetname 'Pioneer'. Ortona also acquired the Arrol-Johnson (XS 93) previously with the Cambridge Motor Omnibus Company, but it was not allowed into the town centre to begin with and was soon re-sold. After a few months two new Scott-Stirlings joined the fleet, one of which was registered CE 691. Ortona also made plans to operate local bus services in Bedford but nothing came of these.

The Ortona buses were far more successful than those of the two earlier operators and the company was officially registered as The Ortona Motor Company Ltd on 28th March 1908. The depot and offices were at the former CMOC premises at 112 Hills Road, with John Berry Walford, (the Founder's son) as Manager. The vehicles displayed the fleetname 'THE ORTONA MOTOR CO LTD' along the full length of the side panels in gold block letters. The rapid decline and fall of the earlier motor buses made some local folk highly sceptical at first and there were fears that operations would have to be discontinued because of a lack of support. However, it soon became apparent that the Ortona vehicles were far safer and more reliable than their predecessors had been and, despite being limited to a speed of 12mph, the buses became extremely popular. After about a year's successful running, double-deckers were authorised. The original buses were rebuilt with top decks and more vehicles joined the fleet. There were two new double-deckers, one of which (CE 1088) was a Commer, along with two more Maudslay saloons (CE 894 and CE 977) with more powerful 25hp chassis, which were also rebuilt as double-deckers soon afterwards. Despite the narrowness of the streets the service was extended through the

Above: Ortona's first new buses were delivered in 1908 and were all double-deckers. They included two more Maudslays, one of which is seen here in Huntingdon Road on service 2 to Mill Road after having been converted to a double-decker. The bus and crew are immaculately turned out, while a choice of entertainment is offered at the New Theatre in St Andrew's Street. *(Cambridgeshire Collection)*

Below: The fortunes of the Tramway Company continued to decline as the buses became more popular, and the first country routes were started. Two more Maudslay double-deckers joined the fleet in 1912, and **DU 1752** on service 3 to Sawston was about to be passed by tram No. **2** when it was photographed in Regent Street. *(Cambridgeshire Collection)*

town centre to Chesterton (Chapel Street), covering one of the former horse bus routes. A new service 2 was also introduced, running from Huntingdon Road to Romsey Town, bringing buses to the recently developed Mill Road, with its many side streets of Victorian terraced houses. The Ortona buses introduced fixed stopping places, whereas the trams picked up and set down anywhere on request, making already slow journeys even slower. The buses also took passengers closer to the station than the trams, which inevitably suffered badly from the competition. The situation was not helped by the fact that the Tramway Company still had to pay the Corporation for the upkeep of the roads, while Ortona did not.

THE FIRST COUNTRY BUS SERVICES

In the early years of the 20th century the only public transport into the towns from the surrounding villages was by carriers' carts, unless the village had a railway station. The 1908 edition of Kelly's Directory for Cambridge lists more than 80 villages with a carrier (or sometimes several). The carriers, who often had other interests, operated once or twice a week to specified public houses in the towns. They provided transport for passengers and goods, for as well as bringing in produce from the country they also delivered goods to the villagers from the town shops. The situation had started to change by the end of 1910, when the first country bus services were introduced. Numbered 3 and 4, they terminated at King's Parade in Cambridge, and Ortona's network thus became:

1 Railway Station - Regent Street - Post Office - Chesterton (Chapel Street)
2 Mill Road (Malta Road) - Emmanuel Street - Post Office - Huntingdon Road (Oxford Road)
3 Cambridge - Trumpington - Great Shelford - Stapleford - Sawston
4 Cambridge - Histon - Cottenham

Further country services would soon follow and, as the motor bus network grew, the carriers either vanished from the scene or became bus operators themselves. A horse bus

continued to run for many years between Wickhambrook and Newmarket but this was withdrawn in 1932, when one of the proprietor's horses died.

THE END OF THE TRAMS

As the buses became more popular, tram revenue fell badly, a situation not helped by road works in Trumpington Street. Permission to install passing loops at Emmanuel Street and Regent Street and to lengthen the double track at the junction of Hills Road and Station Road was initially refused but finally granted in 1909 and another new car, number 8, was purchased from Starbuck's. With seating for 40 (18 inside) it was to be the last addition to the fleet, for the trams were now doomed. By 1913 the financial situation had deteriorated further and the Tramway Company was unable to make its payments to the corporation. A writ was issued in September 1913 and on 6th January 1914 the Mayor and Corporation applied for a compulsory winding-up order. This was duly granted, and after 34 years Cambridge was about to bid farewell to its trams. Posters appeared inviting the locals to make a last trip and on the final day, Wednesday 13th February 1914, the cars carried full loads all day. The final departure from the Post Office carried a number of rowdy undergraduates, including an improvised band, while the last car of all left the railway station at 6.25pm, driven by Ephraim Skinner, the oldest and longest-serving driver. As soon as it entered the depot the doors were locked, for trouble was expected from the undergraduates and a contingent of police was standing by. Trouble broke out at 8.30, when around 30 of the students made their way along East Road, Burleigh Street and Fitzroy Street, turning off street lamps and breaking windows, before attempting to burn down the bandstand on Christ's Pieces.

Six days later the company's assets were sold by auction. There was very little demand for second-hand horse trams and very low prices were paid for the cars. Number 8, which had cost £160 only five years earlier, went for a mere £15. The horses went for higher prices but the whole auction raised only £710, while the total deficit was over £19,000. The East

Above: Too much for one horse? On 13th February 1914 the trams carried full loads all day as the crowds turned out to enjoy a last ride. Whether the horses enjoyed the occasion can only be guessed at. *(Cambridgeshire Collection)*

Below: From November 1912 the Bristol-based manufacturer Straker-Squire supplied many new buses to Ortona. The first three are seen here posed with their crews, ready for action on the pioneering service 1. *(Cambridgeshire Collection)*

Road premises were not sold until 13th May. The Cam Shoe Repair Company moved into the offices, while the depot itself initially became a fish market. It was used later on by a corn chandler, then a motor engineer until 1944 when, still with tram tracks inside, it became Peak's furniture depository. Recently refurbished as offices, it continues in commercial use as 'The Tram Shed'. The stable building eventually became a public house, named 'The Old Tram Depot'.

The last years of the horse tramway in Cambridge had seen unequal competition with the motor buses. The trams were very slow, especially in getting under way, while the stretches of single track delayed them even more. Many Cambridge people said it was quicker to walk and 'racing the tram' was a popular pastime with local children. The other reasons for the company's failure were the uncooperative attitude of the Council and the heavy payments they demanded, the lack of progress and expansion which electrification would have offered and the opposition, particularly from the University, which had been encountered from the outset. Horse trams could still be found in South London until 1915 and in a few other towns for a while longer, while they operate as a tourist attraction in Douglas, Isle of Man to this day. Electric trams have recently made a comeback in several British cities and further schemes are being planned, but whether Cambridge is ever served by a modern electric tramway remains to be seen.

>> Upper right: Straker-Squire also supplied Ortona's first charabanc, with a 36hp chassis and a 28-seat body. Its canvas roof was in place in this posed view outside the garage in Hills Road. *(Cambridgeshire Collection)*

>> Lower right: The outbreak of war in August 1914 led to the requisitioning of many vehicles, including nine new Ortona double-deckers. Replacements were not available until the following year and they included this Straker-Squire 36hp (**CE 4031**), seen at the Newnham terminus of service 6. *(Cambridgeshire Collection)*

Below: The end of the line for the Cambridge trams. A last day view of car **5** with some of the Tramway Company staff. *(Cambridgeshire Collection)*

Bottom: Although Cambridge lost its trams as long ago as 1914, the depot in East Road survives and now houses a suite of modern offices. Behind it the large former stable building is now 'The Old Tram Depot' pub, whose sign shows an attractive but inaccurate picture of a two-horse, double-deck tram with fleet number 5. *(Author)*

2. Ortona Progress 1912 to 1924

THE GROWTH OF A BAT COMPANY

As the fortunes of the Tramway Company declined, Ortona flourished. After a four-year gap, eight more double-deckers were purchased in 1912, including another two Maudslays. These had 40hp chassis, and one (DU 1752) appears to have been a former demonstrator. The first five of many Ortona vehicles built by Straker-Squire of Bristol also entered service, registered CE 480, CE 1996-8 and CE 2153. The earliest Straker-Squire buses were built in 1906 under licence from the German manufacturer Büssing, but the firm was designing its own chassis by the time Ortona's first examples were built. The Ortona buses had 4-cylinder engines rated at 36bhp, with Morse silent chains for the final drive. The bodies had seats for 34 passengers (18 upstairs and 16 down).

In October 1913 the British Automobile Traction Company Ltd (the BET's bus operating division) purchased a 50% shareholding in The Ortona Motor Company Ltd. From then on, the BAT virtually controlled Ortona. The resulting increase in capital allowed further expansion into the towns and villages around Cambridge. In Cambridge new local services 5 (Cherry Hinton Road to Newmarket Road) and 6 (Hills Road to Newnham) were introduced, while from 20th February 1914 Ortona was granted licences for six more buses, mainly to meet the increased traffic arising from the tramway closure. By 1914 buses everywhere had become much more reliable and free of accidents, with most of the original Ortona stock now replaced by new Straker-Squire vehicles. The 1914 intake consisted of three more 36hp Strakers, one of which (CE 2552) was a 28-seat charabanc, the company's first. CE 3001 was another double-decker, while new saloon CE 2894 was used to inaugurate service 8 to Royston in April. Another new country route (7) started in the same month to Willingham via Longstanton. At around this time a new fleetname style appeared on some vehicles. This was "ORTONA" in gold, block-shaded letters, except on charabanc CE 2552 where the inverted commas and shading were omitted. A further development on some vehicles (including CE 2894) was a gold script fleetname.

Travelling or working on these early buses was not for the faint-hearted, for their design was not far removed from the horse and coach era. There was no windscreen and the driver sat in a very exposed position, with only a narrow canopy above his head. For additional protection during bad weather there was a canvas apron, which came right up to his chin and which also covered the steering wheel and controls. Similar aprons were also provided for upper deck ('outside') passengers, although a ride on the top deck was a pleasant experience on a fine day. Slatted wooden seats ('garden seats') were used throughout, and these were not very comfortable. Although vandalism and other anti-social behaviour were less common then, there were instances of high-spirited undergraduates smashing the top-deck seats for firewood on 5th November. Lighting was originally by oil lamps, which flickered as the buses negotiated the cobbled streets and the tram tracks, while acetylene gas was also used before electric lighting became standard. Ortona vehicles had solid tyres (which had very little tread) until well into the 1920s and in icy conditions and snow it could be very difficult to pull away from stops. The camber of the road often made the bus slide down towards the kerb, but with maximum revs and the wheels spinning they would manage to keep going. Starting the buses was also difficult in winter, with two men swinging the heavy starting-handle while a third man very carefully warmed the intake manifold with a blowlamp. Before starting out, drivers had to remove and clean grease-caps, while conductors had to polish the brasswork and see that the seat-aprons on the top deck were in good order. On market days the buses were especially busy, with many extra journeys provided.

Right: Women were employed as 'conductorettes' on Ortona's buses from 1916 as more men left to join the forces. They included Mrs Maskell and Mrs Palmer, whose husbands both served in France. *(Cambridgeshire Collection)*

Below: The Ortona fleet expanded rapidly after the end of the First World War. The first Leyland vehicles were delivered in 1919 and they included four with H-type chassis and 34-seat double-deck bodywork. In this view in Emmanuel Street, **CE 6011** was having a close encounter with a light sports car, of the type known as 'cyclecars', then all the rage but soon to be killed off by Herbert Austin's 'Seven', which brought in cheap 'real car' motoring. *(Cambridgeshire Collection)*

WAR AND PEACE, THE FIRST LEYLANDS

The outbreak of the First World War on 4th August 1914 had several effects on the company. In November the War Department requisitioned the chassis of nine new buses, although Ortona retained the bodies, which were stored for mounting onto later chassis. Replacements came in 1915 in the shape of CE 3773 (believed to have been an Austin 25hp double-decker) and three more Strakers. Of these, CE 3866 (COT5 type) and CE 4031 (36hp) were double-deckers, while CE 3976 was a 'U'-type with a saloon body. As staff left to join the armed forces, women took over their jobs and in 1916 female conductors (known as 'conductorettes') were employed for the first time. The company managed to halve its monthly consumption of 3,000 gallons of petrol by diluting it with suitable additives, known as 'Wital' and 'Petrofin' (probably white spirit or paraffin). One of the new Straker double-deckers was fitted with an enormous gas balloon on its upper deck to allow it to run on town gas and was nicknamed 'The Old Gas Bag'. As the war dragged on there were no further route expansions, and no more fleet additions were made until hostilities ended in November 1918. New vehicles added then (all double-deckers) were three more Straker 36hps (CE 4725/30/9), two Austin 25hps and at least one bus built by the McCurd Lorry Manufacturing Company of Cricklewood, London. These were joined later by four more Straker 24hps, with registrations AN 1058, 1083, 1088 and 1090, which were previously with the London General Omnibus Company.

After the war expansion was very rapid, with no fewer then eleven more new vehicles added in 1919. Still more Strakers comprised CE 5180, a 32-seat single-decker, and CE 6399/6400, which were double-deckers on COT3 chassis. The first Leyland and AEC vehicles, all double-deckers, also joined the fleet. The Leylands consisted of four 'H'-type (CE 5421, 5583, 5962 and 6011) and two S5s (CE 5157, 5213) while the AECs (CE 5098/9) had 'YC'-type chassis. These carried fleet numbers C11 and C10 respectively. Ortona vehicles all carried a chassis number (prefixed C) which was usually on the bonnet of the vehicles, and a body number (prefixed B) near the driver's seat. The numbers were on small metal plates and the earliest bus known to carry one was CE 4031, new in 1915 as C1. The numbers were not used in chronological order and many were re-used. For this reason they will not be quoted in the text, although known 'C' numbers are shown in Appendix A. The double-deckers were all 34-seaters (18 outside and 16 inside) and some are believed to have carried the second-hand bodies removed from the requisitioned buses in 1914. The Leylands and AECs were later rebodied as 46-, 48- or 53-seaters.

A GROWING ROUTE NETWORK

Two more Leyland double-deckers (CE 6806/7) followed in 1920, with RAF-type chassis. They had originally been built for the Royal Flying Corps (retitled the Royal Air Force on 1st April 1918) and were refurbished by Leyland after the war. CE 6806 was originally a double-decker, but received a new single-deck body in 1922. The provision of windscreens on these buses made life a little more comfortable for drivers in cold or wet weather. Also new were three more Straker type charabancs (CE 7023-5), with 33-seat bodies on 'A'-type chassis. These originally carried a grey livery, with a simple 'ORTONA' fleetname in a garter device, although they were later repainted green.

The route network continued to grow and the fleet expanded rapidly. Four more Straker 'A' types were delivered in 1921, three with double-deck bodies (CE 9178-80) and a further 30-seat saloon (CE 8364), believed to have operated the first journey to Haverhill on service 13. The Cambridge Chronicle described the double-deckers as "the last word in bus construction." Another followed in 1922, along with two small 20-seat saloons (CE 9829/30) on Vulcan VSD chassis, built by the Vulcan Motor & Engineering Company of Southport. To cope with the increase in traffic four Tilling-Stevens TTA1 double-deckers were acquired from Tilling's London fleet but they only lasted a year before being withdrawn. They carried registrations LH 8606, 8616, 8617 and 8672 and a further ten similar buses were also hired from Tilling.

Right: Also new in 1919 were two AEC YC double-deckers, one of which is seen here at the Mill Road terminus of service 2. AEC vehicles never formed a very large part of the Ortona fleet, despite their popularity in London and elsewhere. *(Cambridgeshire Collection)*

Below: The three Straker-Squire charabancs of 1920 originally carried a grey livery, as shown by **CE 7023**. Here it prepares to depart from the Cambridge Co-operative Society's Burleigh Street store with a staff outing. *(Cambridgeshire Collection)*

The last Straker-Squire 'A' (ER 1134) was delivered in 1923, with a 35-seat saloon body, the first of many to be purchased from Ransomes of Ipswich. Two more Vulcan VSD 20-seaters also joined the fleet (ER 1022/4) together with three Leyland G7 double-deckers (ER 418-20). Although the Straker-Squire vehicles were fast, they were not always very reliable and the firm ceased production in 1925. All subsequent double-deckers were of Leyland manufacture and early in 1924 Ortona took delivery of two G7 Specials (ER 1812/1813) and an SG7 saloon (ER 1814), while a forward-control Leyland GH7 (ER 3137) followed in November. The new buses featured pneumatic tyres, and these were also fitted to the charabancs. Another vehicle was acquired in the spring with the business of Pioneer Bus, run by a Mr Butler. Few details are available, but Ortona paid £160 for the business and resold the vehicle almost immediately. Yet another fleetname style was now in use, this being ORTONA with CAMBRIDGE in smaller letters below, with the lettering in gold. This remained in use for a number of years.

THOMAS TILLING

Thomas Tilling was originally a dairyman in Walworth, London. In May 1847 he set up as a jobmaster, supplying horses for transport work including horse bus services. This led him to start his own horse bus route in 1850, running between Peckham and Oxford Street. More routes followed and the business grew rapidly. Thomas Tilling died in 1893 but two of his sons, Richard and Edward, continued to run the business. In 1897 it became a public company (Thomas Tilling Ltd), and when motor buses appeared the company bought some Milnes-Daimler vehicles. Competition was fierce, and in 1908 the large London General Omnibus Co Ltd (LGOC) was formed from the merger of three smaller operators. Agreements between Tilling and the LGOC restricted Tilling's London operations to 150 vehicles.

Tilling was responsible for the development of the petrol-electric bus, in conjunction with W A Stevens of Maidstone, who designed the electric transmission. The difficulties in driving early motor buses often led to gearbox damage and to solve this problem the gearbox was dispensed with. A petrol engine drove a dynamo, which provided current for an electric motor driving the rear wheels. Production began in 1911, following successful trials in London with a prototype built three years earlier (this actually had two electric motors). Tilling took over the Stevens business to form Tilling-Stevens Motors and by 1914 the company had built over 170 buses. Many operators continued to buy Tilling-Stevens vehicles after the war but in 1929 Tilling sold its shares in the manufacturing company to concentrate on running its bus companies. After buying mainly AEC vehicles for its subsidiary companies it began its long association with Bristol in 1931. The Rootes Group later took over Tilling-Stevens Motors.

By 1924 Ortona's original premises in Hills Road were too small to house the entire fleet, and work commenced on a garage extension. Vehicles not required for daily use, such as the charabancs, were kept at St Paul's garage further along Hills Road. By then the full list of services started since 1913 was as follows (in Cambridge all the country routes started from King's Parade):

5 Cherry Hinton Road (Hinton Avenue) - Station Road Corner - Regent Street - Post Office - Newmarket Road (Stanley Road)

6 Hills Road (Glebe Road) - Station Road Corner - Regent Street - Post Office - King's Parade - Silver Street - Newnham (Grantchester Road)

7 Cambridge - Girton - Oakington - Long Stanton (St Michael & All Saints) - Willingham

8 Cambridge - Trumpington - Harston - Shepreth - Melbourn - Royston

9 Cambridge - Milton - Landbeach - Chittering - Stretham - Ely

10 Cambridge - Cherry Hinton (Robin Hood) - Fulbourn - Great Wilbraham

11 Cambridge - Barnwell - Quy - Swaffham Prior - Swaffham Bulbeck - Reach - Burwell Market day (Thursday) extension to Fordham - Soham - Stuntney - Ely

12 Cambridge - Trumpington - Great &

Above: Ortona purchased four small Vulcan saloons, with VSD chassis and 20-seat bodies. The first pair arrived in 1922 and **CE 9830** is seen on a Races special. The buses were sold after five years of service. *(Author's Collection)*

Below: From 1923 Leylands became the standard choice for double-deckers. In this view **ER 420**, one of the three G7 buses delivered in that year, is seen at the Chapel Street, Chesterton terminus of service 1. *(John Banks Collection)*

Little Shelford - Whittlesford - Duxford - Ickleton - Great & Little Chesterford - Littlebury - Saffron Walden

13 Cambridge - Gog Magog Hills - Little & Great Abington - Linton - Horseheath - Haverhill

13 Cambridge - Gog Magog Hills - Little & Great Abington - Linton - Balsham

13A Haverhill - Steeple Bumpstead - Radwinter - Saffron Walden - Thaxted Market day (Tuesday) service

13A Haverhill - Steeple Bumpstead Market day (Friday) service

13A Haverhill - Kedington Market day (Friday) service

To encourage travel, the company produced an informative and well-illustrated guide to all its services, containing historical and other details of the places served by each route. Four pages were devoted to Ely Cathedral (described as "a Gothic masterpiece"), while not forgetting that Melbourn was then "the centre of the greengage district" and that Oakington was once described by a Bishop of Ely as "the most scandalous parish in the diocese". The railway companies did not welcome the new services and they sometimes introduced special cheap return fares where there was bus competition.

Operating in the flat, exposed countryside around Cambridge had its problems, especially in the windswept fens to the north, where buses were sometime blown off roads into dykes and fields. When a mishap occurred all the available manpower would be dispatched to the scene. The body would be removed from the chassis, which would be dragged back onto the road. The body would then be refitted before the bus was taken back to Cambridge for inspection and repair. The early buses all

Above: ER 1812 was another of the Leyland G7 double-deckers, this one delivered in 1924. It is seen with its crew on service 1. *(Alan B Cross Collection/W Noel Jackson)*

>> Right: To encourage travel, Ortona produced attractive guides to the places served by its routes. They included full route descriptions, historical notes and photographs of places of interest. *(Author's Collection)*

had chassis which stood very high off the road and after one or two instances of people being run over it became customary from about 1915 to fit horizontal 'lifeguard' rails between the front and rear wheels. They were particularly appropriate in Cambridge, which by now had a very large population of cyclists.

Motor Tours from
CAMBRIDGE
by the Ortona Motor Co., Ltd.

3. Ortona's Competitors

Although Ortona's operations grew rapidly in the post-war period, the green buses did not have the roads all to themselves. The First World War led to the building of many modern, reliable vehicles and many men had learned to drive and maintain them. The ending of hostilities produced a large surplus of these machines and, aware of the growing demand for transport, many ex-servicemen used their war gratuities to set themselves up as bus operators. They introduced services from their home villages into the towns, usually on market days, and often followed the tradition of the village carriers by transporting goods as well as passengers. Some of the carriers also replaced their horses and carts with motor vehicles. The former military ambulances and lorries received new bodywork, built either by the operators themselves or by the craftsmen who were still a feature of village life. The country busmen had lower operating costs than the larger companies. Their labour arrangements were more flexible and their buses started and finished their days at the outer ends of routes, with no expensive 'dead' mileage from or to the town. They also offered valuable, stable employment at a time when agriculture was employing fewer and fewer people, and their staff became respected local figures in much the same way as country railwaymen had done when they first appeared on the scene.

Several of these operators went on to purchase small buses of American origin, built by Chevrolet, Dodge, Ford, Graham and Reo. Chevrolet was a subsidiary of General Motors, which gained control of the English car manufacturer Vauxhall. From 1928 Chevrolets were built at Vauxhall's Luton factory but only until 1931, after which the name Bedford was used for Vauxhall's commercial range. Dodge vehicles were being built in England (at Kew) by 1928, when the company acquired Graham Brothers, and some vehicles appear to have been built under the name 'Graham-Dodge'. Fords were built in America and England, the original British factory being in Manchester. Ransom Eli Olds formed Reo after his original

company (later Oldsmobile) also became part of General Motors. Reos were noted for being light and fast.

THE WHIPPET

Henry (Harry) Lee had been a bicycle engineer in London and was a keen cyclist himself. Before the Great War he sometimes cycled up the Old North Road as far as Graveley, a small village to the west of Cambridge. He was gassed in the war and his doctor advised him to move to the country. Together with his family he settled in Graveley, the village he knew. He worked for a while as a horse dealer, then as a fishmonger and for a while he ran a sweet stall, before providing the village with its first bus service in 1919, using a former American army ambulance. It had a Ford Model 'T' chassis, which received a new, 14-seat body with a bench seat along each side, built by the village wheelwright, Mr Crook. The origins of the fleetname 'The Whippet' are uncertain, but it was intended to give an impression of speed. Mr Lee's first routes ran on Mondays to St Ives via Yelling, Papworth Everard and Hilton, and on Thursdays to St Neots via Toseland and Yelling. He then introduced a service to Cambridge via Papworth, with two journeys on Wednesdays and Saturdays, terminating at the Merton Arms in Northampton Street. At first there were very few passengers and one Wednesday morning a disappointed Mr Lee announced that this would be the last day that the service would run. He changed his mind at Caldecote Turn, where fourteen people were waiting. A similar number were there in the afternoon, and the service has continued ever since. Encouraged by his success, he then introduced an express service from Godmanchester to London. He also ran a taxi service and purchased additional vehicles of Sunbeam, Vulcan and Chevrolet manufacture. By 1924 the original premises next to the school in Graveley were too small for his growing fleet and Whippet's operations moved to a larger site next to the White Horse in nearby Hilton.

Above: Accidents will happen! Staff pause for the photographer before continuing their efforts to rescue Leyland S5 **CE 5157**, which had come to grief somewhere to the north of Cambridge while working service 7 to Willingham. *(Cambridgeshire Collection)*

Below: In 1919 Henry Lee introduced bus services from Graveley to St Neots, St Ives and Cambridge with this Ford Model T. The body was built by Mr Crook, the village wheelwright. The group of onlookers and the buildings in the background suggest that it may have just been completed in this view. *(Whippet Coaches)*

HARSTON & DISTRICT MOTOR SERVICES

South of Cambridge, Norman Charles Pennell Thompson left the Navy in 1918 and worked briefly for another local carrier before starting his own business, using the fleetname 'Harston & District'. He too began his bus operations with a converted ambulance, with bodywork built by Mr Willers, the local carpenter and undertaker. The depot was a converted barn in the High Street in Harston, on the main Cambridge - London road. Few passengers were carried at first, for the locals were afraid of the new-fangled machine and preferred to walk. Then, on a very wet, windy day, Mr Thompson stopped his bus just ahead of a group of people carrying heavy loads back from the market. They clambered on board, convinced themselves that it was safe and became regular passengers. The services then became increasingly busy.

In 1925 Mr Thompson took delivery of a new, 14-seat Ford (ER 4437), followed a year later by a larger Daimler CK (ER 6264), with a 25-seat body. He then purchased several Reo buses, including ER 8976 in 1928, followed a year later by VE 855. They carried in a two-tone blue livery with the fleetname 'Harston & District Motor Services' on a garter device around the letters 'NT'. His main bus service (1) followed a very roundabout route from Royston to Cambridge via Reed, Barley, Chrishall, Fowlmere, Newton, Harston and Haslingfield, with daily buses from Fowlmere. Service 2 ran on Wednesdays from Cambridge via service 1 as far as Fowlmere, continuing via Shepreth, Meldreth and Melbourn to Royston for the market, while service 3 linked Barrington with Cambridge via Foxton, Harston and Trumpington on Wednesdays, Saturdays and Sundays. Mr Thompson also advertised "Saloon coaches for hire - distance no object" and ran excursions and tours from Harston.

DRAYTON'S MOTOR SERVICES

Further south, in the village of Barley on the Cambridgeshire/Hertfordshire border, Arthur Drayton began bus operations in 1920 from the Belle Vue Garage, which still bears the family name. He started as a carrier, covering a very wide area, and regularly used his van for transporting chickens to local markets. He also introduced buses to the village, but although the locals were keen to travel they were less enthusiastic about sharing the vehicle with the chickens. Mr Drayton (who was also a skilled carpenter) accordingly built a 14-seat bus body, which his children would lift onto the Ford 'T' chassis when there were passengers to be carried. The first route was to Royston and, as the business grew, Barley became the centre of a route network stretching as far afield as Cambridge (where the original terminus was Maid's Causeway), Hitchin and Nuthampstead. The dark blue and cream buses ran daily to Bishop's Stortford and via Reed or The Eagle Tavern to Royston, with a service from Chrishall on most days as well. It was very much a family business, in which Mr Drayton's sons Jim and Will and his daughter Elizabeth were also involved. There was competition from Arthur Livermore, another carrier-turned-busman based in Barley. From 1926 to 1929 Mr Drayton favoured Graham vehicles and purchased a new Graham every year. The first three (RO 1763, RO 7160 and RO 8998) had 14-seat bodies, while the last (UR 2407) was a 20-seater. Goods continued to be carried, the 1938 bus timetable including a note that "a lorry for Market Produce leaves Chrishall every Wednesday at 8.30 a.m. via Heydon, Chishill, Nuthampstead, Barkway and Barley." There was also an express coach service from Chrishall to London, which provided direct links to the capital from villages not served by the main railway lines. Drayton also ran excursions and tours from Barley and later from Bassingbourn and Heydon.

HEYDON & DISTRICT

Frederick Ernest Weeden was another village bus operator who started his business in the 1920s, apparently after Arthur Drayton taught him to drive. Originally operating as 'Heydon & District' from the village of that name, one of his earliest vehicles is believed to have been a converted mail van. His first service ran to Cambridge via Chrishall, and he moved his business to the latter village a few years later.

Above: Mrs Maud Mansfield and her sons Reg and Horace stand proudly beside **ER 5087**, the last of three Garner saloons purchased. New in 1926, the bus was sold only four years later for conversion to a lorry. *(J R Neale Collection)*

Below: The first AEC in the Mansfield fleet, **ER 6531** had a 26-seat body by Strachan & Brown and was new in 1926. It lasted until 1930, when it was sold for further service. It is seen here with its crew outside the company's office in Burwell. *(J R Neale Collection)*

In 1926 he purchased an American-built Dodge 14-seater (ER 5365), followed by another (ER 9547) in 1928, by which time Dodge vehicles were being assembled in England. His next new bus (VE 1082) was a Graham, following the takeover of that manufacturer by Dodge. The vehicles wore a maroon and brown livery and operations were similar to (and sometimes in competition with) Drayton's. As well as advertising the carriage of chickens (and eggs) he introduced several more routes from Chrishall, serving the nearby villages of Duddenhoe End, Elmdon and Heydon. Weedon's Bishop's Stortford service ran via Clavering and shared the road with Drayton's buses beyond Manuden. The Cambridge route competed with Ortona services 3 and 12 at Sawston and Ickleton respectively. In around 1927 Mr Weeden introduced two routes (via Clavering and via Littlebury Green) to Saffron Walden, where he established several market-day (Tuesday) services to nearby villages. By then he too had a London express service, which started from Heydon and ran via Langley and Clavering. Excursions and tours were operated from Heydon and later from Saffron Walden and Sawston. Described by those who remember him as a smart, helpful and obliging man, Mr Weeden also had an interest in Lucy's Garage on the main Newmarket - Royston road.

LONG'S SALOON BUS SERVICE

To the south east of Cambridge, between the railway lines to Liverpool Street and Ipswich, lies an area of rolling, open countryside dotted with small villages and crossed by the A11 trunk road. The village of West Wratting lies close to the border of Cambridgeshire and the old county of West Suffolk (as it was until 1974), and it was here that Claude Bertram Long established Long's Saloon Bus Service. Little is known about Mr Long but before starting his bus operations he is believed to have had a Ford lorry (CE9 124) and this probably carried passengers on occasions. He also favoured small, American-designed buses and in 1928 he purchased a 14-seat Reo (ER 9148), followed by a Chevrolet 26-seater (VE 1412). His bus services began in November 1920 and few villages were left

unserved by the network of market-day routes he built up. These ran to nearby Haverhill on Fridays and went slightly further afield to Newmarket via Brinkley on Tuesdays. More significant was the service from Great Thurlow via Great Wratting, Withersfield, Weston Colville and West Wratting to Cambridge. This ran daily and became increasingly busy. Mr Long's timetables also informed the locals that "day excursions are operated during the summer months to seaside resorts (details from the office or conductors)". The vehicles carried a mid-blue livery.

MANSFIELD'S BROWN BUSES

Also close to the West Suffolk border but further to the north, George Mansfield ran a cobbler's shop in the large, straggling village of Burwell in the days before the First World War. He expanded his business to include the sale and repair of bicycles and in 1914 built a house and cycle shop in the centre of the village. He then purchased a motorcycle and sidecar combination, with which he provided transport for the bank clerk on his weekly visit from nearby Newmarket. He progressed to a Ford Model 'T' taxi, which was followed in about 1922 by a larger vehicle on the same chassis. The dual-purpose body could carry passengers or goods and was built by Miller's of Sturton Street, Cambridge. It had tip-up seats along the sides for passengers and a canvas roof, which could be rolled back for large loads. So began a business still remembered with affection by many. The first route, and always the most important one, was from Burwell to Cambridge via The Swaffhams and Quy. This became service 1 and originally ran on Mondays and Saturdays, but by 1924 it was a daily operation. The importance of local markets saw the bus heading for Newmarket on Tuesdays, Bury St Edmunds on Wednesdays and Ely on Thursdays. Friday was maintenance day. The business thrived and the fleet was increased. A second Ford 'T' (ER 3813), with a body by Lambert of Thetford, was purchased in 1925. Garner of Moseley supplied three new buses (CE 9954, ER 2054 and ER 5087) the latter being exhibited at the 1926 Motor Show at Olympia. Yet another former army ambulance

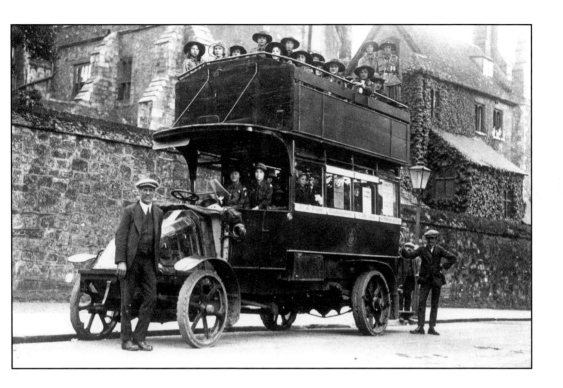

Above: In complete contrast to the other small operators, Jabez Parnell started his Haddenham & District services with a double-decker. It was a Tilling-Stevens TTA1 of uncertain pedigree, but by 1922 had acquired the Isle of Ely registration **EB 3557**. Mr Parnell stands proudly in front of his bus in this view. *(Cambridgeshire Collection)*

Below and page 35 upper: Typical small buses in the Thompson and Drayton fleets show the type of vehicle used by most of the village operators. Will Drayton stands by his bus in the view on page 35. *(Author's Collection)*

to serve the area was ER 4613, which had a Napier chassis. The first of many AEC vehicles was ER 6531, with a Strachan & Brown body, new in 1926, while the first half-cab bus was an Associated Daimler (ER 9437), delivered in 1928 shortly before AEC ceased to be associated with Daimler. It was followed by VE 1050, a Daimler CF6 with a Willowbrook body, and from then on Daimlers were always a feature of the fleet. Vehicles carried a brown and cream livery, with the colours later reversed on coaches.

The company later became well known as 'Burwell & District' but this fleetname was not used at first. Passengers and local bus timetables referred to the company as 'Mansfield's brown buses' or just 'Mansfield.' In the late 1920s several more bus routes were established from Cambridge, to The Eversdens, to The Wilbrahams via Fulbourn and to Caldecote via Hardwick, while the main route was later extended northwards to Fordham on Mondays, Wednesdays and Saturdays. Summer express services were introduced from Burwell to Felixstowe and Great Yarmouth, and excursions were also operated from the village.

HADDENHAM & DISTRICT MOTOR SERVICE

To the north of Cambridge, Jabez Cornwell Parnell ran services from Stretham, a village on the main Cambridge - Ely road. Unlike so many other small operators he first took to the roads with a double-decker, in this case a Tilling-Stevens TTA1 petrol-electric, similar to those which Ortona acquired from Tilling's London fleet. The origins of the vehicle are uncertain but it was reregistered EB 3557 in January 1922. Mr Parnell's main service was from Haddenham to Cambridge via Wilburton, Stretham and Waterbeach. He also had several routes into Ely, and he used the fleetname 'Haddenham & District Motor Service'. He also advertised "furniture removals and general motor haulage". Subsequent vehicles were all

single-deckers, including a pair of Ford Model 'T' 14-seaters EB 4319 and EB 4703. Parnell's usual livery was black, although at least one bus was painted brown.

BARKERS BUS SERVICES (FENSTANTON & DISTRICT BUS SERVICES)

Operating from 'The Chequers' in Fenstanton, William Barker is believed to have borrowed Parnell's double-decker to start his business, before purchasing a new 14-seat Ford Model 'T' (EW 3079). He ran market day (Monday) services into nearby St Ives from Hilton (in competition with The Whippet) and Fen Drayton. Both routes passed through Fenstanton, which was also later served by Brand's service from Elsworth. Mr Barker introduced buses on Wednesdays and Saturdays into Cambridge from Coton and on a circular route via Madingley and Dry Drayton, villages not served by Ortona. He also had a main road service from St Ives via Fenstanton into Cambridge, which additionally ran on Fridays and (in common with Whippet's Cambridge routes) terminated at the Merton Arms. Most of the small buses owned were bought new and offered plenty of variety. A Reo Sprinter (EW 4894) was purchased in 1926, while the Ford was replaced in 1929 by a Chevrolet LP (EW 5701).

MAJOR FRANCIS

In 1922 Major W Francis, who apparently was regarded as the 'Squire' of Quy, introduced a service from Lode to Cambridge via Quy and Teversham. It seems to have been a 'social' rather than a commercial operation, for most of the route was already covered by Ortona's service 11 from Burwell and by Mr Mansfield's service from his home village, which commenced at about the same time. Major Francis used a 20-seat Ford 'T' (ER 2968) painted in a red livery, and this was later followed by a second Ford (VE 81).

Below: National purchased a large number of AEC YC vehicles, fitted with double-deck, saloon or charabanc bodies by a variety of builders. Number **2040** (**BM 8228**), with a body built by the operator, is seen here on service 14 from Bedford to St Ives. *(Alan B Cross Collection/W Noel Jackson)*

4. Ortona's Neighbours

In addition to the village-based operators, other companies introduced services which did not compete but which ran to the edges of Ortona's territory. The market towns around Cambridge often marked the boundaries between Ortona and the neighbouring companies.

THE NATIONAL OMNIBUS &
TRANSPORT COMPANY LTD

The National Steam Car Company Ltd was founded by Thomas Clarkson to operate services in London, originally with steam-powered vehicles which he designed himself. Like the BET and Tilling, National made agreements with the London General Omnibus Company, which limited its London operations and led to the establishment of businesses elsewhere. Starting in Essex, National took over the bus operations of the Great Eastern Railway in Chelmsford in July 1913. Further west, and after the First World War, National exchanged its London operations for the Bedford area services of the LGOC. These had been suspended in 1914, when the army requisitioned the depot and its buses. When National restarted the services in 1919 the company was renamed the National Omnibus & Transport Company Ltd. By 1920 National had a route to St Neots, and this was later extended on certain days to Huntingdon and St Ives.

As well as establishing itself in the Chelmsford and Bedford areas, National opened a new depot in the yard of the Anchor Inn in South Street, Bishop's Stortford in 1921, and introduced three new services. One of these was the 13 via Stansted and Newport to Saffron Walden, where it met Ortona's 12 from Cambridge. Among the earliest vehicles used on service 13 were AEC 'B' type double-deckers acquired from the LGOC. A separate series of numbers was used for the Bedford network. Originally service 2, the St Neots route was renumbered 4 (and later 4A), while the Huntingdon and St Ives extension became 14. The Bedford area became known as the company's Midland area, while the services in

Essex made up the Eastern area. Very much further afield, the company also started to build up a network of services in the West Country.

Until 1920 National specified the AEC 'YC' type, a chassis already supplied in huge numbers to the War Department. National placed nearly 100 in service with double-deck, saloon bus and charabanc bodies, many of which were built in the company's own workshops. From 1921 further examples of the lighter AEC 'B' type were purchased, along with a number of smaller 14-seat buses. Some had American-designed Chevrolet chassis, others were built by Burford, a company set up by National director H G Burford, and which survived until the mid-1920s. National used a mainly off-white livery to begin with, but this was changed early in 1923 to red (similar to the shade used by the LGOC).

HERTFORD & DISTRICT OMNIBUS
SERVICES

The first bus service to reach Royston from the south was provided by the short-lived Hertford & District Omnibus Services, based at Ware. One of the partners in this company was Herbert Arthur Harvey, who was involved on several occasions with bus and coach operations in the Cambridge area. In July 1921 Hertford & District introduced a route from Hertford via Puckeridge to Braughing, where a bus was outstationed. In May the following year the route was extended to Royston via Chipping, and the outstation moved to the Green Man in Royston. In October journeys were introduced via Barkway instead of Chipping, followed in November by a local service, which briefly ran from Ashwell to Heydon via Royston. The buses were mostly Daimler saloons and Straker-Squire double-deckers, which carried a dark brown and cream livery. The business was efficiently run and the buses were well maintained, but the rise and fall of Hertford & District was very rapid. The company disappeared from the scene in June 1924 although Mr Harvey did not, at least for long, as will be seen later.

Above: The early Eastern Counties Road Car fleet consisted entirely of Tilling-Stevens buses. Number **42** (**DX 3443**) was one of two TS3A saloons delivered in 1922, the first in the fleet with Ipswich registrations. The local firm Ransomes built the 36-seat bodies, and the bus is seen on service 27 from Mildenhall to Newmarket. *(Alan B Cross Collection/W Noel Jackson)*

Below: A further ten Leyland double-deckers joined the Ortona fleet in 1925, with the longer GH7 chassis and seats for 53 passengers, five more than the previous year's deliveries. Number **40** (**ER 4922**) waits to leave on service 3 from Drummer Street, which became the main terminus for country bus routes in November that year. *(Alan B Cross Collection/W Noel Jackson)*

THE EASTERN COUNTIES ROAD CAR COMPANY

This company was set up in 1919 by Walter and Thomas Wolsey to bring people into Ipswich from the surrounding villages. The Great Eastern Railway had already established a bus service (in August 1905) from the town to Shotley Pier, while local services were provided by the cars of Ipswich Corporation Tramways, which were electrified in 1903. The Wolsey brothers (who had previously been involved with bus operations in London, Brighton and Folkestone) approached Tilling in London, who arranged for four Tilling-Stevens double-deckers to be sent from Brighton to inaugurate the new services. These began in June 1919 and, after a short period of experimental operation, the new Eastern Counties Road Car Company Ltd was registered on 30th August 1919 to take over the Wolsey brothers' operations, with offices at Dog's Head Street and Lower Brook Street in Ipswich. The company expanded quickly, building up an impressive network of services in Suffolk, and many more Tilling-Stevens vehicles joined the fleet. In April 1922 ECRC took over the Great Eastern Railway's Shotley Pier bus service, together with three Thornycroft double-deckers. An earlier attempt had also been made (in June 1920) to establish operations much further north, when several services centred on the Fenland town of Wisbech were introduced, numbered between 20 and 25. These were not successful and were discontinued in September 1922. By then the company had several routes radiating from Bury St Edmunds, including service 13 to Mildenhall, which was soon extended to Beck Row. A new service 14 was also introduced, initially to Wickhambrook. By 1924 this route had reached Stradishall, with a market day extension to Haverhill. By 1925 the trunk 16 was running from Bury to Newmarket via Barrow and Gazeley, with additional market services to Newmarket (14A and 27) and Ely (13A).

Eastern Counties Road Car continued to favour Tilling-Stevens vehicles, the majority of which were single-deckers. The company also purchased a few small Bean and Dennis saloons, while from 1929 the Leyland TD1 became the preferred choice for double-deckers.

Despite its origins, the ECRC was promoted as a BAT company, although Thomas Tilling had a large shareholding. It became a Tilling & BAT subsidiary from 16th May 1928. A red livery was used, similar to that used by Tilling's fleet in London.

<< Opposite page: An Eastern Counties Road Car Company Leyland Titan TD1. *(John Banks Collection)*

Above: Among the vehicles taken over with Parnell's business in 1926 was Dennis 2½ ton saloon **EB 5893** seen here in its original livery. Fitted with a Dodson 32-seat body, it was numbered **50** by Ortona, lasting until 1931 when it passed to Eastern Counties. *(Alan B Cross Collection/W Noel Jackson)*

Below: A rare make, **EB 4858** was a 20-seat Hawkeye, also new to Parnell. It was numbered **51** and had the distinction of being owned twice by Ortona. It was sold in October 1927 to Gammond of Chatteris and reacquired five months later when the Gammond business was taken over. *(Alan B Cross Collection/W Noel Jackson)*

5. Ortona and National Expansion 1925 to 1930

Ortona's operations grew very rapidly after 1924. In Cambridge another local service (15) was started in February 1925, running hourly from Madingley Road (Storey's Way) via Grange Road, Sidgwick Avenue and the Town Centre to Milton Road (Arbury Road). In the autumn the main terminus for country buses moved from the Senate House to Drummer Street, and over the next two years Ortona's network continued to grow. Some services were taken over from other operators and they included more routes away from Cambridge. Early in 1925 the acquisition of a local operator provided several infrequent rural services and a foothold in Newmarket. The company purchased a plot of land in Fordham Road for the construction of a garage, and introduced a new route (14) to Cambridge via Dullingham, Six Mile Bottom and Fulbourn. The rural services were numbered 14A (to Haverhill), 14B (Brinkley) and 14C (Woodditton), while new routes introduced were the 16 (to Ely via Soham) and 17, which covered the 16 as far as Burwell.

A single vehicle was also acquired from the Newmarket area operator, while the next few years also saw regular intakes of new stock. Ten Leyland GH7 double-deckers with 53-seat Dodson bodies were purchased in 1925 (ER 3137-41 and ER 4918-22), together with the first three SOS vehicles in the fleet. Registered ER 3142-4, these were built by the huge 'Midland Red' company (another BET subsidiary) to the design of its Chief Engineer, L G Wyndham Shire. Mr Shire and his Traffic Manager O C Power had considerable influence on bus designs at the time, and the initials are believed to stand for 'Shire's Own Specification' or possibly 'Science Over Strength'. The Ortona vehicles had 'S'-type ('standard') chassis with the fleetname prominently cast at the top of the radiator. They were 'normal control' vehicles (the driver sat behind the engine) and their 31-seat bodies were built by Brush, also a BET associate.

The year 1926 was a significant one for Ortona. In March the company's territory expanded northwards with the purchase (for £2,500) of Parnell's Haddenham & District business. Five vehicles were included, although the Tilling-Stevens petrol-electric double-decker (EB 3557) was immediately sold to the jam manufacturer Chivers of Histon for use as a staff bus. Two Ford 'T' buses (EB 4319 and EB 4703) also remained for only a few weeks without being repainted. A rare American-built Hawkeye (EB 4858) was retained for further service, along with a Dodson-bodied Dennis 2½-ton (EB 5893). The depot at Stretham remained the property of Mr Parnell, who charged Ortona an annual rent of £25 to use it to operate his former routes. The main Haddenham - Stretham - Cambridge route was numbered 20, while the other services, which served the Ely area, eventually became 20A, 21 and 21A.

The green buses were now very much a part of the local scene but not everyone was happy. In February 1926 householders in Chesterton Road protested to Cambridge Borough Council about the buses, claiming that "the effect of the excessive speed at which these jolting juggernauts are driven is to produce an intermittent earthquake, which is doing great damage to our houses". They added "they should not be allowed to exceed 10mph, increasing to 15mph when pneumatic tyres are fitted. The present indulgence, which allows solid-tyred vehicles to bump along at 20 to 25mph is altogether unreasonable".

Despite the protests passenger numbers continued to grow. In March 1926 Ortona opened an office in the town centre at number 23 Peas Hill, which was rented from the Corporation.

DRUMMER STREET

As long ago as 1905 it was being claimed that during the University terms Cambridge had a

Above: The small size of the buses makes Drummer Street seem remarkably spacious in this view, taken soon after it opened. A Mansfield Garner (**ER 2054**) departs for its home village, passing the Ford T (**ER 2968**) operated by Major Francis to Quy and Lode. Various Ortona saloons are visible in the background, while the car park seems to be well filled. *(Cambridgeshire Collection)*

Below: Ortona purchased two new Ford T saloons, a type more often found in the fleets of the smaller operators. Both had 14-seat Lambert bodies and the first, No. **52** (**ER 6126**), is seen in Drummer Street. *(Alan B Cross Collection/W Noel Jackson)*

worse traffic problem than any other town in England. The narrow streets in the town centre became increasingly choked with traffic after the first motor cars appeared on the scene, and the problem was made worse by horse-drawn carts and animals. In 1925 the Master of a nearby college complained to the Town Council that buses terminating at King's Parade were adding to the traffic congestion there. The Council decided to address the problem, but the plan it rushed through was far from popular at the time and has caused controversy ever since. It was decided that the main terminus for country buses was to be Drummer Street. Originally known as Drusemere (meaning 'muddy pool') this short cul-de-sac once contained a dipping pool from which the public could draw water. It was bounded on three sides by the grounds of Christ's College, Emmanuel College and an ancient open space known as Christ's Pieces. This had been purchased in 1884 by the Council and landscaped as a public park. To cater for 12 country bus routes and to provide free parking for 35 cars the Council now decided to enlarge Drummer Street, resulting in the loss of one-third of an acre of the Pieces' 15 acres. Work started immediately amid a storm of angry letters to the Council and the local press. A mass meeting took place on Christ's Pieces, attended by a crowd of nearly 3,000 indignant citizens. Calls were made for a referendum and even a High Court injunction to stop the work from going ahead, while claims were also made that the noise from the buses would drown the music from the park's bandstand. Speeches were made from a farm wagon and a resolution was passed condemning the Council for its action. The crowd decided to take the protest directly to the Mayor, and the wagon, with a deputation on board and with around 1,000 following on foot, was pulled through the streets to the Mayor's house in Newton Road. The Mayor met the demonstrators and agreed to tell the Town Clerk to call a special meeting, if instructed to do so by the necessary five Councillors. There was no civil disorder and the crowd dispersed. When the Council meeting duly took place the decision was confirmed and, despite strong opposition still being voiced, the work was completed. Many regarded it as an

improvement when the new bus terminus came into use in November. Unaware of all the fuss, some passengers still went to the Senate House, where an Inspector was on hand to redirect them. Access to Drummer Street from the town centre was along the narrow, traffic-free Christ's Lane. On the other side of St Andrew's Street was the archway leading into Post Office Terrace, where in June 1927 Ortona opened a second booking and enquiry office. This was retained by Ortona's successor the Eastern Counties Omnibus Company until 1938, when a new office in Drummer Street replaced it.

NATIONAL TAKEOVERS AND EXPANSION

National was also expanding and in the early months of 1926 acquired Progress Motor Service of Huntingdon and St Ives & District Motor Service. From Progress came five vehicles of Berliet, Daimler, Guy and Thornycroft manufacture along with several routes centred on Huntingdon. The St Ives & District takeover included six vehicles of Fiat, Leyland and Thornycroft manufacture, a network of routes mainly to the north of St Ives and a garage in North Road. The routes taken over were added to National's Midland area operations. St Ives & District had previously operated into Cambridge from St Ives, Papworth and Arrington, but before National took over Mr Course sold the Papworth and Arrington routes to Bedford of Caxton and Piper of Longstowe. Ortona took over these two small operators soon afterwards.

National purchased a few more AEC 'YC' buses in 1925, before switching to Dennis for new vehicles, fitted with double- and single-deck bodies. From 1926 these were followed by a batch of Guy saloons and charabancs, and in the following year by the first of many Leyland single-deckers, fitted with bus and coach bodies. The first had normal-control Lioness PLC1 chassis, while later deliveries were of the forward-control PLSC3 type. A batch of Associated Daimler 416A saloons provided further variety, along with more Guys, this time with coach bodies. A new green livery was introduced for the coaches.

Above: Three SOS S types built by Midland Red (whose name originally appeared on the radiator) joined the Ortona fleet early in 1925. They had 31-seat Brush bodies and No. **37** (**ER 3142**) is seen here in Ely on service 16 to Newmarket. *(Alan B Cross Collection/W Noel Jackson)*

Below: Ortona acquired the operations of a Mr Bedford of Caxton early in 1926, with routes from Caxton and Papworth into Cambridge. These became service 18, on which No. **43** (**ER 5039**), another Midland Red-built S-type SOS, was a regular performer. *(Alan B Cross Collection/W Noel Jackson)*

AREA AGREEMENTS

The BET owned two suburban tramway companies in London (Metropolitan Electric Tramways and South Metropolitan Electric Tramways). When LGOC buses began to compete with its trams, the BET set up the Tramways (MET) Omnibus Co Ltd, with a fleet of Daimler buses. Before long an agreement was reached, similar to that which had been made with Tilling, which limited the size of the BET's bus operations in the capital. Unable to expand in London, the BET/BAT and Tilling set up bus operations elsewhere, initially on the south coast in Brighton, Deal, and Folkestone. Where competition was likely, the two combines agreed not to operate in each other's territories. These agreements defined the operating areas of their new subsidiaries for many years afterwards and many of these 'area agreement' companies were eventually jointly owned. Further bus operations were quickly developed elsewhere, sometimes with joint shareholdings, sometimes not. In East Anglia the BET/BAT acquired a 50% share of the Ortona business in 1913, while the Ipswich-based Eastern Counties Road Car Company, set up by Tilling in 1919, later became a BET/BAT company in which Tilling had a major interest.

AN AREA AGREEMENT AND MORE ORTONA TAKEOVERS

A notable development in March 1926 was the signing of an area agreement between Ortona and National. This established a boundary, starting from Haverhill and running through Steeple Bumpstead and Saffron Walden to Royston. From there it continued along the Old North Road to Caxton Gibbet and on to St Ives, Chatteris and Sutton. Both companies were free to run as far as the towns along this line to turn or to reach a garage, with similar fares on common sections of route, while each could run excursions from anywhere on 'their' side. This continued the process whereby bus and railway company managers divided up the country in order to establish their respective territories.

As already indicated, Ortona also expanded to the west of Cambridge in the spring of 1926

by acquiring the businesses of a Mr Bedford, based in Caxton, and H J Piper of Longstowe along with the sections of route previously run by St Ives & District. Ortona paid £650 for Bedford's two-bus operation with routes from Caxton and Papworth to Cambridge, which became service 18. From Piper came a second, less direct, route from Cambridge to Royston via Arrington and Bassingbourn, which was numbered 19. There are few details of Mr Bedford's vehicles although at one time he ran a Tilling Stevens saloon (ER 938), which later ran for Chivers of Histon as a staff bus. From Mr Piper came an AEC 'Y' (NK 4363) and a Daimler 'CD' (CE 6254).

To the north, Mr Mansfield refused to make a running agreement with Ortona on his Burwell to Cambridge route but offered to sell his business for £5,000. No sale took place and Mr Mansfield continued to compete with the larger operator, adding a new AEC saloon (ER 6531) to his fleet.

OUTSTATIONS

By this time buses were being kept overnight at the country ends of some routes. Cambridge-based vehicles previously had to run empty to (and back from) the outer terminus, but the establishment of outstations eliminated much 'dead' mileage each morning and evening. Cleaning and maintenance could be done during layover time in Cambridge, and the bus could be changed when necessary. As was the case with the smaller bus operators, local crews usually enjoyed a happy relationship with the community and much goodwill was created. By the end of 1926 Ortona had buses outstationed at Royston (two vehicles), Bassingbourn, Cottenham, Caxton and Haverhill (one vehicle each).

With its territory more clearly defined, Ortona continued to modernise and expand. The staff all remained at work during the General Strike of 1926. Town services 5 and 6 exchanged terminals and became Cherry Hinton Road to Newnham (5) and Hills Road to Newmarket Road (6). Fleet modernisation also continued in the early part of the year with the delivery of another three Dodson-bodied Leyland GH7 double-deckers (ER 5305-7) and four more SOS 'S' saloons, two each with

Above: Further SOS saloons joined the fleet in 1927. They had Q type chassis, again bodied by Brush, with seating for 37. The driver now sat alongside the engine, in what looks to be a very cramped cab. Bus **54** (**ER 7107**) is seen on new service 22, which originally ran via Burwell and Soham, but was soon extended to Ely. *(Alan B Cross Collection/W Noel Jackson)*

Below: The only AEC saloon ever operated by Ortona was this YC 24-seater, **NK 4363**. Based on a former War Department chassis, it was acquired from Piper of Longstowe in 1926 and numbered **55**. It lasted only until the following year and is seen here at Cambridge Railway Station. *(Alan B Cross Collection/W Noel Jackson)*

bodies by Brush and Ransomes (ER 5038/9 and ER 5302/3). Also added were a Leyland SG11 saloon (ER 5304) and a 14-seat Ford 'T' (ER 6126). By this stage many of the Straker-Squire vehicles had been withdrawn.

In 1927 seven more Brush-bodied SOS saloons were purchased (ER 7105-10, 8555) and these were of the improved 'Q' type, with longer, lower chassis and room for 37 passengers. They were also forward control vehicles, with the driver alongside the engine. Also new were three small Star Flyer VB3 20-seat saloons (ER 7111-3), a Leyland PLC Lioness (ER 7114) with a 20-seat "all weather" coach body, another Leyland GH7 double-decker (ER 7115) and a further Ford 'T' (ER 7838). Among the vehicles displaced were two Vulcans, the Daimler and the Hawkeye. New services introduced from Cambridge were 22 to Soham via Burwell, 23 to St Ives via Histon and Willingham and 23A to St Ives via the main Huntingdon road. The former Haddenham & District service 20 was extended to Sutton, while alternate buses on local service 2 now continued along Huntingdon Road to Girton Corner. In June the company rented (for £30 per year) a second town centre office at 7 Post Office Terrace, closer to Drummer Street than the Peas Hill premises. A plot of land was also purchased in Ely for the construction of a garage.

1928 - A MEMORABLE YEAR FOR ORTONA

In January 1928 Mr G H Iles was appointed General Manager (he was previously Secretary) and he moved into the house at 110 Hills Road, next to the garage. It was to be a memorable year. In February two all-Leyland PLSC3 Lions arrived (ER 8886/7), with 36-seat saloon bodies, and a month later Ortona's first proper luxury coaches were delivered. Registered ER 8801-3, they also had Leyland Lion PLSC3 chassis but were fitted with 'all-weather' canvas-roofed bodies, built by London Lorries. The company also took delivery of its first covered-top double-deckers soon afterwards. John Walford had been keen to introduce these for several years but the narrow streets of Cambridge prevented their introduction until the new Leyland TD1, with

its low-built chassis, was available. The new buses (ER 8804-7) had Leyland bodies with 51 seats, those on the upper deck arranged in the 'lowbridge' four-in-a-row pattern with a sunken side gangway. Despite the closed tops, these buses had open staircases. They entered service on country routes 3, 4, 7 and 8 and were immediately very popular. The last to be delivered was ER 8806, which arrived in May. In the same month James Berry Walford died. From small beginnings with four second-hand buses he had seen Ortona develop into a thriving and successful business, which by the end of the year had more than 60 vehicles and was still growing. Ortona also purchased a second-hand Dennis single-decker in 1928 from Herbert Harvey, formerly a Director of Hertford & District, who was now running a haulage business in Harston. This vehicle was kept only until the following year.

EXPANSION IN ELY AND ON THE BEDFORD ROAD

Ortona's operations in the Ely area expanded rapidly, with the opening of a new garage there and the transfer of several routes from National. Ortona also acquired the business of G O Gammond of Chatteris (jointly with the Peterborough Electric Traction Company), followed by Bowyer & Topper's Ely & District services and a Reo Sprinter (FE 9094). Bowyer & Topper ran a service from Littleport to Cambridge, which Ortona operated for a short while before the road was left to the local operator Bert Washington. Negotiations also took place with Mr Washington (whose routes mainly served the area to the north of Ely) regarding the possible acquisition of his business, but he declined to sell. However, Ortona became the major operator in Ely and by the end of the year had an impressive local network. In January the extension of service 22 from Soham gave the company three routes to Cambridge (9, 20 and 22). By the end of the year there were also regular services to Newmarket (16), March (24) and St Ives (25/25A) as well as several other routes to the surrounding villages.

Still more new routes were introduced from Cambridge. From 1st October a new joint service 29 to Bedford via St Neots provided

Above: The three Star Flyer VB3 saloons had 20-seat Ransomes bodies. In this view No. **13** (**ER 7111**) waits in Drummer Street to depart for Newmarket Races. *(Alan B Cross Collection/W Noel Jackson)*

Below: Also awaiting racing enthusiasts is **ER 7114**, the solitary Leyland Lioness charabanc. The hood is up, suggesting uncertain weather conditions, while the plain ORTONA fleetname contrasts with the more elaborate version used on the buses. *(Alan B Cross Collection/W Noel Jackson)*

further evidence of the company's good relations with National. It was Ortona's first regular long-distance route and initially ran every two hours. Each company provided one bus and Ortona's contribution was usually a Leyland PLSC1 Lion. In Cambridge the route terminated at Ortona's Hills Road garage, for although Drummer Street had only been in use for three years it was already becoming congested. Whether one additional bus every two hours would have made the situation much worse is open to question, but the new arrangements were not very convenient for passengers wishing to reach the town centre. Service 29 also had a Sunday service, the first to be provided by Ortona. Sunday buses were introduced on most of the other routes soon afterwards, although the town services did not have them until February 1929 and they were not always very profitable. With the introduction of service 29, the local 15 was withdrawn between Madingley Road and Market Street, although the Milton Road section was extended to King's Hedges Road. In November the recently introduced service 23A was diverted between Cambridge and St Ives via Oakington, Longstanton, Swavesey and Fen Drayton and extended from St Ives to Somersham. In the same month the tenancy of St Paul's garage ended following the enlargement of the Hills Road premises. Other new services introduced during 1928 were 18A (Comberton via Grantchester and Barton), while to the south another variation of service 13 branched off at Linton to serve Hadstock, with the main Haverhill service briefly extended to Kedington. The "Haverhill & District" network (as it was referred to in timetables) offered even more variety, with new sections into Haverhill from Balsham (this was soon abandoned), Thurlow and The Camps, as well as from Linton to Saffron Walden. All were referred to as service 13A and for a while Ortona had nine different routes with this number.

TILLING & BAT COMPANIES AND RAILWAY INTERESTS

Ortona's continued growth was helped by an additional influx of capital. On 16th May 1928 the Ortona Motor Company, the Peterborough Electric Traction Company and the Eastern Counties Road Car Company all became Tilling & BAT subsidiaries, following the agreement between the two organisations to formalise all their existing agreements. The main-line railway companies had also agreed to buy shares in the T&BAT bus companies, and from 28th February 1929 the London & North Eastern Railway (LNER) and the London, Midland & Scottish Railway (LMSR) both became shareholders in Ortona and PET. Their involvement led to the purchase of 30 new vehicles, the largest annual intake since operations began, delivered in small batches throughout the year. There were no fewer than 14 more Leyland TD1 double-deckers with covered tops. The first five (VE 301-5) were delivered in January and carried Hall-Lewis bodywork. They were joined in November by Brush-bodied VE 2039-43. All these had highbridge bodywork (with centre gangways on both decks) and seats for 52 passengers, and they featured the usual open staircases. The four delivered in October (VE 1965-7 and VE 1994) were even more interesting. Intended for country routes, they had lowbridge Leyland 48-seat bodies and were the first (and as it turned out the only) fully enclosed double-deckers to be operated by Ortona. Three new all-Leyland single-deckers were VE 306, a 32-seat Lion PLSC3, and VE 309/10 with 29 seats on Tiger TS2 chassis. Dennis supplied five small 20-seat saloons in the shape of VE 307/8 (with Ransomes bodywork on G-type chassis) and VE 1102/3 and VE 1952 (Strachan-bodied GL-types). Ransomes and Brush supplied the bodywork for five more SOS saloons (VE 501-4 and VE 1101), delivered in the spring with chassis type 'M', featuring double rear wheels. 'M' stood for 'Madam', for the improved design featuring 34 individual seats was intended to appeal particularly to discerning lady passengers. Whether or not it succeeded is uncertain, for Ortona purchased no further SOS vehicles. A final trio of Leyland Lion saloons with LT1 chassis (VE 2142-4) were delivered at the end of the year, with Dodson 32-seat bodies. A slight change was made to the fleetname style, which now used a less ornate style of lettering. The new single-deckers also had white-painted roofs, while

Above: Ortona's official view of the solitary Leyland Lioness charabanc, **ER 7114**, appeared in the guide to the company's services, where it was described as "the last word in comfort, speed and safety." *(John Banks Collection)*

Below: In contrast to the new Leylands, the Straker-Squire charabancs looked very old-fashioned. With its hood up, **CE 7025** could have been mistaken for an Army lorry. These vehicles were withdrawn in 1928. *(Alan B Cross Collection/W Noel Jackson)*

VE 301-5 also had white window surrounds, although these were later repainted green.

The involvement of the railway companies allowed the introduction of road/rail interavailability. Passengers with return bus tickets could now make their return journey by train, or vice versa, at no extra charge. Initially available on service 29 between Cambridge and Bedford, this facility was also introduced on service 11 (which followed the Cambridge to Mildenhall branch as far as Burwell) and later on several other routes.

ORTONA REACHES PETERBOROUGH

The new buses replaced the last Straker-Squire and Vulcan vehicles but most were used to increase the size of the fleet as the route network continued to grow. Most important was service 32 to Huntingdon and Peterborough, which started in May 1929. With a journey time of 2¼ hours it was operated jointly with Peterborough Electric Traction, who confusingly used the number 16 for their share of the service. Each company initially provided a SOS saloon but it soon became necessary to allocate double-deckers.

THE PETERBOROUGH ELECTRIC
TRACTION COMPANY LTD

When the introduction of horse trams was being planned in Cambridge, similar proposals were being considered by the City Council in Peterborough. Several schemes were discussed but not proceeded with, and the horse buses already operating in the city continued to provide services. There were no further tramway developments until May 1899, when the BET applied to operate electric trams in the city. After a great deal of debate the construction of the lines began three years later. On 5th August 1902 the BET registered the Peterborough Electric Traction Company Ltd as a subsidiary company, with its depot and offices in Lincoln Road. Services started on 24th January 1903 with the opening of the line from the Market Place to Walton, followed a week later by the line to Dogsthorpe. Trams began operating to Newark in March, completing the network. The total route mileage was 5¼ miles and the gauge used was

3ft 6in. Operations began with twelve open top double-deck cars, built by Brush with seating for 48 passengers (26 upstairs and 22 down) and numbered from 1 to 12. The livery was lake brown and cream, including the BET wheel and magnet device, and the services were an immediate success. Two more cars were purchased from Brush in 1904 and were numbered 14 and 15.

Objections by the City Council and the Great Eastern Railway had prevented the introduction of trams on the south side of the River Nene. In April 1913 the company introduced motor buses on routes to Stanground and London Road, initially with four Straker-Squire single-deckers (two saloons and two charabancs). No more bus services were started until after the First World War, when routes were introduced to Woodston and further afield to Crowland and Whittlesey. The first buses carried the same brown and cream livery as the trams but this was changed in 1924 to red and white, lined in gold. Buses originally carried the fleetname 'PETERBOROUGH ELECTRIC TRACTION CO LTD' but this was later shortened to 'PETERBOROUGH' with 'TRACTION CO LTD' below. By 1924 the company still only had nine buses but in the years up to 1930 the network grew rapidly, particularly after PET became a Tilling & BAT subsidiary in 1928. The company's policy for new vehicles was broadly similar to Ortona's. After buying Straker-Squires, it turned mainly to SOS and Leyland, as well as an assortment of other makes from the fleets of small operators it had taken over. Buses replaced the trams in August 1930, when the Walton tram route was linked with the Woodston bus route to form an important cross-city service. By then PET's country bus routes covered an area stretching from Spalding to Cambridge and from Stamford to Ely and King's Lynn. There were depots in March, Oundle, Whittesey and Wisbech as well as several outstations, and the fleet consisted of around 75 vehicles.

In March 1929 Ortona had acquired two vehicles with the business of Meacham, based in Newmarket, with routes to Stetchworth Leys (which became service 33), Chippenham (34) and Haverhill via The Thurlows (35). In June summer express coaches were introduced from

Above: One of two all-Leyland PLSC3 Lions delivered in February 1928, No. 61 (**ER 8886**) stands in front of Cambridge Railway Station on service 1, showing the simpler lettering adopted soon afterwards for the fleetname. The bus later received a new forward entrance body. *(Alan B Cross Collection/W Noel Jackson)*

Below: Illustrating another fleetname style is No. 23 (**ER 8803**), one of the three Leyland PLSC3 luxury charabancs new in 1928. The 28-seat body was built by London Lorries, whose name would probably not have impressed potential passengers. *(Alan B Cross Collection/W Noel Jackson)*

Cambridge to Hunstanton (service 90), Clacton (91) and, jointly with the Eastern Counties Road Car Company, to Felixstowe (92). Another new country route was the 36 from Cambridge to Steeple Bumpstead. The town network became even more comprehensive, with the introduction of 1A (Newmarket Road - Railway Station), 2A (Coldham's Lane - Post Office), 30 (Great St Mary's - Borough Cemetery) and 31 (Hinton Avenue - Newnham), bringing buses to several previously unserved roads. Service 30A was also introduced as an extension of the 30 to the villages of Fen Ditton and Horningsea. Town service 6 was extended at both ends, from Glebe Road further along Hills Road to Queen Edith's Way, and from Stanley Road to Ditton Walk. On the country routes the Balsham section of service 13 now continued to West Wratting and the 18A to Great Eversden, while service 11 was diverted via Reach. By the end of the year the fleet stood at 77 vehicles, all fitted with pneumatic tyres.

THE EASTERN NATIONAL OMNIBUS COMPANY

In the meantime, National had continued to purchase large numbers of Leylands in the shape of PLSC3 Lions (mostly with bus bodies) and PLC1 Lioness coaches. The first Leyland TD1 double-deckers also joined the fleet, carrying standard Leyland lowbridge bodywork with open staircases. The bus livery changed to two shades of green and white, although Bedford-based buses retained the previous red livery for a while. The summer of 1928 also saw National continue its expansion by acquiring the Biggleswader Blue Bus Service of Mrs M A Atkinson. Most of her routes ran only on market days and included services to Royston and St Neots, which were numbered 35B and 35C. No vehicles were included.

During 1929 the railway companies held discussions with National with a view to taking over their bus operations. Following the negotiations, National's operations in Bedfordshire and Essex passed to the new Eastern National Omnibus Company Ltd from midnight on 31st December 1929, with the LNER and the LMSR each holding a 25%

share in the new company. The Eastern National name had actually been registered on 28th February 1929, when the two railway companies also acquired shares in Ortona and Peterborough Electric Traction. The LNER also held shares in the Eastern Counties Road Car Company. The new Eastern National company continued to purchase new Leylands, adding LT2 Lions and TS3 Tigers to its fleet along with more TD1 Titan double-deckers, while a batch of AEC Regent I double-deckers also entered service. Eastern National continued to use the green and white livery of its predecessor.

MORE ORTONA TAKEOVERS

Modernisation of the Ortona fleet continued during 1930. Sixteen new vehicles were purchased, comprising three Leyland Tiger TS2 saloons (VE 2874-6) with 26-seat Ransomes bodies, an all-Leyland Lion LT2 30-seater (VE 3783) and another twelve Leyland TD1s (VE 3198/9, 4200-9), all with Brush 52-seat highbridge bodies which once again featured outside staircases. Five of the original SOS 'S' types of 1925 were converted by BMMO to 'ODD' specification and fitted with new United 26-seat bodies, which gave them a lower, more modern appearance, the vehicles involved being ER 3142/4, ER 5038 and ER 5302/3.

There was further growth in the Newmarket area, including the introduction of Ortona's second route to Cambridge, which commenced on 26th April 1930. For some reason it was given the out-of-sequence number 62, and at the Cambridge end it ran in competition with Long's service from The Thurlows. The takeover of the business of A E Norman of Exning and some operations of Challice Brothers of Newmarket added four small saloons to Ortona's fleet, including two Chevrolets from Norman (CF 8117 and UT 2055) and a Fiat from Challice Bros. These had very short lives with Ortona. A few older vehicles were withdrawn, and four old Leyland double-deckers were sold to Peterborough Electric Traction.

Early in 1930 the market day buses in the Haverhill and Saffron Walden area, all of which ran as 13A, were renumbered in the

Above: The all-Leyland TD1 had a lower chassis than previous types and allowed Ortona to introduce covered-top double-deckers in 1928, although they retained the traditional open staircases. In this view, No. 2 (**ER 8804**) pauses on the main road service 8 to Royston. *(Author's Collection)*

Below: Two Dennis G 20-seat saloons were purchased in the winter of 1928/9 of which **VE 308** is seen here before entering service. The 20-seat bodies were built by Ransomes. *(Author's Collection)*

range 40 to 48, including a new 43 from Debden Green to Saffron Walden. Other service developments included a city service (84) in Ely, which attracted few passengers and was soon discontinued. In six eventful years Ortona's route network had grown considerably. The timetable for October 1930 shows the following new services in and from Cambridge (all the country routes started from Drummer Street):

1A Newmarket Road (Coldham's Lane) - Mill Road - Tenison Road - Railway Station

2A Coldham's Lane - Vinery Road - Mill Road - Drummer Street - Post Office

14 Cambridge - Fulbourn - Six Mile Bottom - Dullingham - Newmarket

15 Market Street Corner - Milton Road - King's Hedges Road

18 Cambridge - Barton - Comberton - Toft - Bourn - Longstowe - Caxton - Great Gransden - Waresley

18 Cambridge - Barton - Comberton - Toft - Bourn - Longstowe - Caxton - Papworth

18A Cambridge - Grantchester - Barton - Comberton - Toft - The Eversdens

19 Cambridge - Barton - Haslingfield - Harlton - Orwell - Arrington - Bassingbourn - Royston

20 Cambridge - Milton - Waterbeach - Chittering - Stretham - Wilburton - Haddenham - Sutton - Ely

22 Cambridge - Barnwell - Quy - The Swaffhams - Burwell - Fordham - Wicken - Soham - Ely

23 Cambridge - Histon - Cottenham - Rampton - Willingham - Over - Swavesey - Fen Drayton - Fenstanton - St Ives

23A Cambridge - Girton - Oakington - Longstanton - Over - Swavesey - Fen Drayton - Fenstanton - St Ives - Needingworth - Bluntisham - Colne - Somersham - Chatteris

29 Cambridge - Eltisley - St Neots - Eaton Socon - Great Barford - Bedford (Joint service with ENOC)

30 Great St Mary's - Trumpington Street - East Road - Newmarket Road (Borough Cemetery)

30A Great St Mary's - Trumpington Street - East Road - Newmarket Road - Fen Ditton - Horningsea

31 Cherry Hinton Road (Hinton Avenue) - Coleridge Road - Mill Road - Drummer Street - Post Office - Silver Street - Newnham (Grantchester Road)

32 Cambridge - Fenstanton - Godmanchester - Huntingdon - Great Stukeley - Sawtry - Stilton - Yaxley - Peterborough (Joint service with PET)

36 Cambridge - Gog Magog Hills - The Abingtons - Linton - Bartlow - The Camps - Haverhill

62 Cambridge - Fulbourn - Balsham - West Wratting - Weston Colville - Carlton - Brinkley - Dullingham - Wood Ditton - Cheveley - Newmarket

90 Cambridge - Ely - Hunstanton (Summer express)

91 Cambridge - Haverhill - Clacton (Summer express)

92 Cambridge - Newmarket - Felixstowe (Summer express/Joint service with ECRC)

Despite all the takeovers there were still several competitors. As well as providing a challenge to Ortona, some of the smaller operators were also battling against each other and, as will be seen in the next chapter, the competition was not confined to local bus services.

Above: Later in 1929 three Dennis GL saloons arrived. With 20-seat bodies by Strachan and Brown, they replaced the remaining Vulcans in the fleet. *(Author's Collection)*

Below: Further modernity came with the four fully enclosed TD1s. These had lowbridge bodies and entered service on country routes in October 1929. Few photographs of them seem to exist but this one, probably No. **78** (**VE 1965**), is seen in Drummer Street with its crew on service 3. *(Author's Collection)*

6. The Rapid Growth of the Express Coach Network

By the mid-1920s bus services had become a well-established feature of everyday life. From 1925 the development of faster, more comfortable vehicles led to the rapid expansion of long-distance express coach services. Strikes by railwaymen in 1926 led some travellers to look for alternatives, and the development of express coaches was also helped by improvements to the main roads, many of which were being tarmacked for the first time. Two new coach companies (Varsity and Westminster) set up businesses in Cambridge and from the outset they were mainly providers of express services. Both companies had short lives, although one coach operator (York Brothers) remains in business to this day.

THE EASY MOTOR COACH COMPANY

George York originally established a carrier's business in Cogenhoe (near Northampton) with a horse and cart. In 1924 he bought a Ford Model 'T' lorry, which he used to transport general goods and coal. Before long he was carrying passengers on a casual basis and in 1925 he began a regular service into Northampton, for which the lorry was thoroughly cleaned and its body replaced by a passenger one. Loadings increased and a second Model 'T' was purchased, followed by a Chevrolet and a Renault. George was then joined by his older brother Frederick, previously a blacksmith. The purchase of another lorry allowed the original Ford to be rebodied by Waveney of Lowestoft as a 14-seat bus. Soon afterwards, the York Brothers began running excursions to the coast, which were an immediate success. From these beginnings grew a regular express service from Northampton to Great Yarmouth via St Neots, Cambridge and Newmarket, which is believed to have started in 1926. The first luxury coach was not purchased until 1930, this being a Maudslay ML3BC (RP 8768), with a 32-seat

Metcalfe body. New Maudslays then joined the fleet each year until 1936, the most notable being the 1935 pair (VV 3698 and VV 3834) with the advanced SF40 chassis, featuring a set-back front axle although the engine was vertically mounted at the front. They had very modern looking bodywork by Grose of Northampton, who built several coach bodies for the Yorks. The coaches carried a blue livery and were operated as The Easy Motor Coach Company, although the family name was always included on vehicles and publicity material. The service settled down to a Friday to Monday operation from Easter to the end of September (a pattern followed by many summer holiday coach services) and the stop in Cambridge was originally in Maid's Causeway. In 1937 a switch was made to Leyland for new coaches and two Tiger TS7s (NV 9197/8) were delivered, followed in 1938 by a pair of Cubs (ABD 700/1), all with Burlingham bodies. Further second-hand Maudslays, including another SF40 (AOX 698) were purchased in the years up to 1940, when the Yarmouth service was suspended until after the war.

EMPIRE'S BEST COACHES

A few years after York Brothers introduced their Yarmouth service, the splendidly named Empire's Best Coaches joined the already varied selection to be seen in Cambridge. Owned by Webber Brothers and based at Wood Green in north London, Empire's Best already operated a daily service from London to Clacton. In 1930, to make better use of surplus coaches, they began to operate further from home, with a weekend service from Clacton via Haverhill and Cambridge to Rugby, Coventry and Birmingham. It ran from Whitsun until the end of September and during its first summer it was so popular that extra coaches had to be hired from other operators. In 1931 it was rerouted via Market Harborough

Right and below: Highbridge bodies were fitted to the other ten TD1s delivered in 1929, making them more suitable for town services. Numbers **27/69** (**VE 301/3**) were of the first batch, which had Hall-Lewis bodywork. *(Author's Collection)*

and Leicester instead of Rugby, and an additional daily service from Clacton to Northampton via Rushden was also introduced, although this only lasted for one season. From 1932 the service ran to Birmingham on Fridays, Saturdays and Sundays and to Clacton on Saturdays, Sundays and Mondays. As with some of the other summer coach services, the Cambridge stop was well out of the town centre, and the blue Empire's Best coaches called at the Spread Eagle in Lensfield Road. Empire's Best ran a mixed fleet, which included Gilford and Leyland coaches and a Star VB4.

THE VARSITY SALOON COACH COMPANY

The Varsity Saloon Coach Company of Cambridge was established in October 1927. One of the Directors may have been a Mr Longland, while another was W Francis, possibly the same Major Francis who ran the bus service from Lode to Cambridge. The office was initially in Alexandra Street, not far from the Ortona premises in Post Office Terrace, while the coaches were kept at the Merton Arms in Northampton Street.

The Watch Committee authorised Varsity to run a daily express service from the Merton Arms (already a country bus terminus) to London (Langham Place). It followed the main A10 trunk road through Royston and Ware and the first two coaches (ER 8506 and ER 8508) were Reo Pullmans with 20-seat 'all weather' bodywork, built respectively by the Economy Motor Co Ltd (known as Emcol) of Lowestoft and Eaton Coach Works (Taylor) of Norwich. Early in 1928 they were joined by a third Reo (ER 8507) and another coach registered XP 5977, although no further details are known. All carried a livery of light Cambridge blue and white, although a darker blue soon replaced the white. By December there were two daily journeys, increased to three by the following April, with one coach outstationed in London. The garage and office moved to Godestone Road, while Drummer Street became the terminus for the coaches.

The business soon ran into financial difficulties and by October 1928 ownership had passed to a partnership of Arthur Aitchison

Speak, Herbert Arthur Harvey and William Smith. Captain Speak owned premises in Upper Regent Street in London, which became the Varsity offices and waiting room. He had previously worked for United Automobile Services in Darlington and had later set up Reliance Express Motors Ltd in competition with United, apparently with backing from Mr Harvey. Mr Smith, a former mayor of Lowestoft, was a chartered accountant and he became company secretary. Mr Harvey was previously a Director of Hertford & District. After that company ceased trading in 1924 he moved to the north and eventually became involved with East Yorkshire Motor Services. In 1926 he moved south again and set up as a haulage contractor in Harston. He was a skilled engineer and he took responsibility for the maintenance and the day-to-day running of the coaches. He was also something of an innovator and he developed Harvey's Paraffin Attachment. This made it possible for the coaches to run on paraffin, which cost only 4½d a gallon compared to petrol at 1/3d a gallon. The engine was started from cold using petrol, then switched over to paraffin after a few miles. On journeys from Cambridge this operation was usually performed at the AA box in Trumpington, at the junction of Hauxton Road and Shelford Road. It was claimed that fuel costs would be reduced by 60% ("Harvey's Paraffin Attachment pays the driver's wages"), and bring about the end of carbon deposits, pitted or sticky valves, gummed pistons and seized rings. Despite these promised benefits the paraffin sometimes found its way into the sump and diluted the engine oil and, unless the oil was changed frequently, the consequences were very expensive. Manufactured by the Nuswift Engineering Company of Elland, Yorkshire, the attachment was patented and marketed to the motor trade at a cost of £15 complete, and a local depot was set up at 38 New Square. The use of paraffin finally ended when increases in excise duty made it uneconomic.

Varsity's new owners purchased three more Eaton-bodied Reo coaches (ER 9240, ER 9845/6) and these were licensed when new to 'Reliance Express, Cambridge'. The London terminus moved for a few weeks to the Central London Coach Station in Cartwright

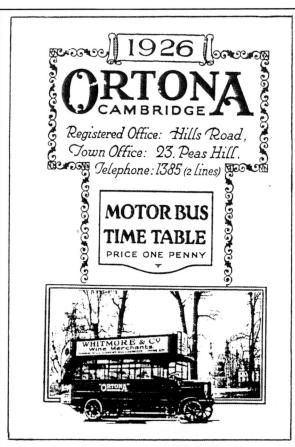

Motor Bus Services and Motor Coach Tours in

EAST ANGLIA

Conducted by the Ortona Motor Co. Ltd.

59

Gardens, off Euston Road. It soon reverted to Langham Place, which was a short distance from the Upper Regent Street premises. The business thrived and traffic quickly built up, especially after the speed limit for vehicles with pneumatic tyres was increased to 20mph from 1st October 1928.

WESTMINSTER COACHING SERVICES

In the meantime, a competitor had taken to the roads. In 1924 three partners (James Rich, Francis Rose and William Coleman) formed the Westminster Omnibus Company. They operated their first bus, a Dennis, on any route where a profit could be made but with the passing of the London Road Traffic Act in that year they had to run proper timetabled services. They chose routes 73 and 76 and ordered four more Dennis buses. Another pair followed in 1927, when the Belgravia Omnibus Company was purchased. At around the same time, the company introduced express coach services and tours to the east and south coast resorts, and these operated as 'Westminster Coaches.' The coaches started from a stand in Arthur Street, just off Charing Cross Road and close to the company's offices.

An application for an express service between Cambridge and London was made, and this started early in 1928. A separate company 'Westminster Coaching Services' of 19, Pentonville Road, London N1 was set up to operate the service, and initially there were two daily return journeys, with an additional coach on Thursdays and Saturdays. After leaving Cambridge, Westminster shared Varsity's route via the A10 to Royston, before heading for Baldock and reaching the capital via the Great North Road (A1). The last coach to arrive back in Cambridge each day made a circuit of the town for the convenience of passengers. The service was started by a Gilford 166SD (UC 5468) and a Dennis F (YU 9391). Both had normal-control chassis with luxuriously-appointed 20-seat 'parlour saloon' bodies, that on the Gilford built by Redhead. In contrast to the firm's London buses (which were red) the coach livery was buff with a brown waistrail and black window surrounds. Garage and office facilities were set up at the premises of Walter Moss in Hills Road. Westminster's

operations expanded very rapidly. In February one journey was extended daily via Newmarket (where a coach was based) to and from Bury St Edmunds. By July three coaches served Newmarket daily, (with two coaches based there) while another served Huntingdon and St Ives. By November six daily journeys were operating between London and Cambridge, three of which diverted via the RAF Station at Duxford. As the network was built up, five more 20-seat Dennis F coaches were purchased between April and October 1928, these being UC 5677, UC 5795, YX 1491 (all with bodywork by Dennis,) YX 5782 and XV 1403.

ACME PULLMAN, AERO EXPRESS, EASTERN IMPERIAL

On 5th October 1928 Acme Pullman Services Ltd introduced an express coach service from London via Epping to Bishop's Stortford. It started from the company's offices in Bishopsgate and was an immediate success. A half-hourly service was provided by the company's fast, comfortable coaches, which were far more popular with long-distance travellers than the parallel London General buses. A few journeys continued northwards up the A11, competing with National's service 13 as far as Saffron Walden and then continuing via Chesterford and Six Mile Bottom to Newmarket, where a booking office was established at number 1 Albert Street. Like all the company's offices, this also included a comfortable waiting room.

Another express service to use the A11 was introduced in the spring of 1929 by Aero Express Coaches of Buckhurst Hill. In the spring of 1929 this operator introduced coaches from London to Cambridge via Bishop's Stortford and Saffron Walden. For a short while both Varsity and Westminster faced competition from this service, which ran three times on weekdays and twice on Sundays. It was soon transferred to Eastern Imperial Motorways, but it did not last for very long.

COMPETITION ON THE ROADS TO LONDON

Soon afterwards, Varsity introduced an

Above: One of the three Leyland Lion LT1 saloons received at the end of 1929, No. **67** (**VE 2144**) waits to depart on the main road service 13 to Haverhill. From 1928 Ortona single-deckers had destination blinds instead of boards, while the roof luggage rack is another notable feature. *(D S Deacon)*

Below: The trio of Leyland Tiger TS2 saloons delivered in 1930 were very attractive vehicles. In this view No. **86** (**VE 2874**) shows off its well-appointed Ransomes body, which had comfortable seating for 26 passengers. *(Cambridgeshire Collection)*

additional service from Cambridge to London via Saffron Walden, Bishop's Stortford and the A11. Traffic built up on this route and on the original service via the A10 and, encouraged by their success, Varsity introduced a daily service from London via Uxbridge, Beaconsfield and High Wycombe to Oxford. After operating from various rented premises, the company eventually had its own garage in Botley Road, as well as renting an office in Gloucester Green Coach Station, where the service terminated. These new services required more coaches, and by September 1929 Varsity had purchased a Studebaker (VE 334) and five 26-seat Gilford 166SD coaches (VE 1154, 1626, 1709, 1797/8), three of which had Duple bodywork. On 31st October the business was formed into a limited company Varsity Express Motors Ltd. The Godestone Road premises were now inadequate for the size of the fleet, which moved to a new, purpose-built garage at 68 Newmarket Road. Two more Duple-bodied Gilford 166SDs (VE 2132, 2296) were added to the fleet at the end of the year.

Varsity's rapid growth also continued in 1930, when five AEC 'Regal' coaches were added to stock. They were 28 seaters with bodywork by Dodson (VE 3031-3) and Duple (VE 3440/1). On June 10th 1930 a second company was registered, in order to extend the Cambridge-London service via Winchester to Bournemouth. The new company was Varsity Coaches Limited, which began operations with six Leyland Tiger TS2 coaches (UL 5354-6, XV 3774-6). These had Dodson bodies and were purchased from Palanquin Coaches, London W3, who had used them on its London-Manchester service. A local office was established at Holdenhurst Road in Bournemouth, and three daily departures were advertised in the summer of 1930, with a return fare of 19/6d (97½ pence). In January 1931 the service was extended to Poole. The Cambridge - London services were also increased, with five weekday coaches each on the routes via Ware (six on Sundays) and Bishop's Stortford (two on Sundays). In addition to its express services, Varsity Express also operated excursions and tours from Drummer Street.

In the meantime Westminster's growth had been equally impressive. The first half of 1929

saw the frequency of the existing services increased, as well as a new daily service in April to Great Yarmouth (where a coach was outstationed) and Lowestoft. The Huntingdon service was diverted at St Ives to run via Chatteris and March to Wisbech, while from May one weekday coach also reached Ely. In June the company introduced coaches between London and Great Yarmouth via Ipswich, Southwold and Lowestoft, with another vehicle based at Yarmouth. The Ely service was increased to twice daily, and by the summer there were up to eight coaches between London and Cambridge, three to Newmarket and Bury St Edmunds and two to Wisbech and Yarmouth. In October yet another new route was introduced, linking London via Newmarket with Norwich, where an office was established. A large intake of new coaches was obviously necessary, and these consisted of two new Gilfords 166SDs with Hoyal bodies (UL 4824/5). These were followed by five more Dennis F vehicles with Dodson bodies (UL 7590, 7692, 9654 and 9813, together with six forward-control Dennis FS types, which also had Dennis bodywork (UU 5144-8, GF 9510). These were the last 20-seaters to be purchased, and were supplemented late in 1930 by larger, 31-seat coaches. These had Gilford 168OT chassis ('OT' standing for 'over type' meaning 'forward control'). These featured Gruss air suspension, which could easily be adjusted to improve the ride quality, and the bodies were built by Gilford's subsidiary company Wycombe. They also had low entrance steps and were luxuriously fitted out with individual leather upholstered armchair seats, curtains and veneered panelling. Further refinement was provided by heaters, though how effective these were is not certain, for Westminster's advertisements of the time also listed travel rugs as being supplied. Registered GK 3401-11, the Gilfords had American-manufactured Lycoming engines and were noted for their speed.

CHALLENGES FROM THE LOCAL COACHMEN

With up to eighteen express departures to choose from on weekdays via three different

Above: The final double-deckers to join the Ortona fleet comprised a further twelve Leyland TD1s with Brush bodywork, similar to the second 1929 batch. Number **89** (**VE 3198**) stands with its crew at the Huntingdon Road terminus of service 2. *(R Warwick Collection)*

Below: Very eye-catching in the 1930s, the York Brothers Maudslay SF40 coaches had Grose 32-seat bodywork and looked quite capable of continuing straight into the sea when they reached Yarmouth. The first one (**VV 3698**) is illustrated, showing 'CAMBRIDGE' and 'NEWMARKET' on either side of the door. The large 'E' (for Easy) is also clear for all to see. *(R Warwick Collection)*

routes (as well as two railway lines), passengers between Cambridge and London had an excellent choice of services. Ortona now had several express routes to the coast but made an agreement with Varsity and Westminster not to introduce any services to London. It is not clear what Ortona gained from this, although the coach companies may have agreed not to compete with Ortona on its bus routes. Despite the agreement with Ortona, the two express coach operators had to contend with additional competition in 1930 from two small Cambridge firms. These were Brown's 'Lord Astor Coaches' and Wheatley's 'Cambridge Comfort Coaches'. Both were mainly involved in private hire work, using vehicles of Gilford, Lancia and Reo manufacture. They now began to organise regular excursions to London during busy periods, when they could be sure of good loadings by undercutting the Varsity and Westminster fares. In those days there were few controlling regulations to prevent their activities, although they could not offer regular departure times or pick up passengers in the London area. Westminster experienced far more serious competition from other established operators running express coaches to London from East Anglia. As well as the Acme Pullman service from Newmarket, these included United Automobile Services, Norfolk Coachways, Hillman, Eastern Motorways and Bush & Twiddy's 'East Anglian Highways', all advertising express coaches from Yarmouth, Norwich, Thetford and Newmarket, with most serving Lowestoft as well. Competition between London and Yarmouth was very

intense, and Westminster's service from London to Yarmouth via Ipswich lasted only until October 1930.

In the face of such intense competition, vehicles and staff were kept extremely busy. A typical Varsity driver's early shift might start at 6.00am, with the first journey on the 6.30 departure to London via Ware. Mr Harvey had a reputation for checking on the punctuality of coaches on the Ware route as they passed his bungalow, and some drivers would deliberately coast past so he could not hear them. Returning to Cambridge at 12.00, the same driver would then take the 1.30pm departure to London via Bishop's Stortford. Back in Cambridge, the coach would be taken into the garage to be prepared for the next day. The driver's day would finish at 7.00pm, although sometimes a third trip to London might be necessary. In those days there were no restrictions on the number of hours worked, and as the competition intensified some Varsity drivers even offered to work a shift for no pay in a bid to keep their jobs. Despite the hardships drivers took a great pride in their work. They were allocated their own coaches and took such pride in them that their appearance was usually immaculate. One driver in particular would spend much of his time in London between trips polishing his coach as though it were his own car, and when flowers were plentiful he would place a posy in every wall vase in the vehicle. Varsity has been described as a friendly company and was very well regarded. Unrestricted competition on this scale was not destined to last for very much longer, however.

Above: A line-up of Varsity Dennis coaches outside the Newmarket Road garage, after operations moved there from Godestone Road in October 1929. *(M G Doggett Collection)*

Below: One of the five Dennis F coaches new to Westminster in 1928. By the end of the year the company had six daily departures to London via Royston, Baldock and the Great North Road. **YX 5782** is on the Emmanuel College side of Drummer Street, which was traditionally used by the smaller operators. *(John Banks Collection)*

7. More Small Operators

Several more village busmen took to the roads in the 1920s. Some competed with the growing networks of Ortona and National, while others provided links from villages not served by the established operators.

F W BRAND

Frederick William Brand started as a carrier in the village of Elsworth and by 1930 he had also introduced two bus routes. These ran from Elsworth via Conington to St Ives on Fridays and to Cambridge via Knapwell, Childerley Gate and Madingley Road on Saturdays, sharing the Merton Arms terminus with Whippet's services from the same area. For most of their existence Mr Brand's operations required only one vehicle. He acquired the Ford 20-seater formerly used by Major Francis of Quy (VE 81) and he also owned a small Chevrolet (EW 4685).

A L WATTS

Another one-bus operator based in Elsworth was Arthur Lewis Watts, with a service to St Ives on Mondays, following a similar route to Mr Brand. He also operated to Cambridge via Boxworth and Huntingdon Road on Saturdays, as well as a route to St Neots. Mr Watts ran his services with the Ford 'T' (ER 2968), which had also been new to Major Francis.

RELIANCE MOTOR COACHES

Leslie Parker ran excursions and tours from Cottenham using the fleetname Reliance Motor Coaches. He was not just a coach operator, for he also provided bus services to Willingham, Histon and Cambridge. The Reliance service into Cambridge ran approximately hourly in competition with Ortona's service 4. By 1929 it was a daily operation, which required up to four vehicles. In addition to the usual parcel service offered by many small operators, Mr Parker would arrange the booking of theatre or cinema tickets "if Patrons place their order by Tuesday

of each week." Timetables informed would-be passengers that Mr Parker was also a motor and cycle engineer and could also supply all wireless sets, finally adding that "courteous consideration, reasonable prices and the convenience of Patrons is my object, and I appeal for your confidence and encouragement." Two second-hand Reo saloons (GD 7875 and FL 5757) were purchased in 1927, and were joined in 1929 by a third Reo (VL 1147) and a larger Gilford 166OT (MT 3569), which had a 32-seat Strachan body.

ASHWELL & DISTRICT BUS SERVICES

To the south west of Cambridge, Ashwell lies at the source of the Rhee tributary of the River Cam, just over the border in Hertfordshire. An attractive village, it is two miles from its railway station (Ashwell & Morden) on the Cambridge to King's Cross line. It was in 1926 that Henry Leverett moved to the village from London. Although he had trained as a hat maker, he had been connected with road transport for most of his life, both as an employer and an employee. Latterly he had a jobmaster's business, but his failing health forced him to sell out and retire to more rural surroundings. His house at the top of Bear Lane had previously been used as a factory and he developed an extensive garden there. Two fierce dogs patrolled his property day and night and rumours began to circulate in the village. Eventually Mr Leverett made it known to the locals that he was building a bus, which duly took to the roads in October 1928. It had a Morris chassis, with its home made bodywork finished in a mixture of red paint and polished aluminium. Registered UR 225, it was variously referred to as 'Ye Olde Tin Can' or 'Leverett's Tin Pot'. It operated from Ashwell via Letchworth to Hitchin, with regular trips to London on Fridays and Bedford on Sundays. The business was an immediate success and larger vehicles were soon needed. In 1928 Mr Leverett purchased two 20-seat Dennis G saloons (UR 1014 and UR 1870) and extended

Above: The rapid expansion on the express routes to London required additional vehicles. **UL 9654** was one of four more Dennis F coaches, fitted with Dodson bodies, which were delivered to Westminster in 1929. *(M G Doggett Collection)*

Right: A Westminster Coaches timetable cover from 1930). *(Author's collection)*

ISSUED FREE.

WINTER SERVICE, FROM OCTOBER 1ST, 1930, UNTIL FURTHER NOTICE.

WESTMINSTER COACHES

Travel in Luxury

THROUGH
EAST ANGLIA.

WESTMINSTER COACHING SERVICES LTD.
19 PENTONVILLE ROAD, LONDON, N.1.

PHONE CLERKENWELL 9602 (10 LINES)

his operations to Royston. In the following year the Hitchin - Royston service was further extended through to Cambridge in competition with Ortona. Three more Dennis vehicles were added to stock, consisting of UR 3520/1 with 32-seat bodies on EV chassis and UR 5379, another 14-seater on a 30cwt chassis. Additional staff were taken on, and two new cottages were built for them in the village. Another EV (UR 6840) followed in 1930, but by then the daily carriage of schoolchildren into Cambridge was causing capacity problems and a Dennis Lance double-decker was ordered. As well as the bus services, Mr Leverett also operated regular excursions to Clacton and Great Yarmouth. He paid for all his vehicles in cash and, in addition to the buses, also owned a Dennis Lancet (JH 2553) which he used as a caravan.

THE CAMBRIDGE BLUE MOTOR SERVICES

John Goates established this small business in the late 1920s at Wimpole. By 1931 operations had moved to Arrington, on the Old North Road to the north of Royston, and Mr Goates was in partnership with a Mr Joiner. They ran a service from Arrington to Cambridge by way of Orwell, Harlton and Haslingfield, but the route was soon extended to run from Biggleswade. Eventually it grew into a daily Bedford - Biggleswade - Cambridge run with a running time of nearly 2 hours, which terminated at Drummer Street in Cambridge. Special cheap return tickets were available on certain days of the week which offered substantial savings, while the vehicles were also available for private hires when not required for bus duties. Two Thornycroft A2 20-seaters were purchased new (ER 9823 and VE 1525). Also owned were a secondhand Chevrolet 14-seater new to Stratford Blue (UE 4189) and another Thornycroft A2 (WO 486).

COACH OPERATORS

In addition to the above, there were three more operators whose main business was initially excursion and private hire work but who tried on several occasions to break Ortona's local monopoly. They were especially keen to have a share of the traffic to the University boat races and the Gogs Fete, which in those days were major attractions attended by large numbers of people, as described in chapter 8.

LORD ASTOR COACHES

Operating from 68 Abbey Road, this business was established soon after the First World War by Mr A G Brown, although several other members of his family were also involved. The first vehicle was a Napier (CE 2108), known as 'The Cambridge Belle' and it was one of the earliest motor coaches to operate regular excursions from the town. By mid-1921 three Daimler charabancs were in service (CE 8246, CE 8247 and CE 8675). A 14-seat Crossley (CE 9893) with an ex-War Department chassis joined the fleet in 1922, followed a year later by another Daimler charabanc (ER 1354). These vehicles were variously licensed to H A Brown, H E Brown, H Brown and Brown Brothers. From 1928 Italian-built Lancia coaches were favoured. These were noted for their speed and over the next two years at least six were added to stock (ER 7319, ER 9199, ER 9748, VE 1222/3 and TW 8149), all but one of which purchased new. A second-hand Bristol 'B'-type (TW 9768) also joined the fleet in 1930. Mr Brown eventually succeeded in operating services to the special events mentioned, and also introduced a summer express from Cambridge (Milton Road Corner) to Lowestoft.

ROYAL BLUE COACHES

This was the fleetname used by Mr H J (Harry) Brown for his coaches. Operations are thought to have started in 1922 but no details of the early fleet have been discovered. Mr Brown ran a taxi business from 149 Chesterton Road but by the mid-1920s he had purchased his first coach and had moved to 169 Chesterton Road. He also had premises in Stone Street. By 1929 his fleet included a 32-seat Maudslay ML3B coach (VE 919). Later additions were two Associated Daimler coaches, one of which (YE 4390) had been new to the London General Omnibus Company. In July 1936 a Ford 18-seat bus (VE 4482) was acquired from

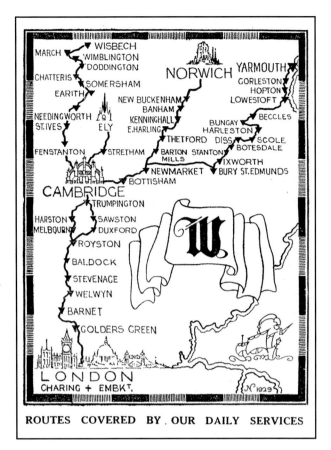

Right: A Westminster route map, also from 1930. *(Author's collection)*

Below: Acme Pullman Saloons ran a half-hourly service from London to Bishop's Stortford, with a few journeys continuing north via Saffron Walden to Newmarket. Acme had 14 Gilford coaches when taken over by London General Country Services, including **UR 5158**, a 168OT with coachwork by Petty. *(The Omnibus Society Collection)*

Papworth Village Settlement, whose activities are described in chapter 11. By then Mr Brown had been authorised to run a summer service from Cambridge (Milton Road Corner) to Great Yarmouth. He also operated on the services to the Gogs Fete and the boat races.

CAMBRIDGE COMFORT COACHES

Percy Wheatley was previously a skin merchant but in April 1929 he purchased a new Graham-Dodge 20-seater (VE 1074) with the fleetname 'Cambridge Comfort Coaches' and he operated from premises in Sturton Street, next to Barclay & Perkins brewery stables and yard. The original coach was soon joined by three more (VE 1075/6, VE 1522) with larger, 26-seat bodies, and a 32-seat Gilford 1680T (VE 1521). Excursions and private hire work formed the basis of operations, but several attempts were made to move into bus and express coach operations. During the summer of 1930, excursions to London were operated at busy times at fares lower than those charged by Varsity and Westminster, the established express operators. A daily summer express service was operated from Cambridge (Drummer Street) to Great Yarmouth and Lowestoft, with additional stops in Bottisham and Newmarket.

PERCIVAL'S MOTORS

Another coach operator who established a presence was Percival Skinner (trading as 'Percival's Motors'), although his main business was in Oxford. In 1928 he set up a subsidiary in Cambridge, managed by his associate Ralph Moore. Vehicles were supplied from Oxford, often by transporting undergraduates between the two ancient seats of learning, and Percival's built up a healthy private hire business. Based in King Street,

Percival's also advertised "good garage accommodation" and "Morris cars to drive yourself".

OTHER OPERATORS

A few other operators provided excursions or occasional services into Cambridge from their home towns and villages. Mr G F Burgoin's 'Grey Pullman Saloons' and Mr H Withers both ran frequent excursions from the Haverhill area in 1929 in competition with Ortona services 13 and 36. Grey Pullman was the more serious challenger, using as many as three vehicles on occasions.

THE NEED FOR REGULATION

Relations between rival operators were sometimes far from cordial. Small buses known as 'chasers' were sometimes employed to overtake the vehicles of competitors and pick up their passengers, and on very busy routes the chasers would operate in pairs. Another tactic was to block the road and prevent a bus belonging to the opposition from passing. Rival drivers would race each other to stops, where conductors would argue about whose bus the prospective passengers should board. Angry words (and sometimes fists) would fly, and one driver ended up in a horse trough at Newmarket during a disagreement between a Mansfield driver and an Ortona driver. Sometimes the police would have to be called, and the battles between Mansfield and Ortona only stopped after an Ortona driver was apprehended by the village policeman, who had been hiding on the floor of the Mansfield bus. Relations improved thereafter, although there was still hostility between many operators and it was clear that the bus industry would soon have to be regulated to prevent matters from getting seriously out of hand.

Above: Varsity took delivery of five new AEC Regal coaches in 1930. **VE 3440** was one of a pair with 28-seat Duple bodies, and was photographed outside the company's Oxford premises. *(Cambridgeshire Collection)*

Below: The small-scale bus operations of Frederick Brand developed from his earlier activities as a carrier, as is evident from the dual-purpose appearance of the vehicle illustrated here. *(Author's Collection)*

8. Regulation - The Road Traffic Act of 1930

Before 1930, local Watch Committees were in charge of licensing omnibuses and motor coaches. Although they were able to impose all sorts of local restrictions for all sorts of reasons, anyone who owned a bus could run on any route. In Cambridge Ortona had a close working relationship with the Corporation and since 1921 had paid them £250 per year for the privilege of being the sole provider of local bus services. All buses operating in the town had to be passed as fit by the local police and after inspection they were stencilled 'Borough of Cambridge (and date)'. Ortona's vehicles had a reputation for being very well turned-out and consequently these inspections were never much more than a formality. From 1928 new Watch Committee licence numbers were allocated to all Ortona buses, corresponding to their chassis numbers. Whatever the legality of these arrangements, they were resented by the smaller operators, for whom there was considerable public sympathy. As the small operators increased in number so too did the competition and, as already described, trouble sometimes flared. The local coachmen also wanted a share of the traffic on the London express services, which had been built up by Varsity and Westminster.

The regulating of buses and coaches began in London in 1924, when the London Traffic Act was passed. This required full details of all routes to be registered with the licensing authorities. Some small operators then decided to move out of London, adding to the 'free-for-all' which still existed elsewhere. Inevitably, this could not last for long, and the Road Traffic Act (1930) became law on 1st August of that year. Although it covered many aspects of road transport, Part IV (sections 61-100) dealt specifically with buses and coaches. Its purpose was to regulate bus and coach service to prevent wasteful and damaging competition. The country was divided into Traffic Areas, each under the control of three Traffic Commissioners. The Ministry of Transport appointed one commissioner, with two Deputy Commissioners provided by local councils. Most Cambridge area operators found themselves under the control of the Eastern Traffic Area, with its headquarters in Cambridge. For many years this was at Sussex House in Hobson Street, before the move to its present home at Terrington House in Hills Road. Operators based in Huntingdonshire came under the jurisdiction of the East Midlands area to begin with, although the area boundaries changed on 1st January 1934. The county of Hertfordshire, which included some of the Royston area operators, was in the Metropolitan Traffic Area. This differed from the others in having one Commissioner appointed by the Metropolitan Police and one deputy.

LICENCES FOR EVERYTHING

Everything was to be regulated. Licences would now be issued to buses and coaches (referred to as 'Public Service Vehicles' for the first time) and also to drivers and conductors, who were required to wear the long-familiar PSV badges in case their roles were in doubt. Each traffic area had a reference letter and these soon became familiar on the badges. Eastern area badges displayed FF and those issued in the East Midlands EE, while the letter N identified staff living in the Metropolitan area. Age limits were also introduced, and some very young conductors employed by the smaller operators had to find other work until they were eighteen years old. All existing services had to be licensed by 9th February 1931, and after that date any operator wishing to start a new service or to amend or curtail an existing service had to apply to the Traffic Commissioners. All applications then appeared in the regular publication 'Notices & Proceedings' which gave the opportunity to object to interested parties. These might include other operators already offering a similar service, and usually did include the railway companies, unless they had a financial interest in the operator proposing the new service. Applications were presented and objections were raised in Traffic Courts, and licences were granted or refused after all the

Above: Henry Leverett favoured Dennis vehicles for most of his fleet, all paid for in cash. His final purchase was this EV, seen here before being registered as UR 6840. The strangely styled body was built by Wilton, and had seating for 32. *(John Banks Collection)*

Below: A W H Barker timetable heading. *(Author's Collection)*

Fenstanton and District BUS SERVICES
TIME TABLE.

Saloon Coaches for Hire.   Special Terms for Private Parties.

Proprietor: W. H. BARKER "THE CHEQUERS," FENSTANTON, Hunts.

Parcel and Booking Offices :   Miss V. Thackray, Market Hill, St. Ives, and "Merton Arms," Northampton Street, Cambridge.

evidence was presented at these public hearings. Any operator proposing a new service had to prove that there was a demand for it by calling suitable witnesses. If the application was granted, a 'primary' licence would be issued for the service. An additional 'backing' licence would have to be obtained if the service was to pick up or set down passengers in another traffic area (or a 'corridor' licence for long-distance services just passing through).

Although the Act eliminated some unnecessary competition, it also made it more difficult for the small operators to compete with the large, territorial companies, especially on the roads covered by the Cambridge local services. For many years the independents, with a few exceptions, were not allowed to carry passengers on journeys wholly within the Borough boundary. For example, the last picking-up point for Burwell & District buses coming into town was the Borough Cemetery, although their main routes served most of Newmarket Road. The Mansfields also had to give up their established services to Caldecote and The Wilbrahams, while further afield Varsity was unable to obtain the necessary licences for its service to Bournemouth and Poole. On the other hand, the Act did safeguard the position of the smaller operators on the routes they retained. The independents alone continued to provide the buses in several villages, while the larger operators gave up some competing market day services in the 1930s. However, many small operators soon gave up altogether and sold out. Only the strongest and most persistent survived.

THE BATTLE OF THE BUMPS

The Cambridge University Boat Races are known as 'The Lent Bumps' and 'The May Bumps', (although the latter actually take place in June). They were a major local event in the 1920s and remain popular today. Each takes place over a period of four days, and Ortona ran special express buses for spectators from the corner of Market Street to the 'Pike and Eel' beside the River Cam at Chesterton. The services were so well-used that some ordinary services had to be curtailed or even cancelled to provide enough buses, but applications by

the local coach companies to operate on the route were refused several times on the grounds that Ortona already provided an adequate service. The Watch Committee eventually issued special licences to Percy Wheatley's 'Cambridge Comfort Coaches', Brown Brothers 'Lord Astor Coaches' and Harry Brown's 'Royal Blue' to run non-stop to Chesterton from Drummer Street. To give everyone a share of the traffic, Ortona were also instructed to run their special buses from Drummer Street instead of Market Street. To counter this, Ortona placed stickers reading "To The Races" on buses running to Chesterton on service 1, which continued to serve the Market Street stop. Matters became very heated one day in June 1930, when a procession of six coaches owned by the small operators tried to pick up passengers waiting for the Ortona buses at Market Street. When one coach driver was ordered to move on by a policeman, he refused and was arrested. He was soon joined in custody by the other five, although they were all released on bail soon afterwards. Returning to their vehicles (which had been driven back to Drummer Street by the police) the six drivers were then prevented from driving slowly through the town centre in convoy. The small operators complained to the local press about Ortona's "illegal, unjust and dishonest monopoly" and there was a great deal of public sympathy for the coachmen and their drivers. The offending stickers were soon removed from the Ortona buses, while the small operators were later allowed to pick up at Market Street. After the passing of the 1930 Act, the local coachmen were all granted licences to operate to the boat races, which continue to be an annual event, although the special bus services ceased many years ago.

THE GOGS FETE

Another very popular local event was the Gogs Fete, held every August Bank Holiday at Wandlebury House. In July 1933 the Cambridge Chronicle reported that a good-humoured crowd of 18,000 people had attended the event and had enjoyed ten hours of fun in blazing sunshine. As well as taking part in treasure hunts and various sports, they were entertained by five bands and "The Great

Risko", a famous aerial gymnast. The first prize in the raffle was "a Morris Minor Motor Car", a luxury which relatively few of those who attended could then expect to own. As Wandlebury is several miles south of Cambridge on the Haverhill road, the event obviously offered plenty of potential passengers for the local bus and coach operators. Ortona, Lord Astor Coaches and Royal Blue Coaches all operated special services to the fete, subject to several restrictions. Passengers could only be picked up and set down at designated stops and each operator could only use a certain number of vehicles on the services, which ran until midnight. The Gogs Fete was suspended when war broke out in 1939 and was not resumed afterwards.

<<< Page 75: An advertisement leaflet put out by Cambridge Comfort Coaches. *(Author's Collection)*

Right: Similar publicity material from Reliance Motor Coaches. *(Author's Collection)*

Below: The Eastern Counties takeover did not diminish the pride taken by the former Ortona crews in their work, as shown by the crew of this former United Leyland TS3, posing with their vehicle on a short working of service 103 to Shelford. *(M G Doggett Collection)*

Above: In 1928 Percival's Motors set up an operation in Cambridge, using coaches from its main fleet based in Oxford. Typical of the vehicles used in the early days was this Gilford AS6 (**GN 9389**). Percival's did a good deal of private hire work for both Universities. *(Author's Collection)*

Below: The Cambridge Blue Motor Services run by John Goates was based at Arrington Bridge, and ran a lengthy route between Cambridge and Bedford via Biggleswade. One of the vehicles used was this Chevrolet (**UE 4189**), which had been new to Stratford Blue. *(Author's Collection)*

9. Ortona - The Final Years

The passing of the Road Traffic Act removed some of the excessive competition from the local bus scene. Ortona remained the sole provider of local buses in the Borough of Cambridge and, emphasising the railway interest, Ortona's timetable now included details of LNER train departures from the town. The presence of the LNER office at Market Hill allowed Ortona's Peas Hill premises to close in 1930, although the office in Post Office Terrace continued to operate. Outside Cambridge many roads were still shared by more than one operator's buses. One example was the village of Barton, which was served at various times by Ortona, Burwell & District, Harston & District and Cambridge Blue. Suspicion and mistrust continued to exist between some rival operators and their crews.

A JOINT TAKEOVER

Small businesses continued to be taken over by larger ones and in December 1930 Ortona joined forces with Eastern National to acquire the Ashwell & District business. By then Mr Leverett employed three drivers, two conductors and one fitter, sometimes assisting with the maintenance himself. His buses were well loaded on market days and at school times, and two more drivers had just been taken on to train for a planned expansion of services. This included a more direct route from Hitchin to Cambridge, for which the timetable was already prepared. However, Mr Leverett now decided (for the second time) that his health was too poor for him to continue working and he advertised his business for sale. It was the first takeover by Eastern National, who allocated the number 41 to the main Hitchin - Royston - Cambridge route. This continued to terminate at Gonville Place in Cambridge and was jointly operated with Ortona, who referred to their share as service 52. Eastern National added five assorted Dennis saloons to its fleet, and numbered Leverett's other routes from Ashwell as 41A (Hitchin via Newnham) and 35E (Stotfold -

Letchworth - Baldock works service), adding the route to Royston via The Morderns to its existing service 35B. They outstationed two buses at The Drive in Ashwell until its new garage in Hitchin was opened in 1936. Ortona's share of the vehicles was a solitary Dennis EV (UR 6840) with strangely styled Wilton bodywork. The order for a Dennis Lance double-decker was cancelled.

END OF AN ERA

The ex-Leverett vehicle was almost the final addition to the Ortona fleet. In March 1931 the Cambridge Chronicle reported that "a big East Anglian bus merger" was about to embrace the Ortona Motor Company and three other concerns. These were the Eastern Counties Road Car Company of Ipswich, the Peterborough Electric Traction Company and the Norfolk and Suffolk parts of United Automobile Services. The railway companies had interests in all four companies and now decided to combine them as the Eastern Counties Omnibus Company Ltd, with its headquarters in Norwich.

In the same month Ortona took delivery of its last new vehicles, in the shape of six Leyland saloons. There were three each on Tiger TS3 (VE 4802-4) and Lion LT2 chassis (VE 4805-7), all with Leyland 30-seat bodywork. Developments continued during Ortona's last few months. Two more coastal express services linked Cambridge with Great Yarmouth (93) and Southend-on-Sea (94), while several routes were renumbered. Town services 1A and 2A became 29 and 32, the original 29 to Bedford becoming 50 and the 32 to Peterborough becoming 51. From Monday 2nd February 1931 regular passenger trains ceased to run between Ely and St Ives. They were replaced by service 25A (Ely - Haddenham - St Ives), which was increased and extended to the railway station in Ely. Two new services introduced early in 1931 also passed through villages which lost their rail service, these being the 37 (to Chatteris via Wilburton and Haddenham) and market day

Above: Lancia Pentatoia coach **VE 1222** is removed from Drummer Street because its owner, Lord Astor Coaches, did not have a licence to pick up there. Six drivers employed by local coach companies were briefly held in custody in June 1930 when they took part in a protest against new stopping arrangements for the May Races. *(Cambridgeshire Collection)*

Below: Before the advent of mass motoring there was fierce competition to carry passengers to popular local events. The notice in the window of Ortona No. **32** (**ER 1134**) reads 'ALL ROUTES GOGS FETE' as the bus waits for customers in Drummer Street. New in 1923, it was the last Straker-Squire to be delivered to Ortona, and was withdrawn six years later. *(Alan B Cross Collection/W Noel Jackson)*

37A (to Ely via Wilburton and Stretham). The success of service 37 was such that in January a 37-seat SOS 'Q' operating the service was stopped by a policeman and found to be carrying more than 60 passengers. Country bus crews were very reluctant to leave regular passengers behind, especially on infrequent services. Another innovation was service 12A, from Hinxton to Ickleton and thence via service 12 to Cambridge. One bus and crew were outstationed at Hinxton. The modernisation and rebodying of the 1925 SOS 'S' types (which had commenced during the previous year) was completed.

UNITED AUTOMOBILE SERVICES LTD

Founded by Ernest Boyd Hutchinson, this company began its East Anglian operations on 4th April 1912 in Lowestoft with secondhand charabancs, which competed with the Great Eastern Railway buses on the route to Southwold. The railway company soon withdrew, and United started other routes to Beccles (soon extended to Bungay) and Oulton Broad. Mr Hutchinson also started services in the north east of England, originally centred on Bishop Auckland. After the First World War the company expanded rapidly and introduced new routes from Cromer, Great Yarmouth, Kings Lynn and Norwich, and by the mid-1920s had a network stretching all the way from Suffolk to Northumberland. Large numbers of AEC and Daimler vehicles were purchased from the War Department and the company's workshops in Lowestoft began building bodywork, initially for its own vehicles but later for other operators. Mr Hutchinson was also involved with East Midland Motor Services, which was formed in 1927 from the business begun seven years earlier by Mr W T Underwood of Clowne.

United remained independent until June 1929, when it was jointly purchased by Tilling & BAT and the London & North Eastern Railway. Mr Hutchinson then resigned and the new owners decided to split up this very large company. The services in the north east continued to operate under the United name, with the Head Office initially in York (although it later moved to Darlington), while the Lincolnshire area was transferred to the recently formed Lincolnshire Road Car Company. The East Anglian area formed the largest part of the new Eastern Counties Omnibus Company, which also took over the coachbuilding factory in Lowestoft.

United originally used a grey livery, by 1927 changed to a very attractive combination of yellow, cream and brown. East Midland used this scheme for many years afterwards, although from 1930 the United livery changed to red and off-white. United's routes never met those of Ortona, although service 37 (King's Lynn - Denver) was extended to Ely after the formation of Eastern Counties.

The new Eastern Counties Omnibus Company came into being on 14th July 1931, although Ortona's final timetable was actually published four days later and made no mention of the fact! The Ortona fleet then stood at 94 vehicles, all with pneumatic tyres and 73 of which were under five years old. The company had built up a proud reputation for good service and the staff were highly regarded by management and passengers alike. Staff relations were friendly, although discipline under Mr Iles was strict. Drivers and conductors were inspected regularly and it was not unknown for a man to be sent home if his collar was not clean or his boots were dirty. There was, however, an element of paternalism in the company's attitude to its workforce and the management seems to have had genuine concern for the busmen and their families. Staff dinners were held in March each year and on Christmas Eve, when all services were stopped for a few hours so that everyone could attend. The busmen also enjoyed the use of a Sports & Social Club at 12 Regent Terrace. Crews normally worked from around 6am to 2pm and from 2pm to 11pm or later. There were also some split duties. In an average 53-hour week a driver could earn from 1/3d up to 1/6d (7½p) per hour and a conductor from 11d to 1/4d (7p). Staff who reported 3 minutes late lost a quarter of an hour's pay. Any staff on early turn who were 15 minutes late lost all pay due before breakfast. The maintenance men (known as 'inside staff') started at 6am and worked to very high standards. Every vehicle received a major overhaul and repaint every two years and re-entered service in immaculate condition, with its paintwork sparkling. Even

Above: When Leverett's Ashwell & District business was taken over in December 1930, most of the fleet passed to Eastern National, including this Dennis EV (**UR 3520**), which was numbered **3058** by its new owner. It is seen here in Royston on the main Hitchin to Cambridge, service 41, which was operated jointly with Ortona. *(Alan B Cross Collection/J F Higham)*

Below: The final additions to Ortona's fleet were made in March 1931, when six more Leyland saloons were delivered. All had 30-seat Leyland bodies and No. **96** (**VE 4803**) was one of three with Tiger TS3 chassis. It was a regular vehicle on the new service 93 to Great Yarmouth. *(Cambridgeshire Collection)*

the cab interior would be varnished! Each bus was allocated to one or sometimes two regular crews, who took great pride in their steed and objected very strongly if, for any reason, they saw it being used by a different crew.

It all worked very well and the new management was content to leave well alone, although many of the men were far from happy when Eastern Counties took over. Their wives were no longer allowed free travel on the buses, while another unwelcome development was a reduction in the pay rates. The starting hourly rate for a driver went down to 11d and for a conductor to 9d, and for the first time a Trade Union was formed.

GROWING UP WITH THE BUSES - A DRIVER REMEMBERS.

For many in the Cambridge area working on the buses was a way of life and sometimes sons (and daughters) followed in their fathers' footsteps by going 'on the buses'. Derek Carter grew up with Ortona and subsequently enjoyed a long career with Eastern Counties.

"I was born in Landudno in 1920 and my family moved to Cambridge in 1922. From 1923 we lived in Stonehill Road, off Shelford Road. My father Alec Carter worked for BP in Ditton Lane but before that he'd driven Royal Blue coaches. He joined Ortona as a driver in 1928 and to start with he was on the Newnham services, 5 and 31. They both went to Hinton Avenue but later on they were extended. Then the 5 went on to Mowbray Road and later still to Strangeways Road and the 31 went to Fishers Lane in Cherry Hinton. The first closed double-decker he drove was VE 4200. His badge number was FF 1117 and his regular conductor was Alf Dant.

"I grew up with the buses and I've never lost my interest in them. As a small boy I loved to stand and watch them coming out of the garage. I remember seeing one once with flames coming out from the engine - I suppose the petrol had caught fire. I also used to sit on the steps of the Bank [on the corner of Hobson Street and Sidney Street, one of the main stops in the town centre] and watch the buses while Mother was shopping in town. I liked riding on them too and I can remember going out to Girton Corner, soon after they extended some

of the service 2 buses from Oxford Road. It was a cold day for riding on an open-top double-decker and my nose was as red as a rear light by the time we got there.

"Later on Father transferred to the Hinxton outstation. His conductor was Albert Lindsell, who lived in Hinxton. The first bus he had there was ER5039, one of the 'SOS' 31-seaters. After that he had a Leyland, VE 306. Eastern Counties numbered it AL66 when they took over, but then they put a new body on it and renumbered it AL1. It was the only one with servo brakes. Then he had NA19 (VF 2847), that was a 36-seater Daimler, and then AL3 (ER 8802), which was a Leyland Lion. It had been a charabanc but it was rebodied as a bus. It was kept in a wood yard at Hinxton and worked on the service to Cambridge. On schooldays they started their shift with the 7.10 from Ickleton to the school at Duxford. The first run into Cambridge was the 9.20, arriving at 10.15, back to Hinxton at 10.30, back to Cambridge at 12.30 when they went to the garage for fuel and to clean the bus. Then back to Hinxton at 2.15, another school run and a last trip to Cambridge at 5.15, returning at 6.15. That was their shift from Monday to Saturday. On Wednesdays they also did a late run to Cambridge but on Fridays they finished after the afternoon school run.

"Mr Iles was a good manager and a nice man. Freddie Fulcher was the foreman. Discipline was strict: there was one inspector who would have booked his own mother and who very nearly caught Father in the Wheatsheaf at Duxford on one occasion. But they looked after the staff. On Christmas Eve all the buses were in by 6.30pm so everyone could go for a Christmas dinner at The Dorothy restaurant. That all stopped under Eastern Counties, along with the free passes for wives. The buses were always on the same runs and each bus had its own crew, or pair of crews, who looked after them very carefully. On routes with more than one bus, they always worked the same journeys and that carried on after Eastern Counties took over. For a while the buses on service 101 were A16, A17, A68, A208, A207, A90 and A69. On the 102 they had A9, A12, A3, A70 and A71, always in that same order. Then they moved A70 onto the 139 and A71 onto the 132."

Above: One of the buses driven by Alec Carter on service 12A was No. **65** (**VE 306**), a Leyland Lion PLSC3, seen crossing the Catholic Church junction. The shelter and underground toilets were removed many years ago. In October 1902 the Manager of the Tramway Company had received a summons for "damaging, injuring and spoiling the public convenience" after he scribbled on the woodwork with a pencil. Graffiti is not a new problem! *(Cambridgeshire Collection)*

Right: The new regime takes over. Eastern Counties numbered the ex-Ortona routes from 101 upwards and continued to place Leyland TD1s in service, with bodywork built in the company's own factory. Numerically the first, fleet number **A176** (**NG 1911**) has its 'bible' indicator changed at Green End Road before it returns to the Railway Station. *(Cambridgeshire Collection)*

10. Eastern Counties Takes Over

For the citizens of Cambridge the most obvious change to their local buses was the adoption of red instead of green as the main livery colour. Ortona's bus routes had 100 added to their service numbers, with letters for the express routes 90 to 94. These became respectively V (Hunstanton), part of X (Clacton), D (Felixstowe), part of N (Great Yarmouth) and Y (Southend). The routes of the other constituent companies were numbered from 201 (Eastern Counties Road Car) and 301 (Peterborough Electric Traction), with the United services retaining their original numbers below 100. The former Ortona and PET networks made up the new company's Western area, while those of United and ECRC formed the Eastern area. Eastern Counties numbered each type of vehicle in a separate series commencing at 1, and Ortona's fleet numbers were retained with the addition of class letters. For saloons these were AC, AL and AT (Leyland), D and DE (Dennis), Q, S and SM (SOS) and T (Star). The double-deckers, all Leylands, were classified A (TD1s) and AA (older G, SG and GH types). Some of the latter were withdrawn in 1932, when Eastern Counties received its first new vehicles but, of course, not all of these were allocated to the Cambridge area. Ten TD1 double-deckers (A176-85, NG 1911-20) maintained Ortona's Leyland tradition (although they had actually been ordered by United), along with fourteen TD2s (A186-99, NG 2721-34). All had lowbridge bodies with enclosed staircases built at Eastern Counties' own Lowestoft factory, except for the first five TD1s, which had Leyland bodywork. They were distinguished by their NG- Norfolk registrations and were followed by another sixteen TD2s in 1933 (A200-15, NG 3861-70 and NG 5401-6) and some Leyland TS4 coaches (AT127-36, NG 3871-80). The company also purchased ten Tilling-Stevens B39A7 saloons (P166-75, NG 5801-10). All had ECOC bodywork except AT136, which is believed to have had a Bush & Twiddy body.

The practice also began of transferring buses between depots throughout the company's large territory. A few former Ortona vehicles ended up at Norwich, Cromer and Ipswich, while several TD1s new to the Eastern Counties Road Car Company came to Cambridge. A notable arrival was A149 (DX 8424), the first local bus with an oil (diesel) engine. It was given a trial run on town service 101, where it failed to impress crews or passengers. The use of a lowbridge bus on such a busy route was not popular, while the noisy, rough-riding engine produced a great deal of smoke. Despite these initial problems, oil engines were eventually found to be more economical and were greatly improved over the next few years. Many Eastern Counties vehicles subsequently had their petrol engines replaced by diesels, including nearly all the former Ortona double-deckers. Other former Road Car Company TD1s drafted in were A143, 150/1 and 173 (DX 8358, 8425/6, 9025).

More old vehicles were withdrawn and by the end of 1934 all the open-top Leyland G7, SG7 and GH7 double-deckers had gone. There were a few extensions to the newly renumbered services, mainly on the town network. The pioneering 101 was extended in Chesterton from Chapel Street to Green End Road and the 106 from Ditton Walk further along Newmarket Road to the Borough Cemetery, initially on Sundays only. A new 139 started in September 1932 from Mowbray Road (Glebe Road) to Histon Road (Gilbert Road), avoiding the town centre but bringing buses to Burleigh Street and Fitzroy Street for the first time. On the country routes the 110 was extended from Great Wilbraham to Little Wilbraham. A significant change in 1933, for reasons unknown, was the end of joint operation on the services to Bedford (150) and Hitchin (152). Eastern National became solely responsible for these services, using their numbers 29 and 41, and outstationed two buses at the Eastern Counties garage in Cambridge. Eastern Counties introduced a new service 149 to Teversham via Cherry Hinton church, while on the town routes occasional buses on the 130 were extended from the Borough Cemetery to

Above: After a few years of frantic competition, the Westminster and Varsity names disappeared from the scene in 1933. This former Westminster Gilford 168OT (**GK 3403**) was numbered **GB5** by Eastern Counties. It had a Wycombe 28-seat coach body, but had received bus livery and lost some of its earlier splendour by the time this photograph was taken. *(J F Higham)*

Below: The Westminster and Varsity takeovers made Eastern Counties the sole provider of coaches to London. There was also an impressive network of express services to other destinations, and Leyland TS4 coach **AT136** (**NG 3880**) is seen here leaving Drummer Street on service N from Birmingham, which covered the former Ortona 93 between Cambridge and Yarmouth. *(Author's Collection)*

service into Cambridge. The Reliance business was absorbed along with five vehicles, with the new company trading as Comfort & Reliance Coaches. The company clearly had expansion in mind, for soon afterwards an impressive six-wheel Karrier DD6/1 double-decker (BU 5553) was added to stock. It had been new to Oldham Corporation Tramways and had a 66-seat English Electric body, but it was soon sold. In January 1934 Comfort & Reliance took over Brown's Lord Astor Coaches, including five luxurious Lancias and a Gilford. Soon afterwards a second large double-decker was obtained, this time a Guy FCX with a Hall-Lewis open-top body (YU 7457), which had been new to the London Public Omnibus Company. Only a few months later, however, the rapid growth ended when Eastern Counties took over the business, retaining the licences for excursions and tours from Cottenham and Cambridge but not the stage services, which served roads already covered by the company's 104, 137 and 137A. Eastern Counties had no use for the vehicles and these were quickly sold for further service elsewhere.

EASTERN NATIONAL PROGRESS

Eastern Counties was not alone in buying out its competitors. Having become a Tilling company in 1931 Eastern National was pursuing a similar policy, and in October 1931 took over the bus operations of the old-established J & S Hinsby of St Neots, along with five buses. Hinsby's main routes ran from St Neots to Bedford (jointly with Eastern National) and to Huntingdon. These were incorporated into existing services 4 and 4A, which were extended to Huntingdon and St Ives in December 1933, when the use of the service number 14 ceased. In August 1934 Eastern National acquired Goates' Cambridge Blue Motor Services of Arrington and allocated the number 29A to his daily Bedford - Biggleswade - Cambridge service. This was Eastern National's third route into Cambridge and it now terminated in Gonville Place, along with service 41 from Hitchin. No vehicles were taken over but Eastern National continued to outstation two buses at Arrington until a new garage was built at Biggleswade in

1937. Service 29A was diverted via Wrestlingworth village in 1935, replacing the former 21 route from Biggleswade. Until 1935 Eastern National updated its double-deck fleet with AEC Regent and Leyland Titan double-deckers, the Leyland chassis type progressing from TD1 to TD4, and all carrying lowbridge bodywork. New single-deckers were nearly all of Dennis manufacture, mostly with 'Lancet' chassis although there were some smaller 'Ace' buses.

FIRST BRISTOL VEHICLES

Eastern Counties continued to develop its route network in 1934 and 1935. The Balsham section of the 113 was extended to Streetly End. A new 150 to Horningsea replaced the occasional extensions on town route 130, which was amended to run from Coldhams Lane (Cromwell Park) via East Road and the town centre to Trumpington. Service 109 was diverted via Waterbeach following reductions on the 120. This was withdrawn north of that village except for school buses to Chittering, which were numbered 120A, although by 1937 use of the 120/120A numbers ceased altogether and Waterbeach became the terminus for short-workings on service 109. On the town network 1935 saw the extension of the 102 from Malta Road to Brookfields. The 106 was extended from Queen Edith's Way to Red Cross Lane, with all journeys at the Newmarket Road end now terminating the Borough Cemetery, while a further extension to Meadowlands was made in 1937.

The Eastern Counties fleet was steadily updated and, in common with other Tilling-associated fleets, the company switched to Bristol vehicles. These were felt by some to be less refined than the Leylands but they soon gained a reputation for reliability and ease of maintenance, although the Gardner engines normally specified were rather noisy. The first examples arrived in the summer of 1935, these being ten 32-seat coaches on JJW chassis (LJ1-10, NG 9901-10) and an equal number of JNW 36-seat buses (LN1-10, NG 9911-20). Ten Leyland TD4 double-deckers also joined the fleet and although most of these were for tram replacement services in far-off Norwich, at least one (A232, AAH 136) is believed to have

Above: From 1935, in line with other Tilling companies, Eastern Counties received Bristol vehicles. Among the first were ten JJW coaches, with 32-seat bodies. Originally numbered LJ5, **NG 9905** is seen at Victoria Coach Station in London, with its post-war fleet number **LJ435**. *(C W Routh)*

Below: A further 28 Bristol coaches were delivered in 1936 including **LJ12** (**AVF 362**), a JO5G with a 30-seat body, built in the company's own Lowestoft factory. It is seen on a South Coast Tour. *(C W Routh)*

operated from Cambridge for a while. All the new deliveries had ECOC bodies. In December 1935 Eastern Counties absorbed the vehicles and services of the Norwich Omnibus Company (formerly the Norwich Electric Tramways Company), owned and operated since 1933 as a separate subsidiary. The takeover included a total of 32 buses of AEC, Bristol and Leyland manufacture, with some of the Leylands later moving to garages in the Cambridge area.

The first double-deck Bristols delivered new to Eastern Counties entered service in 1936, with GO5G chassis and highbridge, Lowestoft-built bodywork, with seats for 56 passengers. Some received their bodies just after the factory had been renamed Eastern Coachworks (ECW) and the new buses were numbered LG9-18 (AVF 351-60). (A batch of Bristol double-deckers numbered LG1-8 had already been delivered to the Norwich Omnibus Company.) Also new were ten JO5G coaches, numbered LJ11-20 (AVF 361-70), with 30-seat ECW bodies. In 1937 four more GO5G double-deckers materialised as LG19-22 (BNG 201-4), at least three of which (LG19-21) were allocated to Cambridge. A further eighteen coaches were LJ21-38 (BVF 101-18). Six of these had JO6A chassis with AEC engines, the others having the more familiar Gardner-engined JO5G chassis. Six new 35-seat buses (LD1-66, BVF 631-6) unusually had JO6D chassis, with Dennis engines. Various engine swaps were later made, including the replacement of the Dennis engines by Gardner units.

Eastern National also switched to Bristol vehicles, after several years of favouring Dennis and Leyland for new deliveries. In 1936 the company received nineteen JO5G saloons, with front entrance ECOC/ECW dual-purpose bodywork, along with twelve GO5G double-deckers with bodies built by Brush. The following year saw the delivery of another twenty JO5Gs (four dual-purpose and the rest rear-entrance buses) and sixteen K5Gs, all with ECW bodies. The link with Leyland was not completely severed, however, for the company also received a total of 21 TD4 and TD5 double-deckers and three TS7 coaches.

EASTERN COACHWORKS

The former United coachbuilding factory in Lowestoft continued to be run by Eastern Counties and from 1931 it became increasingly important as a supplier of bodywork to Tilling & BAT companies. By 1936 it was producing an average of ten bodies per week and it was decided to form a separate company to run it. From 1st July the factory was taken over by a new company called Eastern Coachworks, still under the control of Eastern Counties and with a workforce of 950. A high proportion of the new company's products continued to go to Tilling & BAT companies but for the first time it also built bodywork for operators outside the group. Many of the bodies supplied to T&BAT companies were mounted on Bristol chassis.

MORE BUSES FROM BRISTOL

Ortona had been an enthusiastic user of Straker-Squire vehicles, built in Bristol until the firm ceased production in 1926, although by then Ortona had switched to other makes. In the same city, The Bristol Tramways and Carriage Company (BTCC) started building buses for its own use in 1908, initially at the Filton aircraft works. From 1920 Bristol vehicles were also supplied to other operators from the company's new factory at Brislington. After the BTCC became a Tilling company in 1931 Bristol vehicles were increasingly used by Tilling-associated companies. Bristol built both chassis and bodies, although the products of Brislington Body Works (BBW) were never as widespread as those built by Eastern Coachworks (ECW). The Bristol-ECW combination became increasingly common in Tilling fleets and the first examples entered service with Eastern Counties in 1935. Most of the Bristol vehicles in the Eastern Counties fleet had Gardner engines.

Above: Here is the nearside-front angle of the handsome Eastern Counties-bodied 30-seat Bristol JO5G coach fleet number **LJ24** (**BVF 104**). It was photographed at Victoria on the main Norwich - Cambridge - London service E. *(Alan B Cross)*

Below: The company's first Bristol double-deckers had GO5G chassis and highbridge bodywork. Of the 1937 batch, three (LG19-21) were allocated to Cambridge, where they regularly performed on town services 102 and 106. By the time of this post-war photograph, fleet number **LG19** (**BNG 201**) was working the long service 137 to March. *(Author's Collection)*

11. Independent Progress in the 1930s

Throughout the 1930s most of the independent operators followed a similar purchasing policy as they updated their fleets. To begin with they still favoured small, American-designed vehicles, usually seating around 20 passengers. The products of the Gilford Motor of High Wycombe then became popular until the demise of the manufacturer in 1935. Examples of the normal-control Gilford AS6 featured in several fleets and as loadings increased these were followed by the larger 166OT, 168OT and later by the Hera, with room for up to 32 passengers. The Varsity and Westminster fleets already contained Gilford coaches, while Burgoin of Haverhill and Thompson of Harston also purchased new examples. Several other local operators purchased secondhand Gilfords which had started their careers in Scotland, in the large fleets of Alexander of Falkirk (168OT chassis, with WG- registrations) and Western SMT of Kilmarnock (Hera chassis, with CS-registrations). All had 32-seat coach bodies by Wycombe (Gilford's associate company) and they served their new owners well, some lasting until the early 1950s. As the decade progressed Bedford became the most popular make for small buses and coaches, with seats for up to 26 passengers. The usual choice for larger vehicles was AEC or Dennis, typically seating up to 32, and in the late 1930s the flagship coach in several local fleets was a new Dennis Lancet.

The 1930 Road Traffic Act made it harder to establish a small, rural bus and coach business. Eastern Counties and Eastern National acquired many of their competitors but newcomers continued to appear. Some had only short lives, while others grew from humble beginnings into major concerns, whose vehicles were a familiar sight for many years.

BLUE BELLE COACHES

Mr A V Worsdell and his brother established their business in 1932 in Earith, a village on the Cambs-Hunts border. The first vehicle was a new Bedford WLB with a 20-seat Duple coach body, registered EW 7227, with the fleetname Blue Belle Coaches. Market day buses were provided from Earith to Ely (these started at Willingham) and to St Ives, competing with Eastern Counties 125A. This route had replaced the passenger trains on the Ely - St Ives line, which served Earith Bridge station. Blue Belle also operated a Saturday bus to Huntingdon, while a more frequent service from Bluntisham to Cambridge via Earith offered facilities not provided by the larger operators. Subsequent purchases were all secondhand. A 26-seat Gilford AS6 bus (EW 6764) joined the original Bedford in 1934. A former Varsity 20-seat Reo Pullman coach (ER 9846) and an additional WLB with a bus body (UT 9568) were obtained in 1935, followed by a bus-bodied Reo Sprinter (HM 9773) and a larger, 32-seat Gilford 168OT coach (KF 513). As well as the bus services, a licence was also held for excursions and tours from Earith.

PROGRESSIVE MOTOR COACHES

Albert Edward ('Paddy') Harris worked as a driver for Brown's 'Lord Astor Coaches' until 1934, when he started his own business. His first coach was an Associated Daimler 419 (YE 4379) with a 28-seat Allweather body, new to the London General Omnibus Company. It was used on private hire and contract work and was followed by a varied selection of second-hand machines, some of which lasted only a short time. As well as several Bedfords, these included a 14-seat Chevrolet (VW 9015), a pair of Gilford 166OT coaches (VY 679, 999) and a Leyland TS1 (WX 3260). By the summer of 1939 his fleet stood at four vehicles, with the Head Office in Cavendish Road. The fleetname Progressive Motor Coaches was adopted and the vehicles carried a livery of pale green and white.

UNDERGRADUATE ROADWAYS

The third new operator in the early 1930s was unusual in that it never owned a single vehicle.

Above: Several local operators purchased Gilford coaches, both new and secondhand, in the 1930s. Norman Thompson added this Duple-bodied AS6 (**VE 8761**) to his Harston & District fleet in 1933. The coach passed with the business to the newly formed Premier Travel on the first day of 1936. *(J F Higham)*

Below: This was the unpromising start to the express operations of Undergraduate Roadways on 15th March 1933. Varsity AEC Regal **VE 3032** operating 'on hire' is seen at Skegness, complete with 'PETERBOROUGH-SPALDING' label in its front indicator. Braving the elements are the driver and Arthur Lainson. Apart from Charles Klapper of the Omnibus Society they were the only people on the first journey. *(The Omnibus Society Collection)*

In 1932 a group of University students (still referred to in those days as 'undergraduates') decided to enter the field of passenger transport. Weary of study and sport, they each contributed £5 in capital and appointed themselves as Directors. Their leader was Suffolk-born Edward Arthur Lainson, a Harrow and St Catherine's man, who was an enthusiast for all forms of transport. The business was registered as Undergraduate Roadways, with its Head Office at The Hermitage, Silver Street. This was a St Catherine's College lodging house, where Mr Lainson was one of the residents. Official stationery was printed and representatives were appointed in other colleges. Coaches were hired from several local operators, including Comfort & Reliance, Drayton, Varsity Express Motors and Weeden and they were used 'on hire to Undergraduate Roadways' to provide transport for several sports clubs and other societies within the University. By charging slightly less than the owners of the vehicles would have charged for the same work, a modest profit could be made.

The business did not find favour with the University authorities and before long Mr Lainson was summoned by his outraged tutor and reprimanded for "commercialising the college." Following this, the Head Office was hastily moved to a new address outside the University (45 Jesus Lane) and new stationery printed which named no names, but the enterprise continued. After concluding that there was very little to do in Cambridge on Sundays, the young gentlemen then decided to start a scheduled service to the coast. Most of the nearby resorts were already served, but Traffic Manager H D L Beauchamp (of Jesus College) noticed that Skegness was not. The Directors of Undergraduate Roadways accordingly submitted an application in March 1933 to run a Sunday express service from Cambridge to Skegness via Peterborough, and began the necessary search for witnesses to prove that the demand for such a service existed. To help them they engaged an enthusiastic young solicitor and visited, among others, the Dean of Peterborough Cathedral, who agreed that the new service would indeed make it easier for Cambridge folk to attend Sunday services there. Their plans were not welcomed by the London & North Eastern Railway, whose publicity department had just discovered the "bracing" qualities of the Lincolnshire resort and was advertising them in its famous poster, featuring a jolly fisherman. The Eastern Counties Omnibus Company also objected but, to many people's surprise, the licence was granted. A grand launch was planned, featuring the popular singer Jessie Matthews, but the introduction of the service was a rather more modest affair, the only passengers on the first journey (on 15th March 1933) being Charles Klapper of the Omnibus Society and Mr Lainson himself. The service operated on Sundays throughout the summer of 1933, with additional services at Easter and Whitsun. The usual coach was Varsity Express Motors AEC Regal VE 3032 operating with a regular driver on hire, which was rather surprising. When Mr Lainson first offered Varsity the contract, Mr Harvey had informed him (in his typically abrasive way) that he would "never get a licence to Skegsness (sic)." Later in the year a further application was made to operate Sunday afternoon excursions via two routes from Cambridge to Overcote Ferry, but this was refused. It was also admitted at the hearing that the Skegness service was not proving to be very successful. On the other hand, Undergraduate Roadways had built up a considerable private hire business and had carried out several large contracts. The company had several agents in other areas and had even obtained work in London. Undergraduate Roadways had also become agents for a number of express coach operators, including Empire's Best.

PREMIER TRAVEL LTD

Undergraduate Roadways continued to function until 1937 under the management of Messrs W G Crisp and A T Stockings, who handled the private hire business within the University. Mr Lainson 'went down' in 1934 with a degree and a burning ambition. Armed with his boundless enthusiasm and some capital which had unexpectedly come his way, he cycled round the area visiting local bus and coach operators and offering to buy into their businesses, as well as advertising in the trade press for additional financial backing. Some of

Above: Another ex-Harston & District vehicle in Premier Travel's fleet was this Reo (**VE 3002**), new in 1930. It had a 14-seat body and is seen here on a darts club outing from Haslingfield. Driver Sid Pennell, who remained with Premier for 44 years, is on the right of the picture. *(Cambridgeshire Collection)*

Below: The pride of Premier Travel's pre-war fleet was this Dennis Lancet 2 (**CCE 568**), new in 1937 with an opulent Duple body. It is seen here on service 5 from Birmingham to Clacton at the original stop opposite the Spread Eagle in Lensfield Road. The licence for this service was later acknowledged to be the best purchase Premier ever made. *(Author's Collection)*

this eventually came from Sir Christopher Magnay, formerly a Director of the Premier Omnibus Company in London, which had been compulsorily taken over by the London Passenger Transport Board. Two local operators were also suitably impressed, and from 1st January 1936 Norman Thompson's 'Harston & District Motor Services' and Harry Brown's 'Royal Blue Coaches' formed the basis of Premier Travel Ltd.

Many years later Sid Pennell, a former Harston & District driver, recalled "I remember the first time I met Mr Lainson, although I had seen him about the place often enough. We had the first staff meeting at the Marquis of Granby, Norman's pub. All of us were there." He goes on "Mr Lainson was a typical 'grad' - bike clips over his heels, short trousers, good manners. He was only four years older than me, a bit taller, some fair hair. Anyway, we drank our pints and smoked his De Reske cigarettes. He told us that he intended to build up, with our help, a network of express services covering the whole country. We sniggered a bit and got down to the real business of the meeting - money and wages. Mr Lainson said 'Your wages will be the same as hitherto.' Well I didn't agree with that, so we began to have a go at each other (not for the last time either)." Sid Pennell remained with Premier Travel for 44 years, latterly as Manager of the Drummer Street office.

Sir Christopher Magnay became Chairman of the new company, with Mr Lainson as Company Secretary. The Head Office was at 15 Market Hill, Cambridge, with operations based at Harston. A two-tone blue livery was used, with the lighter shade known as 'Premier blue' and mixed to special order. This was clearly a company with ambition but the initial fleet consisted of a motley assortment of small vehicles, some of which were not in the best of health. Mr Thompson had continued to update the Harston & District fleet in the early 1930s. A third new Reo (VE 3002) with a 14-seat body was delivered in 1930 along with another new vehicle, registered VE 4386, of which no further details are known. Subsequent additions were all Gilfords, starting in 1931 with a 168OT (VE 4993) with a Beadle 31-seat coach body, followed in 1933 by a Duple-bodied AS6 (VE 8761). The final acquisition

(WG 334) was one of the former Alexander 168OT coaches referred to earlier. Premier retained the Reo and the three Gilfords. From Mr Brown's Royal Blue fleet came a former LGOC Associated Daimler 419, similar to the Progressive vehicle (YE 4390) and a Maudslay (VE 919), together with a Ford 18-seater, which was immediately sold. Of the routes taken over, the most frequent was the daily service 1 (Fowlmere - Harston - Haslingfield - Cambridge) which was extended on market days to serve Royston. In Harston & District days the buses followed a very roundabout route via Reed, Barkway and Barley but after Premier took over they ran direct via the A505 between Royston and Dotterall. The slightly more direct service 2 ran to Royston via Melbourn on market days, while Barrington's link with the outside world was provided by service 3 to Cambridge. Spurred on by members of the local Women's Institute, Mr Lainson applied to divert this service via Hauxton, saving villagers the long walk to the main A10 road. He entertained the ladies to afternoon tea on the day of the hearing, where objections were received from Eastern Counties, whose service 108 stopped on the main road at Hauxton Gap. Premier's application was nevertheless granted and Hauxton now had a bus service for the first time, though it ran only on Saturdays and Sundays to begin with. In October 1938 services 2 and 3 were linked (as service 2) to provide a through Cambridge - Barrington - Royston facility on Wednesdays.

A DREAM STARTS TO COME TRUE

Premier Travel's other local route was the former Royal Blue service to the May Bumps, which ran for four days in June each year. Mr Lainson's enthusiasm for long-distance coaches has already been noted but in 1936 Premier's express work consisted only of the former Royal Blue service to Great Yarmouth, now numbered 4, which ran on Saturdays from July to September. In 1937 the express operations were given a considerable boost, for the Empire's Best fleet was now unable to cope with the loadings on its two routes to Clacton. The licence for the Birmingham service was accordingly sold to Premier Travel for £505,

Above: The splendid Duple-bodied Dennis Lancet 2 **CCE 568** again, photographed on service 5 from Birmingham to Clacton, after the Cambridge stop moved from Lensfield Road to Drummer Street. The licence for this service was later acknowledged to be the best purchase Premier ever made. *(Author's Collection)*

Below:. One of Long's AEC Regal coaches, **CER 16** was new in 1937. It is seen here in Drummer Street on one of the services to the West Suffolk border villages. The body had 32 seats and gave a very comfortable ride. This was clearly a wartime picture: the AEC had been fitted with headlamp masks, but was strangely devoid of white markings, present on the double-decker behind. *(Cambridgeshire Collection)*

probably the most important purchase in Premier's history. Service 5 (as it became) was a very valuable cross-country route, linking Birmingham, Coventry and Leicester with Clacton-on-Sea, by way of Northampton, Bedford, Cambridge and Haverhill. Empire's Best continued for many years afterwards to operate from London to Clacton, a popular holiday destination for Londoners and Midlanders alike. Premier's timetable promised the "latest type of sun-saloon coaches" with "courteous and efficient drivers." Booking agents were established over a wide area, ready to "gladly give details of connecting services." Service 5 initially ran on three days of the week throughout the summer and became so busy that it was necessary to hire coaches (some of which were definitely not of the latest type) from far and wide to handle the loadings. On busy summer Saturdays as many as twenty coaches were sometimes needed, drawn from operators stretching from Essex to the Midlands. Premier had two new coaches of its own, the first of which was a Bedford WTB (BVE 668) with a 25-seat Duple body, delivered in December 1936. In May 1937, a larger Dennis Lancet 2 (CCE 568) became the company's flagship vehicle. Its Duple body had seats for 35 passengers in opulent, art-deco surroundings and it was source of great pride to its owners.

DOWN BUT NOT OUT

A less up-market purchase was a second ex-Alexander Gilford 168OT (WG 1284), while a disused Harston & District Reo Pullman (VE 855) was returned to service after six of its seats were removed. This created an empty area, devoid of handrails, across which passengers had to dash in order to reach the remaining seats. This modification was necessary to provide a one-man bus, for which the maximum legal capacity was then 20. Economies were now necessary, for Premier was in financial difficulties. Following a trading loss in 1937 Sir Christopher Magnay resigned, along with his associate Captain C G P Kirk. Mr Lainson became Chairman and, assisted by Mr Thompson, set about improving the financial position and saving the company.

Further new coaches were now out of the question but two more Gilfords were obtained. One (HX 3464) was another AS6 20-seater, while the other (TM 8465, known as 'Tom Mix') had a 30-seat Strachan body on a 168OT chassis. It had served several previous owners, including Eastern National, and was bought for £50 from a travelling salesman. Money was also saved by the very flexible use of the vehicles. For example, the coach working the Saturday express to Yarmouth operated into Cambridge as a service 1 bus from Fowlmere. Two other coaches were able to combine a Saturday and Sunday excursion to Clacton with timings to and from Birmingham on service 5, covering 250 miles, all in revenue-earning service. The combination of hard work and the loyalty of its staff saved Premier Travel, along with the determination of the British public to enjoy themselves. Unrest in Europe was giving rise to a feeling that war was in the air, and many people wanted have a last fling before the inevitable happened. The summer of 1939 was a particularly profitable one for Premier's express services, as the crowds headed for the sea and the sun. By then the fleet stood at eight vehicles.

OTHER INDEPENDENTS 1930-1939

The established village operators continued to expand and modernise. There was a small-scale takeover in March 1932 when Brand of Elsworth took over the operations of Watts of the same village. This gave Mr Brand additional journeys into St Ives and to Cambridge via Boxworth, but Watts' St Neots service was discontinued.

LONG'S BUS SERVICE

At West Wratting, Long's Bus Service (as it had now become) successfully applied to operate a second route into Cambridge. This ran from Burrough Green via Brinkley and Weston Colville to West Wratting, from where it followed the existing route via Balsham and Fulbourn. The full list of services then being run by Mr Long is as follows:

  1 Thurlow - Withersfield - Weston Colville - West Wratting - Balsham -

Above: A splendid Burwell & District line-up in around 1930. The leading vehicle is **VE 1050**, a Willowbrook-bodied Daimler CF6 ready to work service 2 to Ely. It is followed by **ER 9457**, an Associated Daimler also with a Willowbrook body, the AEC (**ER 5431**), and what appear to be a Garner and a Ford 'T'. *(J R Neale Collection)*

Below: As well as the Daimlers for which it later became famous, Burwell & District purchased several other makes of vehicle. This AEC Regal (**VE 7148**) was purchased in 1931 from Bush & Twiddy, who also built the body. After seven years of service it was rebodied by Watson of Lowestoft and repainted in the 'reversed' cream and brown livery. *(J R Neale Collection)*

Fulbourn - Cambridge (see note)

2 Balsham - West Wratting - Weston Colville - West Wickham - Horseheath - Haverhill (Fri)

3 West Wratting - Weston Colville - Brinkley - Burrough Green - Thurlow - Haverhill (Fri)

3a Thurlow - Withersfield - Haverhill (Fri)

4 West Wratting - Weston Colville - Brinkley - Westley Waterless - Burrough Green - Dullingham - Newmarket (Tues)

5 Burrough Green - Weston Colville - West Wratting - Balsham - Fulbourn - Cambridge (Mon-Sat)

The Weston Colville to Cambridge section of service 1 was a daily operation, with the extension from Thurlow running on Mondays, Wednesdays and Saturdays. Services 1, 3 and 4 were coordinated with Ortona routes in the area.

Mr Long purchased two more new Reo saloons, comprising a GE (VE 3696) in 1930 and a Speedwagon (VE 6672) early in 1932, while a Commer Centurion (ACE 246) followed two years later. All had 20-seat bodies, that on the Speedwagon featuring a two-door layout. The need for larger vehicles led to the purchase of two AEC Regals, with luxurious 32-seat coach bodies. The first (AVE 543) was delivered in the spring of 1935 and was followed two years later by a Regal II (CER 16).

COUNTRY BUSES IN THE 1930s - A PASSENGER REMEMBERS

An idea of rural bus travel in those far-off days can be gained from the recollections of Mr Richard Covill, of West Wratting, who was a regular passenger on Long's buses.

"I travelled on the school bus from Westley Waterless to Cambridge from 1932 to 1937, although for a while I cycled to Dullingham and caught the train from there. The bus ran empty from West Wratting to Burrough Green, and the driver would usually hoot as he passed my house. That was my signal to get out of bed. The bus would turn round at the rectory in Burrough Green and wait for any latecomers. I caught it on its way back. The

journey to school in the morning was sometimes very subdued, with boys and girls often finishing their homework. We would stop at the depot in West Wratting while the crew had a cup of tea, and in the summer we would all reach out through the windows and pick as many apples as we could. This did not amuse Mrs Long, who was very strict and would deal with anyone who did not behave properly on the buses. Mr Long was a very nice man, short and dark with a moustache, and he was a bit of a joker. He sometimes drove the bus, and he would entertain the passengers by playing the latest songs on a harmonica. Another regular driver was Charlie Jaggard.

"The journeys home from school in the afternoons were always much noisier. One of the conductors was called Percy Radford and Mrs Long was definitely not amused when we decorated the back of his jacket with coloured chalks. Another conductor was George Britchfield. One day we had a learner driver (no L-plates!) and we met a steam-roller near the old school in Brinkley. The bus went into a ditch and tilted over to about 45 degrees, but the steam roller pulled us out.

"The buses were blue, and the earliest ones I can remember were 14-seaters, with seats on either side of the rear emergency exit and two seats facing inwards. There was also a 26-seater with lots of chrome on it. It was rather noisy and not very comfortable. He also had two 32-seaters - I think they were AECs - they were very luxurious."

After Premier Travel acquired Long's Coaches in 1949, Charlie Jaggard remained with the company. A driver for many years before he became a school bus attendant and then a garage man, he remained with the company until he was well past retirement age. Very much a country busman, he was still with the company when he died in 1978.

Richard Covill now lives in West Wratting, not far from the site of the former Long's Coaches depot, which is now occupied by houses.

BURWELL & DISTRICT MOTOR SERVICE

By 1930 the Mansfield buses were operating six daily journeys into Cambridge, with an additional late bus back to the village on

Above: Whippet's Dennis Lancet 2, **EW 7709**, was new in 1933 and looked less coach-like than those operated by Premier or Burwell & District. The Willowbrook coachwork was nevertheless very well appointed and the whole ensemble purposeful and comfortable. In this view it sparkles outside its home depot when new. It served its owners well, lasting until 1950. *(Whippet Coaches)*

Below: Weeden was another operator to favour Gilford coaches, and was one of several local firms to acquire second-hand examples from the Alexander fleet, including this 168OT (**WG 1275**). The vehicle was equipped with the familiar (for Gilfords) Wycombe coachwork. The destination blind reads 'ICKLETON SAWSTON GT SHELFORD'. *(Author's Collection)*

Saturdays. The fleetname 'Burwell & District Motor Service' was adopted and a fascinating selection of new and secondhand vehicles joined the fleet. Private hire was becoming an increasingly important part of the business, and most of the new arrivals were coaches. A GMC T30 (VE 2289) with a 20-seat Waveney body was delivered in December 1929, followed by a second Daimler CF6 (MT 3957), this time with a 31-seat Duple coach body, which had been new to Empire's Best of Wood Green. This replaced the last of the three Garners (ER 5087). The Daimlers were quiet and smooth running vehicles and another new CF6 with a Willowbrook bus body (VE 5551) was purchased in the spring of 1931, although the next few years saw the purchase of no fewer than six other makes of chassis. An AEC Regal (VE 7148) arrived in 1932. This had been built as a demonstrator in 1931 and had a 31-seat Bush & Twiddy body. A small Albion Victor (VE 9010) in 1933 was followed by a larger, 32-seat Valliant from the same manufacturer (ACE 764) in 1934, along with a rare Star Flyer VB4 (UA 6581), and a Bedford WLB 20-seater (HA 9797). The bus network saw further expansion. Service 4 was extended northwards from Fordham to Soham and became a daily operation, while a new service 11 continued from Fordham to Isleham and Mildenhall on Mondays, Wednesdays, Saturdays and Sundays.

George Mansfield died in 1935, but his widow Maud continued the business, assisted by her sons Horace and Reg and daughters Elsie and Doris (Dolly). The updating of the fleet had continued and a second WLB (AVE 549) was purchased new, while the former Empire's Best Daimler (MT 3957) received a new Duple coach body. January 1937 saw the delivery of an impressive Dennis Lancet 2 (BVE 872) which was very similar to Premier Travel's newest vehicle, followed later in the year by another Albion Victor (CCE 768) and a 20-seat Leyland Cub (CK 4790). A larger, 26-seat Cub SKPZ2 (CVE 551) was added in 1938, together with a Dennis Ace (AKR 937) with a 20-seat bus body, previously with London Transport. In the same year the AEC Regal (VE 7148) received a very modern-looking new body built by Watson of Lowestoft. Another vehicle to be rebodied also

started life in London. This was a six-wheel Leyland Titanic (AGH 149) which began life as a 62-seat double-decker but received an impressive new Harrington coach body before it entered service at Burwell in 1939. Both of these coaches carried a 'reversed' livery of cream and brown, and by the summer of 1939 the fleet stood at ten vehicles, half of which were less than five years old.

Additional journeys between Lode village and Cambridge were introduced in December 1937 after Major Francis withdrew his service. Burwell & District continued to operate market day services to Ely (2), Bury St Edmunds (7) and Newmarket (8), with an additional bus (6) from Upware and Wicken into Ely. Despite the loss of the routes from Cambridge to Caldecote and The Wilbrahams, the company retained its Saturday only service (3) to The Eversdens.

WHIPPET COACHES

Now settled in Hilton, Whippet also purchased a new Dennis Lancet 2 coach (EW 7709) with a luxurious Willowbrook body, although it was more bus-like in appearance than the Premier Travel and Burwell vehicles. It joined a 20-seat Gilford CP6 bus (EW 6507) and a Bedford WLB coach (EW 7078). Mr Lee purchased three more secondhand Gilford coaches as traffic built up on the express service (4) from Huntingdon to London. These comprised UT 5286, with a 166SD chassis, and 168OT types WG323 (which had started its career in Scotland in the Alexander fleet) and GJ 5293. Service 1 from St Ives to Cambridge only operated on Saturdays and (via Fenstanton) on Sundays, although the section from Hilton additionally ran on Wednesdays. The circular route (2) via Caldecote and Toft also ran on Wednesdays and Saturdays, and both routes continued to terminate in Cambridge at the Merton Arms. Most of Whippet's other routes provided links from Graveley, Papworth and Hilton to Huntingdon (service 3), St Ives (5) and St Neots (6), while service 5a linked the isolated village of Woodhurst with St Ives. An extension of service 3 from Warboys was started in 1934, but this lasted only a few months. Whippet's bus route network then remained largely unaltered for many years.

Above: Drayton's vehicle policy was similar to Weeden's. In 1930 this Gilford AS6 (**GK 9111**) was acquired. Believed to be a former demonstrator, it is seen here on the main route from Bishop's Stortford to Royston. *(J F Higham)*

Below: In 1932 Gill's Bus Service purchased this new Bedford WLB (**EW 7332**). It had a 20-seat Duple body and is seen here outside the operator's garage in Godmanchester. *(Courtesy A Gill)*

WEEDEN'S MOTOR SERVICES

To the south, Mr Weeden had moved his operations by 1930 from Heydon to nearby Chrishall. By 1936 his service 1 was running on Mondays, Wednesdays, Saturdays and Sundays from Great Chishill to Cambridge via Chrishall, Ickleton and Sawston. Service 2 ran to Bishop's Stortford via Clavering on Thursdays, Saturdays and Sundays, with a choice of routes on Tuesdays from Chrishall to Saffron Walden, via Clavering (4) or Littlebury (5), the latter also running on Fridays, Saturdays and Sundays, usually continuing to Linton via Little Walden and Hadstock. Service 7 was a Tuesday circular from Saffron Waldsen via Ashdon, Radwinter and Seward's End, while the Friday coach to London, originally numbered 3, was now referred to as service 6 after several revisions. The ever-popular Clacton was also served by a summer express from Great Chishill. This ran on Wednesdays and Saturdays and offered a direct journey to the Essex resort from Saffron Walden and several nearby villages.

After taking delivery of two more small Dodge buses (VE 3022 and VE 4422) in 1930, Mr Weeden built up a fleet of secondhand Gilfords, starting with a pair of second hand AS6 coaches (GH 9947 and GO 9556). A new Albion 530 (BCE 372) was delivered in 1935, fitted with a Watson 20-seat coach body, followed by three former Alexander Gilford 168OT coaches (WG 333, WG 1273 and WG 1275). The last arrived in 1937 along with another new Albion, this time a PK114 (CUR 921), with a Waveney body. For front-line coach work Mr Weeden purchased a splendid Dennis Lancet 2 (CVE 12) and a Bedford WTB (CVE 424), both with Duple bodies. By mid-1938 nearly all the small Dodge and Graham buses had been replaced along with the first two Gilfords, although a small, second hand Reo (DO 8042) joined the fleet in the summer of 1939.

DRAYTON BROTHERS MOTOR SERVICES

At Barley, Mr Drayton's sons Will and Arthur were now fully involved with the business and the above title was adopted. The fleet intake

was very similar to Weeden's and in 1930 comprised a Dodge (UR 7961) and a Gilford AS6 (GK 9111, believed to be a former demonstrator). A second AS6 (JH 4429) followed two years later and another Dodge (AJH 107) was delivered in 1935. No more new vehicles were added to stock until 1938 when a very rare Dennis Pike (DRO 972) was delivered. It was one of only fifteen built and carried a 20-seat Duple body. Drayton's also acquired two of the ex-Alexander Gilford 168OTs (WG 332 and WG 1286). Fleet modernisation was completed by three Bedford WTB coaches (BAJ 161, BFD 955 and CWD840) and the almost inevitable Dennis Lancet 2 (ENK 387), with a Duple coach body which tried (unsuccessfully) to look fully fronted. The Graham and Dodge vehicles were all withdrawn by 1939.

By then Drayton's service 4 into Cambridge was running on Mondays and Saturdays, with one return journey from Nuthampstead via Barley, Fowlmere and Newton. Buses on service 1 were provided daily to Bishop's Stortford and on most days to Royston, with additional buses into Royston from Nuthampstead on market days. Services 2 and 5 ran on market days and Sundays to Hitchin and via various routes to Royston. The Chrishall - Heydon - Barley - London express service also operated on Fridays and was also numbered 6. A Drayton coach left Chrishall and a Weeden coach left Heydon at 8.30am Friday morning, passing each other in the short distance between the two villages as they travelled in opposite directions to the capital.

CHIVERS & SONS LTD

Better known for jams and jellies than buses, this company became a PSV operator following the passing of the Road Traffic Act in 1930. Steven Chivers founded the business in 1873 to use up spare fruit from the family's orchards in Histon, and the Orchard Factory opened soon afterwards. It expanded rapidly, drawing staff from a very wide area and eventually employing 3,000 people. The factory was beside the Cambridge to St Ives railway line, and some of the workforce arrived by train, while Ortona was already providing three special buses in the years up to

The policy followed by Eastern Counties of fitting new bodywork to older chassis began in 1935 and continued for many years. Former Ortona **AH89** (**VE 3198**), new in 1930, is seen *(above)* on service 132 with its original Brush open-staircase body and *(below)* at the Railway Station on service 101 after a new Eastern Coach Works body had been fitted in 1938. The bus survived in this form until 1950. The immaculate appearance of the conductor, complete with cash bag and TIM correctly worn, is notable though not uncommon for that era of pride in work and appearance. *(C W Routh; Author's Collection)*

1914. After the war Chivers began to operate its own buses, and acquired a large number of Tilling-Stevens vehicles from a variety of sources. Some of these were rebuilt to a very high standard in the company's own workshops for use as lorries and vans, while others retained their original bodywork for use as staff buses. Most received new registrations, early examples being CE 9174/5 and ER 4147, all with TTA1 chassis. In 1926 they were joined by similar EB 3557 from Haddenham & District, and TTA2 saloon ER 938, previously with Bedford of Caxton. The same year saw the purchase, from Eastern Counties Road Car, of the first of many Tilling-Stevens TS3s. The Chivers workshop transformed one of these (XB 8389) into a huge 89-seat covered top double-decker, the first to operate in Cambridge. It lasted in this form until the 1930 Road Traffic Act came into force, after which it was rebuilt as a tanker. With the passing of the Act, Chivers was granted a PSV operator's licence and was allowed to charge the staff for using is services. By 1934 there were fourteen Tilling-Stevens TS3, TS3A and TS6 double-deckers in service. These had been new to Brighton, Hove & Preston United (later Brighton, Hove & District), East Kent, Maidstone & District and North Western. By then Chivers also had factories at Ely, Huntingdon and Wisbech (with others further afield), while the company's own fruit farms covered a very wide area. Tilling-Stevens remained the usual choice for buses for many years, notable exceptions being a pair of Leyland TD1s and an Albion saloon. Chivers continued their PSV operations for many years, although the number of buses gradually declined as Eastern Counties took over the routes. Several other local firms also purchased buses (usually old ones) for use as non-PSVs to transport their workers, but none were as inventive as Chivers.

PAPWORTH VILLAGE SETTLEMENT

In January 1938 another service was licensed as a PSV operation for the first time, although the operator had already been providing a service for many years. This was Papworth Village Settlement, established in 1919 when the Cambridge Tuberculosis Society treatment moved its local treatment centre from Bourn to Papworth. A Peerless 5-ton lorry initially met the need for a direct service to Cambridge, and six nurses, patients and visitors could usually be accommodated along with the coal and other supplies for the settlement. No fares were charged, and priority was given to nursing staff.

The first bus had a home made body built on the chassis of a Straker-Squire car, donated by Chivers of Histon. Far more luxurious was a Lancia ambulance, which served throughout the First World War and was donated by the Canadian Red Cross. Registered CE 5987, it had pneumatic tyres and reputedly could reach a speed of 70 mph. More sedate was a 14-seat Morris (ER 5621), which was followed by several small Fords, including an 18-seater (VE 4482) in 1930. This lasted for six years, after which it was sold to Harry Brown's 'Royal Blue' coaches. The replacement vehicle was a 20-seat Dennis Ace (BER 783), which faithfully maintained the service for twenty years. The only route ever operated was from Papworth to Cambridge, terminating at the Railway Station. Although regarded mainly as a works service, it also carried schoolchildren from Caxton Cross Roads and Knapwell Turn, but no other stops were allowed between Papworth and the Cambridge boundary. Fares could be charged after the service was licensed, although pre-booking was essential and a list of passengers had to be available for inspection by the Traffic Commissioners as required. The little brown Papworth bus was a regular sight in Cambridge, with three return journeys on Mondays to Saturdays. The normal terminus was later changed to Drummer Street, although the Railway Station was still served by request.

L D QUINSEE

When Eastern Counties acquired the Comfort & Reliance business in 1934, one of the Lancia coaches (ER 9748) passed to Mr L D Quinsee, who operated from Mr Wheatley's former premises in Sturton Street, Cambridge. Mr Quinsee appears to have operated under the fleetname 'Comfort Coaches' and he also owned a former LGOC Associated Daimler

Above: Also at the Railway Station is **NA15** (**VF 2826**), an Associated Daimler 423, which began its life with United Automobile Services. Known to crews as 'nannies', they too received new Eastern Coach Works bodywork. *(The Omnibus Society Collection)*

Below: The regular saloon on the 'back road' service 119 to Royston was this all-Leyland Lion LT2 (**VE 4805**). It was one of the last buses delivered to Ortona, and was numbered **AL20** in the Eastern Counties fleet. Driver Holland once carried 119 passengers on a service 119 bus, but not this one! *(C W Routh)*

(YE 4373), although no further details of his activities have so far been discovered.

FORDHAM & DISTRICT

Ernest George Palmer started his operations in the 1920s under the above name. His early fleet consisted of small single-deckers, including a Chevrolet (CF 9874), a Reo (PY 7383) and a larger Gilford 168OT (KX 7843). He then purchased several Bedfords, with WLB or WTB chassis. He ran market day buses from his home village to Newmarket, Ely, Bury St Edmunds and Mildenhall, the most frequent being the service to Newmarket. By 1930 he had started a service from Chippenham to Cambridge via Fordham and Burwell. One return journey was provided, on Saturday afternoons, although most of the route was already covered by Ortona services 111 and 122 and Burwell & District's main route. The Cambridge service was discontinued in 1937 but the market services continued.

GILL'S BUS SERVICE

Albert James Gill had been in business since 1904 as a cycle and motor cycle engineer in Offord Cluny. In 1914 he moved to premises in Cambridge Street in the centre of Godmanchester. He extended his activities to include cars and in about 1920 decided to enter the bus and coach business. Like many pioneering busmen he began operations with a former Word War 1 ambulance, in this case a De Dion, which was noted for its speed. With the help of his brother-in-law, a carpenter, Mr Gill converted the body for use as a bus. In 1923 it was joined by a 27-seat Leyland S (registered HE 8), new to Barnsley & District but purchased from Peterborough Electric Traction. Subsequent purchases included a new Chevrolet 14-seater in 1929, followed three years later by a new Bedford WLB (EW 7332), with a 20-seat Duple body. Three larger Gilfords then joined the fleet, including yet another former Alexander example (WG 329). All carried a livery of light blue and cream with the fleetname 'Gill's Bus Service'. Several infrequent bus routes served the thinly populated area to the north of Huntingdon. Most ran only on market days, serving Oundle, St Ives, St Neots and Bedford. The Oundle route was cut back in January 1937 to run as a circular from Godmanchester and Huntingdon to Upwood, following the opening of the aerodrome there. The early 1930s also saw the start of a Saturday evening express service from Huntingdon and Godmanchester to Cambridge for cinema performances, usually at the Central or Victoria cinemas. This continued until around 1938, when a similar service to Peterborough was introduced, although Huntingdon by then had its own cinema. Mr Gill also advertised excursions from Godmanchester.

Left: Philip 'Laddie' Holland is at the right of this trio during the 1937 strike by Eastern Counties and Eastern National crews, when the employers offered the equivalent of an increase of 0.05 pence an hour. The public were sympathetic but the pay rise the crews hoped for was not forthcoming. *(Courtesy P Holland)*

Below: In a scene familiar after 1940, an Eastern Counties double-decker, complete with wartime 'clippie', heads down Sidney Street on a local service. The soldier crossing the roads reminds us that uniforms were everywhere; unfortunately, being just there at just that moment, he obscures the identity of the bus. *(Author's Collection)*

12. Major Operators 1936 to 1939

EXTENDED LIVES

As well as the new Bristols, Eastern Counties was still operating a large number of former Ortona vehicles. Many of these very well maintained machines were comparatively modern and it was decided to extend their lives by fitting new bodywork, starting in December 1935 with the Leyland PLSC Lions. Charabancs AL21-3 (ER 8801-3) and buses AL61/2/6 (ER 8886/7, VE 306) all received new ECOC bus bodies with rear entrances and were renumbered AL2-6 and AL1 respectively. In April 1936 Leyland TS2 saloons AT76/7 (VE 309/10), previously fitted with Leyland 29-seat bodies, were rebodied by ECW (as it had now become) as 56-seat highbridge double-deckers and renumbered AH242/3. In December similar bodywork (but with 54 seats) replaced the open staircase Hall, Lewis products on Leyland TD1s VE 302/3, which were renumbered from A68/9 to AH68/9, the letter H denoting highbridge vehicles. In the years up to 1939 all the former Ortona TD1s were given new ECW bodies, some highbridge and some lowbridge.

A further modification (which included the TS2s) was the replacement of the Leyland petrol engines by Gardner diesel units, while some of the double-deckers also received new chassis frames in 1945. Other former Ortona vehicles were less fortunate and were withdrawn. These were Dennis G saloons D52/3 (VE 307/8) and the SOS 'ODD' rebuilds, along with all the remaining Gilford coaches acquired from Westminster and Varsity. Many other vehicles, which started life with Eastern Counties Road Car, Peterborough Electric Traction and United, also received new bodies and some were allocated to Cambridge. As well as the ex-Eastern Counties Road Car TD1s they included former United vehicles with chassis by Associated Daimler (NA class) and Tilling-Stevens (P class). These received new bus bodies between 1935 and 1937, and the Tilling-Stevens vehicles were also fitted with Gardner diesel engines. Eastern National also started a rebodying programme, and from 1933 a number of Leyland PLSC3 Lions received new saloon bodies built by either ECW or Beadle.

THE 1937 BUS STRIKE

One other event of 1937 was the strike by Eastern Counties and Eastern National crews. This started in May in support of a claim for higher wages and went on for several weeks after the Union rejected the increase offered by the Management. Not all the crews favoured strike action and some tried to take buses out. Pickets at the garage tried to prevent this and on one occasion a brick was thrown at a bus. The smaller operators did not wish to take sides but they were anxious that some services should be maintained, fearing a loss in passenger numbers if no buses at all were provided. Premier Travel applied to operate more buses between Cambridge and Royston via the main road (covering Eastern Counties 108 and Eastern National 41) and between Cambridge and Cottenham via services 104, 137 and 137A. The latter application was refused but the Premier buses were well filled on the Royston road. Whippet Coaches gained a short-term licence to operate a daily service from Cambridge to Bedford as a replacement for Eastern National 29, with the agreement of the Bedford & Cambridge Drivers' and Conductors' Strike Committee. The independents also enjoyed increased loadings on the country roads they shared with the larger operators. Some buses were still provided over all or part of Eastern Counties 103, 112 and 112A (covered by Weeden); 110, 114 and 162 (Long); 111 and 122 (Burwell & District). Parts of the 118, 118A, 119 and Eastern National 29A were covered on various days by Burwell & District, Premier Travel and Whippet, while Barker, Blue Belle and Whippet filled gaps left by the suspension of the 123, 123A and 151. At Trumpington (and possibly elsewhere) striking Eastern Counties crews were on hand to check that the independents did not run any unauthorised

Above: With headlamp masks in place and white edging on its mudguards, Burwell & District's Leyland Titanic (**AGH 149**) shows the wartime modifications required on all buses. The coach started life in London as a 62-seat double-decker in 1933. It joined the Burwell fleet six years later and received a new Harrington coach body. *(The Omnibus Society Collection)*

Below: In 1941 the shortage of buses led to the hiring by Eastern Counties of three AEC Regents from Westcliff-on-Sea Motor Services. They had Weymann lowbridge bodies complete with roof route number boxes, a feature more familiar on London buses although not used by Westcliff. The three buses remained with Eastern Counties until 1945. **JN 4748** is seen in Drummer Street. *(M G Doggett Collection)*

extra journeys. The crews eventually returned to work, although the Management did not improve on its original offer.

A DRIVER LOOKS BACK - PHILIP 'LADDIE' HOLLAND

"I was born on 7th July 1911 at Melbourn, near Royston and I went to the village school. My first job after I left was on a poultry farm and my wage at the end of the first week was 6 shillings [30 pence]. Dad said "Go back and tell them you're worth 8 shillings!" I did, and that became my wage until I left six months later. After that I worked for four and a half years in a grocer's shop. I got married in 1930, when I was 19 years old - we were together for 67 years until my wife passed away in 1997.

"In 1936 I joined Eastern Counties as a conductor, based at the Royston outstation. To begin with I used to go to work on my bike, but later on we moved to Royston. My regular mate was Joe Varney, whose father Jack was also a driver, and we worked the services to Cambridge. The 108 went along the main road, with every other bus through Meldreth and Shepreth, and the 119 went the 'back road' way through Bassingbourn. They kept one saloon bus there with a regular crew, Charlie Stewart and Ted Gillham. In Royston the buses used the High Street, Market Hill and Barkway Road, where we had to reverse and stop outside the Green Man. The buses were kept in the yard behind the pub. In 1937 I moved up to being a driver. They had to bring a chap down from Scotland Yard for the test because Royston was in the Metropolitan Traffic Area. My first conductor was Reg Townsend, whose parents kept the Green Man. His previous driver Arthur Northrop had joined the RAF. One of the first buses I drove was A2 (ER 8804) and I can also remember A80 (VE 1967). The Leylands were good performers but their engines had been modified to try to save fuel. When they replaced the petrol engines with diesels the first ones were very rough and noisy. They also had to cut away some of the floorboards in the cab, so that the pedals would fit. This made them so draughty that I used to wear my bike clips in the winter. After that they changed to Bristols, which slogged along but they weren't nearly as lively. We had one, LL6 (CNG 206) that couldn't have pulled a hen off her nest. [This bus had a 4-cylinder engine.] Another thing that happened in 1937 was the strike. The Union in Cambridge put in a pay claim and we were offered a rise of one eighth of an old penny an hour [0.05 pence]. We weren't having that but they wouldn't increase their offer so we had to accept it in the end. There was no strike pay so we had to go round collecting. One conductor, who came from 'up north' disappeared back there, and took quite a lot of the strike fund with him."

In the years leading up to the Second World War there was a large intake of new vehicles into the Eastern Counties and Eastern National fleets. In January 1938 Eastern Counties received the first of a batch of eight Dennis Ace 20-seaters (D1-8, CAH 921-8), while delivery began in March of 36 Bristol L4G saloons (LL1-36, CNG 201-36). The first twelve were dual-purpose 32-seaters the rest being 35-seat buses. All the new vehicles had ECW bodies. A start was also made on rebodying the 1932 Leyland TD1s and TD2s. New Gardner engines had already replaced their original Leyland units, and in the years up to 1940 a total of six TD1s and seven TD2s received new ECW bodies, some highbridge and some lowbridge.

WASHINGTON AND BARKER TAKEN OVER

A small, more varied selection of vehicles also joined the fleet in 1938 following the takeovers of three local operators. Bert Washington of Littleport sold his business in January along with seven vehicles, although Eastern Counties only used three of them. These were a Commer PN3 with a 20-seat Duple bus body (JE 2780) and a pair of Dennis Lancet 32-seaters (EB 9897 and JE2 510). Eastern Counties numbered the vehicles C6, DL3 and DL4 but the former Washington services were not given numbers until November.

In March Barker's Fenstanton & District services were taken over. They were numbered 151A (St Ives - Fenstanton - Cambridge), 153 (Cambridge - Madingley - Dry Drayton - Cambridge circular) and 154 (Cambridge - Coton). There was no room for them in

Above: The first double-decker in the Burwell & District fleet was **KJ 1912**, all-Leyland TD1, new in 1931 to Maidstone Corporation. With an official seating capacity of 48, it was found on occasions to be capable of carrying more than 100 airmen, who preferred the crowded conditions to the long walk home. It is seen in Drummer Street, with the troublesome AEC 'Q' lurking in the background. *(J R Neale Collection)*

Below: The members of the US Armed Forces who arrived in 1942 made the local buses even more crowded, but were irresistible to some of the local female population. With one headlamp masked and the other probably with its bulb removed, Premier Travel Gilford AS6 **HX 3464** is seen adding to the war effort. Its Duple body officially had seating for 20, but undoubtedly carried more when the need arose. *(The Omnibus Society Collection)*

Drummer Street and they continued to terminate at the Merton Arms. Two 20-seat buses were retained, these being a Commer Centaur (EW 7406) and a Dennis G (XS 2284), which received fleet numbers C7 and D32. In the same month, the acquisition of the Worsdell Brothers' Blue Belle Coaches further strengthened Eastern Counties' position in the area. The Bluntisham to Cambridge via Earith service was initially numbered 107A and the Earith to Huntingdon route became 123B, with the Ely and St Ives journeys absorbed by service 125A. Eastern Counties had no use for the Blue Belle vehicles, three of which were immediately resold to Whippet. These were Gilfords EW 6764 and KF 513 and Bedford WLB EW 7227.

Eastern Counties received another large intake of new vehicles in 1939, starting with ten more Dennis Ace buses (D9-18, CVF 809-18). These were followed by no fewer than 50 Bristol L5Gs, this time with larger 5-cylinder engines. Most were 35-seat buses (LL37-74, CVF 837-74) but ten had 32-seat dual-purpose bodies (LL75-84, CVF 875-84), while the final two were 26-seat coaches with forward entrances (LS1/2, DAH 161/2). Among the former Ortona vehicles displaced were all the remaining Dennis GL and SOS 'Q' and 'M' types. Other withdrawals included the ex-Barker Dennis and the three former Washington machines.

Eastern National added further new Bristol/ECW vehicles to its fleet in 1938, comprising 28 L5G saloon buses and 20 K5G double-deckers. The company also continued to buy the businesses of small operators in its area, along with many non-standard vehicles. Among the fleets taken over were Harold Donne's 'Huntingdon Coaches' and F Lewis Slade's 'Offordian Coaches' of Offord D'Arcy in February. These takeovers gave Eastern National additional services in the Huntingdon and St Ives area, while in April the acquisition of Herbert Wilson's 'Clavering & District' business included more services into Royston and Saffron Walden.

STORM CLOUDS GATHERING

The last of the new vehicles were not delivered until August 1939. By then it was clear that events in Europe would soon lead the nation into another war, an early effect of this being the construction of airfields throughout the region. The flat East Anglian terrain was ideal for this and, even before the RAF began to expand in the mid-1930s, a number of airstrips had been built. These included the aerodrome at Duxford, which dated from the First World War. It was one of the earliest RAF stations and in the summer of 1938, as the international situation worsened, it was the first to be equipped with the new Spitfire. Bus services from Cambridge to the aerodrome were initially provided on Saturdays, by the extension of journeys from Sawston on the 103 and by diverting occasional journeys on the 112 (Saffron Walden) route. Another airfield was under construction at Oakington, and by the late summer of 1939 the surrounding land was being developed into the RAF station which would remain active for more than 30 years. Its construction closed the direct road from the village to nearby Long Stanton, and as a result service 107 (Cambridge - Willingham) was re-routed at Girton Corner to run via the main Huntingdon road. A new local service 152 from Market Hill via Newnham to Girton had started in 1938, and this was duly extended to Oakington in place of the 107. As preparations for war continued, the region's bus and coach operators were about to face their greatest challenge yet.

Above: Will they all fit in? The chassis of this Premier Leyland Tiger TS1 (**TF 1555**) was new in 1930 but the origins of the Alexander body are unknown, although it did not always seem to be very firmly attached. Purchased from Ribble but new to the Furness Omnibus Company, it was Premier's first Leyland. Despite its shortcomings, it served the company until 1951. *(The Omnibus Society Collection)*

Below: **EER 549** was a Daimler CWA6 with highbridge Brush bodywork. It entered service in 1945 as the third utility double-decker in the Burwell & District fleet. Despite their lack of refinement, they were reliable machines, this one lasting until 1956. *(Alan B Cross)*

13. War 1939 to 1945

On 2nd September 1939, as a long, hot summer was coming to an end, Driver Fred Barker was Clacton-bound on Premier Travel service 5 with a full load of holidaymakers. On arrival they learned of Neville Chamberlain's ultimatum to Hitler and, after a brief consultation, decided to return immediately to the Midlands and prepare for war, without even opening the boot of the coach. The next day Britain declared war on Germany, and everyone was encouraged to stay at home until their country needed them.

IS YOUR JOURNEY REALLY NECESSARY?

Preparations for the anticipated conflict had been going on for some time. Eastern Counties had already given an undertaking that vehicles would be available to transport service personnel at one hour's notice. Now, as gas masks were issued, buildings sandbagged, windows taped and Air Raid Precautions finalised, the region's bus and coach operators were faced with all sorts of new regulations, forms and work. Transport for evacuees was an early priority, and on the first day of hostilities a large number of buses and coaches were ordered to Cambridge railway station to meet the new arrivals and carry them on to their destinations. Mr Lainson was at Cambridge with Premier Travel's entire fleet, while across its large operating area Eastern Counties had over 200 vehicles in attendance at 30 stations. Extra buses and coaches were also needed to transport men and women engaged in essential war work, including the construction of more aerodromes. In Cambridge itself, Marshall's had opened their airfield on Newmarket Road in 1938 and the company became increasingly involved in maintaining and repairing aircraft. For security reasons the main road past Marshall's was closed during the early part of the war and traffic was diverted via Fen Ditton. After the road was reopened all buses passing the aerodrome had to stop, while passengers on board had their ID cards checked. The extra

traffic generated by the airfields resulted in several new bus routes. Eastern Counties introduced service 119A, which provided up to ten additional buses on weekdays between RAF Bassingbourn (opened in 1938) and Royston, while existing service 117A (Newmarket - Cowlinge) was extended to RAF Stradishall. Mr Weeden introduced new services from Whittlesford station and Cambridge to RAF Duxford, which were "extended to the WAAF HQ at Thriplow Turn when required." As the Royal Air Force increased its presence in the area, bus and coach operators sometimes found it difficult to provide enough vehicles. For a while the supply of new buses stopped completely as factories were turned over to war production, although Eastern National managed to take delivery of 25 more Bristol K5Gs, the last of which did not arrive until 1941. The vehicle shortage was made worse as buses and coaches were commandeered for military use, often at very short notice. Across the Eastern Counties fleet 21 vehicles were taken by the War Department, with a further 71 reserved for use by the ARP and the Home Guard, should the need arise. The RAF also took the pride of the Premier Travel fleet (Dennis Lancet CCE 568) but returned it after its engine failed.

At Cambridge 29 elderly single-deckers were converted for use as ambulances. These were Associated Daimler, SOS and Tilling-Stevens vehicles, which had originated in the Ortona, Peterborough Electric Traction and United fleets. On 29th September 1939 the introduction of fuel rationing added to the difficulties and service reductions were unavoidable. Eastern Counties withdrew or suspended seventeen express coach routes. In the Cambridge area, bus services 117C (Burwell - Bury St Edmunds), 129 (Railway Station - Coldham's Lane), 133 (Newmarket - Stetchworth Leys), 135 (Newmarket - Haverhill), 149 (Cambridge - Teversham), 163B (Ely - Littleport St Mary's) and 213A (Bury St Edmunds - Ely) all disappeared from the timetables. The village of Teversham continued to be served by a diversion of the

Above: The Eastern Counties wartime double-deckers looked very austere alongside the company's prewar vehicles. This postwar view shows **LKH3** (**FAH 103**), a Bristol K6A with a Park Royal body. It ran in this form until 1953, when it received a new ECW lowbridge body. The bus is on service 119, which in 1950 offered three buses to Royston on Wednesdays, although on other days most journeys ran only as far as Bassingbourn. *(Alan B Cross)*

Below: Delivered to Premier Travel in August 1945, **EER 570** carried the first non-utility body on a postwar Bedford, although it had the wartime OWB chassis. It originally carried a maroon livery but was repainted blue soon afterwards. Arthur Lainson stands second from the right in this view. *(The Omnibus Society Collection)*

114 (Cambridge - Newmarket). Other services were reduced on Saturdays and in the evenings, with no buses at all before midday on Sundays. In October Eastern National withdrew service 39 (Chelmsford - Saffron Walden), while December saw the end of the former Clavering & District 40 (Arkesden - Royston) and the Royston - Cambridge section of service 41. The independents also suspended their express routes, although in the case of the coastal services they would have done so anyway, the summer season having just ended. On Premier Travel service 5 the last coach was driven by Driver Sid Pennell, referred to earlier. In addition to its Felixstowe and Yarmouth express routes Burwell & District also withdrew service 11 (Mildenhall to Cambridge) and its market day buses to Ely. The London services of Weeden and Whippet also disappeared from the timetables.

THE END OF THE PHONEY WAR AND FURTHER REDUCTIONS

After all the initial excitement, very little seemed to be happening. Where was the war? As the nation waited for it to start and hopefully come to an early end, everyone settled down to enjoy an unexpected reprieve, a period known as the 'phoney war'. The RAF dropped leaflets over Europe and soldiers dug trenches, but the only casualties were caused by the blackout. Street lighting had ceased and headlamps had to be masked, with extra white areas painted on the front wings, side and rear panels and platform edges of buses. The work of bus crews became very difficult. Driving in the blackout was far from easy, and conductors sometimes had to walk in front of the bus to guide drivers, especially in foggy weather. Interior lighting was at a minimum: in Eastern Counties and Eastern National buses reduced to a single, hooded bulb suspended from the ceiling by a wire, which was pulled along inside the bus by the conductor.

The winter of 1939/40 was one of the worst of the century. The RAF was grounded and troops were called in to keep trains running. Life still proceeded calmly but was made harder by the introduction of food rationing on 8th January 1940. The severe winter gave way to an early spring and, still uncertain about what the future held, the crowds flocked to the seaside for what would be the last time for several years. The York Brothers express service to Yarmouth continued until 11th May, while Premier Travel and Midland Red planned reduced coastal services for the summer, although by then much of the coastline would be out of bounds to civilians. On 14th May, Chamberlain's unfortunate claim that "Hitler has missed the bus" was quickly followed by the fall of Denmark, Norway and France. The Dunkirk evacuation brought the 'phoney war' to an end and the threat of an invasion increased. Signposts were removed along with railway station name boards, while church bells were not to be rung unless the enemy invaded. Eastern Coach Works moved its production from the vulnerable east coast town of Lowestoft to a former United Counties bus garage at Irthlingborough in Northamptonshire. The war had arrived at last.

The first bombing raid on Cambridge took place on the night of 18th/19th June 1940, when two bombs severely damaged eight houses in Vicarage Terrace, killing ten people. With so many aerodromes in the region an additional hazard came from crashing aircraft. When a damaged bomber came down at Somersham on the night of 5th/6th October, seven houses were destroyed and eleven people lost their lives. Three people were killed when another bomber came down on a house in Histon Road. Amidst the destruction the bus operators struggled to maintain services. As well as vehicles and fuel, spare parts were in short supply and, before long, so were staff. By May 1940 so many men had been called up that Eastern Counties once again began to recruit women conductors and garage staff. Conductresses also appeared for the first time on Premier Travel buses. Although transport management was a reserved occupation, Premier had to struggle on without Mr Lainson, who departed for the Royal Naval Patrol Service. The day-to-day running of Premier Travel was left to Norman Thompson, now assisted by Mrs Lainson. Much to his dismay Mr Thompson (who had sold Harston & District in 1936) now found himself back in charge of a larger business. The maintenance of the fleet became increasingly difficult, although from 1942 this

Above: The takeover of the Weeden business added another Duple-bodied Dennis Lancet 2 to the fleet. Despite being known to staff as 'The Old Thumper' **CVE 12** was very comfortable to ride in, and is seen here at King's Cross coach station in London. It served Premier well, lasting until 1958. *(Alan B Cross)*

Below: Also acquired from Weeden were two small Albion coaches, the only vehicles of this make ever owned by Premier Travel. **CUR 921** had a PK114 chassis and a 26-seat Waveney body, and it lasted until 1952. In this snowy scene in Drummer Street it still wears Drayton's dark blue livery. *(Author's Collection)*

improved with the arrival of a suitably experienced driver (Mr M J Gifford) who eventually became the company's Chief Engineer. During the following year Mr R A Howard transferred from Eastern Counties to take up the post of Traffic Manager.

Eastern Counties withdrew two more express coach routes in April 1940, but despite all the difficulties life had to go on, and a few route changes took place on the buses. On the Cambridge local services the 105 was extended from Mowbray Road to Strangeways Road and the 139 from Gilbert Road to Roseford Road, with some buses continuing to Histon Railway Station. Service 130 was extended along Coldhams Lane to a new terminus at Stourbridge Grove. This partly replaced the 132, which was surprisingly withdrawn although it had only recently been extended to Newnham via Storey's Way. On the country routes the extension of part of the 107 to Earith absorbed the former Blue Belle 107A, while a new 116B for factory workers was introduced from Ely via Soham to Snailwell.

Plans to rebody more double-deckers were cancelled but most of the buses concerned had their bodies extensively rebuilt by ECW over the next three years. In an attempt to save fuel, Eastern Counties converted some of its buses to run on producer gas. Each one towed a two-wheeled trailer, which burned anthracite. The trailers were produced in the Bristol factory, and by April 1942 fourteen vehicles had been converted, including Cambridge-based LJ2 (NG 9902), a 1935 Bristol JJW. Several Eastern National vehicles were also converted but they did not run in the Cambridge area.

UNFROZEN BUSES AND THE END OF THE BEGINNING

By 1941 the shortage of new buses was so desperate that the Government temporarily lifted the freeze and allowed manufacturers to complete vehicles from parts already in stock. The buses were referred to as 'unfrozen' and six were allocated to Eastern Counties. They all had ECW bodywork built to pre-war standards, and comprised two more Dennis Ace 20-seaters (D19/20, DVF 519/20, although five had been ordered), together with five Bristol L5G buses (LL85-9, EAH 685/6,

787-9). In 1942 no fewer than 40 similar buses were received, numbered LL90-129 (with EAH and ENG registrations). They were intended to be 35-seaters but, along with several older saloons, soon had the seating reduced to 31 with all the seats facing inwards, so that 29 standing passengers could be crammed in. This arrangement was very unpopular and the buses soon became known as 'cattle trucks', but the company was only doing its best to make use of the resources it had. Three AEC Regent double-deckers (JN 3230/4297/4748) were also borrowed from Westcliff-on-Sea Motor Services. They had Weymann lowbridge bodies and stayed until 1945, at least one of them finding a temporary home in Cambridge. There were further raids by enemy bombers in the early part of the war, and the garage in Hills Road suffered minor damage. A far more serious incident took place in Newmarket on the afternoon of 18th February 1941, when several buildings on the north side of the High Street were severely damaged and 27 people were killed.

From 30th June Eastern Counties withdrew its remaining four express routes, including service E (Norwich - Cambridge - London). There were further bus service reductions from 4th November, although a new service 166 was introduced from Newmarket to Cambridge via the main road. It passed Marshall's and ran daily, although on Sundays it was restricted to "workers holding passes." To the south of Cambridge, one express route did not disappear completely. This was Drayton's London service, which continued to run from Chrishall to Anstey, continuing to Bishop's Stortford to connect with the 0930 train to Liverpool Street. The return journey was made by a similar connection from an evening train.

In October 1942, the Ministry of War Transport issued a directive to the effect that all PSV operators with fleets of 150 vehicles or more were required to convert 10% of their total fleets to run on producer gas. As far as Eastern Counties was concerned, this would have meant that some 55 vehicles would have been involved. In the event the number of conversions only reached 26, but no further examples were allocated to Cambridge.

Above: The Albion PK114 **CUR 921** in a photograph taken after it had been repainted in Premier livery. *(Author's Collection)*

Below: The last pre-war vehicle delivered to Weeden was **CVE 424**, a Bedford WTB with Duple 20-seat coachwork. Seen here on a works service after repainting in Premier Travel livery, it lasted for a further ten years with its new owner. *(Author's Collection)*

A WARTIME CONDUCTRESS RECALLS

Many bus operators had employed women as conductors during the First World War, and from 1940 history repeated itself. As more and more men left to join the forces, women were drafted in to replace them, working behind the scenes in garages and on the road. Most became conductresses and, despite some opposition from the remaining men to begin with, the women were soon accepted.

Gladys Caston became a conductress in 1941 and achieved fame soon afterwards when she won the 'Miss Cambridge' title. Known to colleagues and passengers as 'Glad', she loved her job and stayed with Eastern Counties for 42 years, becoming a familiar and popular figure on the local buses. In November 1948 she married Driver William Hughes, who had previously worked for London Transport. They sometimes worked together as a crew, although for many years Bill was the Driving Instructor at Cambridge, as well as being actively involved with the local branch of the Transport & General Workers' Union. Here is Glad's story:

"I was born Gladys May Caston on 8th December 1923, in Old Chesterton. We later moved to Brooks Road, on the other side of town. Every day I had to walk to Chesterton Girls' School in Gilbert Road - it was several miles there and back. I left school when I was 14 and my first job was at Pye's in Newmarket Road. Then I went to work in a laundry but I only stayed there for about a month. After that I had a job in Williams' fruit shop in Mill Road, where I stayed for six months before moving next door to the Arcadia newsagent and sweet shop. One day in March 1941 I received a letter from the Government, telling me that I was needed for war work. I was 18 years old and I'd thought about joining the WRNS but I went along to the interview, where I was given the choice of being a railway porter, working in a hospital kitchen or going on the buses. I chose the buses and I was sent to a doctor in Newnham for a medical. I'd been used to starting work at 5am and I was often out socialising until after midnight, but I still managed to pass. We didn't get much training and I was always a bit of a duffer at arithmetic, but I learned how to use the Willebrew

machines, got my conductor's badge (number FF8420) and was ready to start. We had to work on all the routes and I enjoyed going out into the country, but my favourite was always the 101 from the Station to Chesterton, where the buses turned round at Kendal Way. I liked the 139 too, but lots of the others didn't.

"It wasn't easy working in the blackout. We only had one very dim light in a cylinder, rather like a cocoa tin, which we could slide along the ceiling on the end of a wire. It didn't always stay there when the bus was full of servicemen. They often paid their fares with half-crowns instead of pennies, even though I always called out to them to "scrape the edges"'. [Half crown 2/6d (12½p) coins had ridged edges, unlike the similar size penny (1d) coins, which did not.] The buses were often packed, especially the 'cattle truck' single-deckers, but most of the passengers were wonderful. I called them 'my public!'

"We had one of the gas powered buses with trailers, and one mechanic was in charge of it. We didn't have to do anything to the trailer while we were out on the road, but it was hard to turn it round. One day we had it on the 139, and when the driver started reversing the bus went one way and the trailer went the other. Some drivers would drive further on until they came to a roundabout and turn round there. We also had the 'Westcliffs' on hire. Lots of drivers didn't like them because they were so unstable. One of these buses fell over on a factory journey into town from the Short Brothers factory on Madingley Road.

"One day I was sent out to work at Royston. They said I'd be there all day (but they never mentioned anything about meal breaks). I worked the last bus to Bassingbourn, which was packed with Canadian airmen. They were as drunk as lords! Back in Royston I sat down on my ticket box in the Market Place to wait for someone to come out from Cambridge to take me home.

I sat there until 3 o'clock in the morning, because they'd forgotten all about me in Cambridge, but eventually someone remembered and came out to fetch me. The same policeman had walked past several times but he hadn't said a word!

"On another occasion I was on the 101. There were lots of 'boys in blue' (injured

Above: This Dennis Pike (**DRO 972**) was one of only fifteen built and was acquired by Premier with the Drayton business. Its 20-seat Duple body made it suitable for use as a one man bus and it is seen here at Chrishall depot, after working the former Weeden service from Cambridge. *(J F Higham)*

Right: A 1947 Premier Travel timetable. *(Author's Collection)*

servicemen) staying at Chesterton Hall and a crowd were waiting at the stop. One had both his legs in plaster and could hardly move. It took me and four of his mates to get him onto the platform, and I told him to stay there, be my 'unofficial assistant conductor' and ring the bell when I called out. This worked until we got to Bridge Street, where I got down to help another passenger off the bus. For some reason my unofficial assistant conductor rang the bell and the bus set off without me. I had to run right through the town centre as far as the University Arms Hotel before I caught it."

THE END OF THE BEGINNING?

After two more hard winters and an extension of food rationing, the spring of 1942 was also notable for the arrival in the area of the first servicemen from the United States. Some local residents later claimed, perhaps unfairly, that the newcomers did more damage than the German air raids, which seems strange in a town used to the antics of high-spirited undergraduates. The locals gradually learned to accept the Americans, although their presence made the local buses even more crowded. Cambridge offered many attractions, including the American Red Cross Club in Trumpington Street at the former Bull Hotel. Drummer Street became very busy as everyone rushed to catch the last buses home after an evening in town. In November the Allied victory at El Alamein prompted Churchill's statement that this was "not the end, not the beginning of the end but perhaps the end of the beginning." This at last gave the country something to celebrate. The daily sight of convoys of Allied aircraft provided signs that the tide of the war was turning, although the construction of further airfields shattered the peace of many tranquil villages in the region.

In the meantime the ownership of the Eastern Counties Omnibus Company had changed. The relationship between Tilling and the BAT had not always been harmonious and the directors eventually decided to break up the joint company from 29th September 1942. Eastern Counties accordingly passed to Tilling Motor Services Ltd, which already owned Eastern National. Further afield, other former Tilling & BAT companies became part the

BET group, which now ceased to have any involvement in local bus services in East Anglia, although after the war the express coaches of several BET operators regularly passed through on their way to and from the coast.

As the stocks of pre-war bus parts ran out, so did the supply of unfrozen buses, and Eastern Counties received no more new vehicles until 1944. The Eastern Coach Works factory continued to refurbish the bodies on older vehicles and dealt with over 150 Eastern Counties vehicles, some of which had been damaged by enemy action, although it was not possible to build new bodies. Some buses were painted grey, partly because of a shortage of red paint but also to make them less visible to enemy aircraft. A large number of Eastern National vehicles also received new or refurbished bodies, the work being carried out mainly by Beadle, although some buses were dealt with by ECW or East Lancashire Coachbuilders.

The independents also enlarged their fleets to cope with the demands of the war and, in complete contrast to the standardised Eastern Counties intake, obtained a fascinating assortment of secondhand machines. Despite the withdrawal of its London service in 1940 there was plenty of work for the Whippet fleet, which gained Bedford, Dennis, Gilford, Leyland and AJS vehicles, the last-named manufacturer being far better known for its motorcycles. The Progressive fleet, which in 1939 stood at five coaches, almost doubled in size with the arrival of a former LGOC AEC Regal (GF 541, which joined a similar coach purchased just before the war), a 20-seat Morris bus (OD 3237), a Commer Invader (VX 8653) and a Gilford 168OT (HX 7571). Mr Long replaced his Reo Speedwagon with an AEC Regent (TV1631), which began its career as a double-decker with Nottingham Corporation but later acquired a Harrington coach body.

LADDIE HOLLAND'S WAR

"During the war they took on women as conductors and I worked with Ida Rosendale, from Bassingbourn. She was a 'Knight of the road'! It wasn't easy conducting in the

Above: New in 1946, **FNG 816** was a Bristol K5G with the lowbridge version of the standard postwar ECW body. It was also one of a small number of buses in the Eastern Counties fleet to have the early style of opening side windows shown here. It is seen in Drummer Street waiting to work a short journey on service 109 to Waterbeach, the terminus for alternate buses on the main road service to Ely. Delivered as LK19, it was renumbered soon afterwards as **LK49**. *(C W Routh)*

Below: Eastern Counties received a large number of Bristol L5Gs fitted with the standard saloon body. They were used on local services such as the 129 and 139 but were more often found on country routes. Displaying a short-lived style of blind lettering, **LL641** (**FPW 512**) is seen in Drummer Street on the 'back road' route to Haverhill via The Bumpsteads. Service 136 was renumbered 13A in 2003. *(The Omnibus Society Collection)*

blackout and with hardly any lights it was murder driving. No lights at all were allowed on the aerodrome at Bassingbourn, which was even worse. One night we met a big crowd off the midnight train at Royston station. We were supposed to do a double run but I'd had enough for one day so I said "Pile them all on!" When we got to the camp I counted 119 passengers get off the bus. I thought I felt it swaying about a bit on Kneesworth Hill! Sometimes we had to go and cover work in Cambridge if there weren't enough spare crews. One day when I was there the crew foreman sent me out on the local service 115 and then forgot all about me. I had to phone up to remind him that I wanted to catch the last bus back to Royston, which left at 10.15. I very nearly missed it! I must have been backwards and forwards from the Market Hill to the Golden Hind fifteen times that day.

"I stayed on the buses for a while after the war and I can remember when we had the first 8 foot wide buses. We really noticed the difference, especially in Royston High Street, which in those days was the main road to London, although it was quite narrow. When I eventually left I was on the top pay rate of £3. 1 shilling and 9 pence a week [£3.09]. I went to work in a rubber factory in Letchworth. Although I missed the buses I doubled my wages, and I stayed there until I retired."

Glad Hughes and Ida Rosendale both stayed on the buses after the war. Ida continued to work from Royston until the late 1960s, latterly with Driver Bill Chapman, on one of the two remaining crew duties. Laddie Holland died in May 2004 at the age of 92.

UTILITY BUSES

Burwell & District's buses were also very busy and in 1940 Mr Mansfield managed to have one his surviving Daimler CF6 coaches (VE 1050) fitted with a new, 32-seat Thurgood coach body. More significant was the purchase of B&D's first double-decker, for the opening of RAF Bottisham in January 1941 had made it clear that larger vehicles were needed. The bus was a 1931 Leyland TD1 (KJ 1912), new to Maidstone & District but latterly with London Transport. It had a Leyland highbridge body with seats for 48 passengers, although on at least one occasion it carried over 100 airmen back to Bottisham on a late-night journey, once again indicating the reluctance of country bus crews to leave passengers behind. Even larger loads were possible with the AEC Renown six-wheeler (VO 7884) purchased a year later. It had been new to the Ebor Bus Company of Mansfield and, with its 66-seat Strachan body, seemed huge beside other members of the Burwell fleet. More unusual still was an AEC 'Q' (KY 5141) which started its career with Bradford Corporation. This was purchased in 1943 and had room for 60 passengers in its Metro Cammell body, which featured a front entrance, a feature never before seen on a double-decker in Cambridge. Unfortunately its side-mounted engine suffered from overheating problems and the 'Q' was soon sold. Another secondhand addition was a Leyland Tiger TS2 (BU 6465), which received the nearly new Thurgood body from VE 1050, the Daimler chassis being finally retired.

By the spring of 1943 the Royal Navy had effectively ended the submarine threat to merchant shipping. Some imports of previously unobtainable materials were resumed, providing relief to operators and passengers alike. There were small-scale increases to services and a few new buses were also delivered. Only three manufacturers continued to build bus chassis throughout the war and, fortunately for Burwell & District, one of these was Daimler. The first of three AEC-engined CWA6 buses (ECE 869) was received in August 1943. Although none of B&D's routes passed under low bridges it had a 55-seat lowbridge body, built by Duple but definitely not to pre-war standards. Bus bodies now had to conform to a rigid utility specification, as laid down by the Ministry of Supply with the intention of saving aluminium, steel and other scarce materials. Elegant curves and comfortable upholstery gave way to square corners and (in some buses) slatted wooden seats, while there were few opening windows to provide a breeze on warm days.

The other manufacturers who continued to build chassis for buses were Guy and (for single-deckers) Bedford. Eastern National was allocated ten Guy Arab double-deckers with Brush bodies but they are not known to have operated in the Cambridge area. Both Premier

Above: Twenty saloons received by Eastern Counties in 1947 had new Bristol L4G chassis, fitted with 1938 ECW bodies removed from older Associated Daimler chassis. They were a strange mixture of old and new, their prewar bodies with 'bible' indicators contrasting with their lower, postwar radiators. Complete with chalked service numbers, **LM489** (**GNG 519**) heads for the station on the 101, a service on which every type of vehicle occasionally appeared. *(W J Haynes)*

Below: Several operators took delivery of lightweight, integral vehicles in the early post-war years. Most had bodies by Beadle and reconditioned engines from withdrawn prewar vehicles. Eastern Counties **D999** (**FNG 818**) was the fourth prototype, with the engine from a withdrawn United Counties Dennis Ace. It is seen here at Newmarket on service 116 to Ely. *(J F Higham)*

Travel and Weeden received new Bedford OWB saloons, starting in 1943 when ECE 794 was delivered to Weeden and ECE 879 to Premier Travel, with very basic 32-seat bodies by Mulliner and Duple respectively. Their wooden seats were uncomfortable if passengers could stay on them, although they sometimes slid off as these noisy, petrol-engined machines hurtled along winding country roads. By 1943 revenue from Premier's bus routes had doubled, despite a 25% cut in the scheduled mileage and the withdrawal of the profitable express and excursion traffic. Some of the additional income came from the transport of service personnel, aerodrome construction workers and, more recently, prisoners-of-war. Coaches were still hired when other operators could spare them, and the hire of a double-decker from London Transport was also negotiated. The use of such a vehicle would never have been considered before the war, as it would have been impossible to use it for coaching work. The loan never took place, for Premier's garage and maintenance arrangements were not up to the standard required by LT. Another possible solution to the staff shortage was to train some of the conductresses as drivers, but this also never happened.

Progressive added seven more vehicles to its expanding fleet during 1943, some of which were Tilling-Stevens C60A7 buses with 32-seat Beadle bodywork (KJ 6881/2, AKJ 49/50) which had been new to Maidstone Corporation. Three additional coaches were a Dennis Lancet (EX 3987) and two AEC Regals (NG4828 and CMJ 447). A pair of AEC Reliances (MY 538/43) from Nottingham Corporation (with dual-entrance bodies by Short Brothers) provided further variety soon afterwards. Whippet also obtained a pair of Dennis Lancet coaches (DOP511 and BAA 392), the last vehicles acquired until after the war.

In January 1944 Premier Travel received a second Bedford OWB bus (ECE 948) and another followed in August (EER 242). A similar bus (EER 99) was allocated to Weeden, who also acquired Burwell & District's Dennis Ace (AKR 937). The new Bedfords all had 32-seat Duple bodywork. Premier also acquired an elderly second-hand Dennis F coach (MO 8513). A further Daimler CWA6 double-decker (EER 102) joined the Burwell & District fleet in May, this time with a Brush lowbridge body, while a secondhand Albion Valkyrie coach (CS 1998) was also obtained. In November Eastern Counties took delivery of its first new vehicles for two years and its first new double-deckers since 1937. They had Bristol K6A chassis fitted with utility bodywork, three with highbridge bodies by Park Royal (LKH1-3, FAH 101-3) and the fourth with a lowbridge version by Strachan (LK1, FAH 107).

THE BEGINNING OF THE END

The bombing raids continued to take place until 1944, and on one occasion the Eastern Counties garage was damaged, although Cambridge did not suffer as badly as many other towns and cities. A few V1 flying bombs fell in the region, while the fear of attacks by V2 rockets resulted in a second wave of evacuees from London in July. By the autumn, however, life began to return to normal, as streetlights were switched on again and blackout restrictions were eased. Oil supplies started to improve after September 1944 and the use of producer gas buses ceased. As the war drew to an end there were revisions to several local services in Cambridge. Services 102 and 106 exchanged terminal points, 105 and 131 were shortened, the Newnham section replaced by the 115, with a new 115A providing additional local buses to Trumpington. The new services were as follows:

102 Perne Road (Brookfields) - Mill Road - Town Centre - Newmarket Road - Meadowlands

105 Strangeways Road - Mowbray Road - Cherry Hinton Road - Hills Road - Drummer Street

106 Red Cross Lane - Hills Road - Town Centre - Huntingdon Road - Girton Corner

115 King's Hedges Road - Milton Road - Town Centre - Newnham (Grantchester Road)

115A King's Hedges Road - Milton Road - Town Centre -

Above: New in 1947, **LK50** (**FNG 817**) was a Bristol K5G with the standard style of opening windows on its lowbridge ECW body. The new standard bodies featured large and very clear 48ins-wide destination blinds, shown here with a later style of lettering. The bus is leaving a strangely deserted Drummer Street for Sawston on service 103, a route on which it would encounter no low bridges. *(W J Haynes)*

Below: The much deeper roof contour of the standard highbridge ECW body is shown in this view of **LKH64** (**FNG 826**). It is seen at the awkwardly sited bus stop outside Christ's College, which remained in use until 1960. The busy local service 101 ran every 7½ minutes from Green End Road to the Railway Station, although the destination blind appears to have slipped on this occasion. Buses of this type performed faithfully on Cambridge local services until 1970. *(M G Doggett Collection)*

Trumpington (Bishop's Road)
131 Cherry Hinton (Fisher's Lane) -
Cherry Hinton Road - Coleridge Road -
Mill Road - Drummer Street

Eastern Counties took delivery of another twelve new Bristol K6A double-deckers during 1945, numbered LKH4-6 (FAH 104-6) with Park Royal highbridge bodies) and Strachan lowbridge-bodied LK2-10 (FAH 108/9, FNG 141-6, FNG 398). Some of the new buses were allocated to Cambridge and LKH5/6 regularly performed on the 115 and 115A. Their AEC engines made them lively performers and they were popular with drivers. By the time the last were delivered in December the war was over, although some manufacturers continued to supply austerity bodies. Burwell & District's third Daimler CWA6 (EER 549) was delivered in August with a highbridge body, once again built by Brush. In contrast, Premier Travel received a final Duple-bodied Bedford OWB (EER 570) which had the first non-utility body built after the war. Premier also gave a good home to a characterful old Leyland TS1 (TF 1555), which for a while had been owned by Ribble.

THE END - VICTORY AND PEACE

The end of the People's War, like the beginning, was a time of confusion. Eventually the announcements came that 8th May would be Victory in Europe Day and 15th August would be Victory over Japan Day. For the crowds who celebrated VE Day at Market Hill in Cambridge and elsewhere in the region, there were feelings of relief that it was all over mixed with uncertainty about the future. Up to 85% of the nation's women had been engaged in some kind of war work and many were very reluctant to give up their jobs (and their newly-found independence) as the men returned from the war. In some places the women were obliged to leave their jobs on the buses but this did not happen in the Cambridge area, where they have been employed ever since. The 1945 general election resulted in a landslide victory for the Labour Party, under Mr Attlee. The new government had ambitious plans to nationalise all forms of energy, power and the transportation of goods and passengers. As the victory parades were held and servicemen and women started to come home, the local bus operators prepared to enjoy an unprecedented boom in traffic, but were unsure of what the future had in store for them.

Below: One of the older vehicles acquired by Premier Travel with the Burgoin business was this Bedford WLB, previously in the Burwell & District fleet although its original owner is not known. It had a 20-seat Willmott body, and is seen here on Burgoin's express service from Thurlow to King's Cross. *(Author's Collection)*

Above: In the early postwar years operators believed in making the most of what was available. One of two Daimler CVD6 coaches delivered to Burwell & District in 1947, **FVE 526** carried the Duple body built in 1935 to rebody an earlier Daimler CF6. As one of the company's 'luxurious Daimler saloon coaches', it remained in service until 1962. *(Author's Collection)*

Below: New to Burwell & District in 1950, **HER 784** was a Daimler CVD6 with a handsome highbridge body by Massey. Photographed on the company's main route in Drummer Street, with the old Eastern Counties booking office in the background, it gave almost 21 years of faithful service. *(Alan B Cross)*

133

14. Postwar Challenges 1945 to 1947

In the autumn of 1945 Britain's bus operators faced enormous challenges. Their fleets contained many elderly buses which, had the war not intervened, would have been replaced long ago. Vehicles requisitioned by the forces had sometimes been treated very badly and returned in poor condition. New buses were once again being built but they were still in short supply, as manufacturers were being encouraged to export much of their output to help the economy to recover. Spares and skilled staff were also scarce, for not all the men had yet returned from the war. Against this background passenger loadings were breaking all records. Rationing was still in force, some items remaining on ration for a further nine years, so that those with money to spare spent it on leisure and travel. Bus services were being restored as fast as the delivery of new vehicles allowed. Express coach services also reappeared, enabling many people to enjoy their first seaside holiday for several years. All this provided scope for one local operator in particular to greatly increase its operations.

PREMIER'S POSTWAR EXPANSION BEGINS - WEEDEN TAKEN OVER

The early part of the war had been a difficult time for Premier Travel. Mr Thompson, assisted by Mrs M M E Lainson, did his best to keep the business going, encouraged by Mr Lainson's regular letters and telephone calls and occasional visits home on leave. Mrs Lainson became a Director of the company in 1943 and, following the departure of Mr Thompson in July of that year, well-known local businessman W F (Fred) Matthews purchased a large shareholding in the company. This provided a much-needed boost for Premier's ailing finances and in June 1944 Mr Matthews became a Director. Two of his three sons, Messrs F N (Frank) and J A (John) Matthews, subsequently joined the company and the names of Lainson and Matthews were synonymous with Premier Travel for many years afterwards.

The company's great expansion now began. Discussions had started in March 1945 with Mr Weeden on a possible takeover of his business, and this happened in the May. By the time Mr Lainson returned in September his company had a second depot at Chrishall (with Mr Weeden as Manager) and seven more vehicles. These were two nearly new Bedford OWB buses (ECE 794 and EER 99), a Bedford WTB (CVE 424), two Albions (BCE 372 and CUR 921), a Dennis Lancet (CVE 12) and a Gilford (WG 1273). Eight more bus routes centred on Chrishall and Saffron Walden were added to Premier's network, along with three additional express services. The routes were numbered from 6 to 16 by Premier and included service 9 (formerly Weeden 1) from Great Chishill to Cambridge via Chrishall, Ickleton, Hinxton and Sawston. Until the takeover this had run on Mondays, Wednesdays, Saturdays and Sundays but Premier introduced daily buses. A Friday service was introduced on service 10 to Bishop's Stortford (served on Thursdays, Saturdays and Sundays by Weeden 2), while the London express, suspended for the duration of the war, was restored on 9th November 1945 as service 7.

'IT'S ALL ABOUT PEOPLE'

The activity continued. Coach excursions were reintroduced and the private hire business was rapidly built up. Works services were introduced to Pye's factories in Cambridge, initially from Harston, Oakington and Buntingford, the Harston service appearing in the public timetable as service S1. Other services were soon introduced as Pye's business grew, and these became an integral part of Premier's operations. School contracts also became increasingly important, and the first two (to Sawston and Royston) appeared briefly as services S2 and S3. Premier's timetables always had a very professional appearance and, as well as being a firm believer in effective publicity, Mr Lainson was also very fond of slogans. "Our aim is to give

134

Above: Rare in East Anglia, Crossley coaches became popular with Whippet Coaches in the early postwar years. **GEW 272**, seen at RAF Wyton, was new in 1948 and had a Strachan 35-seat body. Whippet eventually built up a fleet of eight of these coaches. *(Alan B Cross Collection/D C Fisk)*

Below: Percival's Motors (Cambridge) Ltd became a separate concern in May 1946 but was still associated with the Oxford-based company. This Gilford Hera (**CS 115**) had been new to Western SMT of Kilmarnock and had a 32-seat Wycombe body. *(J C Gillham)*

you the best possible service" was the claim, along with the exhortations "help us to help you" and "support independent enterprise". Much of Premier's success was the direct result of staff loyalty, which was helped by regular meetings between the Directors and Staff Representatives. The message was clear: "you work with us, not for us" and for many years few chose to belong to an official trade union. Mr and Mrs Lainson and their fellow Directors never forgot that "it's all about people" and the welfare of the staff and their families always remained high on the agenda.

GILL'S BUS SERVICE TAKEN OVER

By the end of the year the company's financial position had improved dramatically and in January 1946 there were discussions with Mr Brand regarding the possible purchase of his business. Nothing came of this but very soon afterwards negotiations began for the takeover of the bus and coach operations of A J Gill of Godmanchester. This duly took place in March and included seven vehicles, four of which were kept. The Gill routes were isolated from the rest of Premier's network, consisting of infrequent services from Godmanchester and Huntingdon to St Ives, St Neots and Bedford, which were numbered from 17 to 20.

Another acquisition in the same month was the Clacton to London express service of Mr W H Thorne of Clacton, a one-way operation for passengers who had made the outward journey by steamer. Service 5 (Birmingham - Cambridge - Clacton) was restored on 7th June, along with the York Brothers Yarmouth service. Premier's own service (4) to the popular Norfolk resort reappeared a month later, along with the former Weeden express from Great Chishill via Saffron Walden to Clacton, now numbered 6. The fitting of upholstered seats made the utility Bedfords more suitable for long-distance passengers, while the fleet was increased by the purchase of two rather elderly, but still serviceable, Leyland Tigers (AG 6221 and GJ 5124).

DRAYTON BROTHERS TAKEN OVER

Premier Travel's first new post-war vehicle was delivered in February 1947, in the shape of a Bedford OB (FER 241) with a 32-seat Dupl bus body. Another eight vehicles joined th fleet soon afterwards when the business o Drayton Brothers of Barley was taken ove Although five modern vehicles had bee purchased in the years up to 1939 there ha been no fleet additions during the war. A secondhand Leyland Cub SKP3 (FD 9601 with a rear entrance coach body was acquired late in 1946 and a new Dennis Lancet coach was on order. The Cub joined the Premier flee along with two Gilfords (JH 4429 and WG 1286), the Dennis Lancet (ENK 387) Dennis Pike (DRO 972) and three Bedford WTBs (BAJ 161, BFD 955 and CWD 840) The former Drayton routes were numbered 12A and 26 to 29 and they established Premier as the main provider of buses on the Saffron Walden to Royston corridor. Cambridge was reached on Mondays and Saturdays by service 27, which ran from Nuthampstead via Barley, Great Chishill, Fowlmere and Newton.

There were several more extensions to the network in 1947. In response to public demand service 23 was introduced from Stapleford and Sawston to Saffron Walden, along with several more routes in the Godmanchester/Huntingdon/St Ives area, numbered 21, 22, 24, and 25. A new express service 3 revived the pioneering Undergraduate Roadways operation to Skegness, offering a direct coach from Cambridge, St Ives, Ramsey and several surrounding villages. Premier also provided coaches for students travelling between Cambridge and Oxford on the new 'Varsity Express' route, which was operated in conjunction with Percival's Motors.

With the threat of nationalisation still in the air, many operators were now deciding to sell out while the going was good. Although the compulsory takeover of bus and coach services had not been mentioned in the King's speech in November 1945, it was clear that the politicians had not changed their minds. Premier's Directors took the view that the Government would pay compensation for its assets, even those which had been other peoples' assets until very recently. Further expansion plans were made and in May 1947 talks were held with Mr Lee regarding the possible takeover of Whippet Coaches. This

Above: Kenzie's Coaches commenced operations in 1947 and purchased this Bedford OB with Duple 'Vista' 29-seat coachwork (**HCE 426**) in December of the following year. It was later described by Cyril Kenzie as "the one we should have kept" after he started his collection of preserved coaches. *(Courtesy C Kenzie)*

Below: The Progressive fleet was updated in the early postwar period by fitting new bodywork to several older coaches. **NG 4828** was a prewar AEC Regal purchased in 1943, which received a new Burlingham body after four years with Progressive. *(J F Higham)*

would have greatly strengthened Premier's position to the north west of Cambridge, but there was to be no sale. One of the former Weeden Bedford OWBs (ECE 794) was sold in November, but by the end of the year the Premier Travel fleet had grown to 30 vehicles, operating from three depots.

MAJOR OPERATORS - THE TILLING APPROACH

While Premier Travel was busy expanding, Eastern Counties and Eastern National began the long-overdue modernisation of their fleets. Both operators received large numbers of new vehicles over the next few years, but it must be emphasised here that they were not just for use in the Cambridge area. Some new types were evenly distributed, while others were confined to certain parts of their owners' territories. In January 1946 Eastern Counties received a final pair of Bristol K6As with Strachan lowbridge bodies (LK11/12 FNG 399/400) before returning to ECW for most of its bodywork requirements. This was very much in accordance with Tilling group policy. Towards the end of the war ECW had built two double-deck prototypes for its post-war designs (one of which was fitted to an Eastern National K5G) and from 1945 moved back to Lowestoft to begin full-scale production. The new ECW bodies were intended mainly for Tilling group companies and the new range included highbridge and lowbridge double-deckers, with 56 and 55 seats respectively. Single-deckers had seating for 35 in the bus version or 31 in the dual-purpose model, which featured coach seating. The styling was less rounded than on pre-war bodies but was still smart and attractive. The Tilling approach was very standardised, and allowed only two standard livery styles for buses. These were the red and cream adopted by Eastern Counties or green and cream used by Eastern National. The uniformity extended to the upholstery, which featured an attractive pattern with the Tilling shades of red and green on a grey background.

NEW TECHNOLOGY

Another standard feature of the new bodies was the provision of very large and informative destination indicators with roller blinds. Ortona's newer vehicles had been equipped with blinds but they were new to Eastern Counties, who had continued to specify a 'bible' indicator on the front of each bus. Under this system, which was inherited from United, each destination display was shown on boards, hinged horizontally across the middle like the pages of a book, which fitted into a frame illuminated at night from each side by two small lamps. To change the display the driver or conductor had to scale the front of the bus to turn the page. Additional displays showed RELIEF (with provision for chalked service numbers) and PRIVATE. Mountaineering skills were not needed to alter the display at the rear, where a board at the bottom of the window provided the necessary information. The last new bus delivered with a 'bible' indicator was LK12.

The new-fangled screens had a destination blind above a second blind, which featured up to three intermediate points and the service number. The rear blinds were reset from halfway up the stairs, where small spy holes gave the conductor a view of the last few letters (or the number) of each display. It was not uncommon to see conductors hanging precariously from the rear platforms of double-deckers as they looked up to check their handiwork. Side blinds were also provided to begin with, identical to the front and rear displays on double-deckers, reduced on saloons to a destination box just forward of the entrance. These did not last long and on double-deckers the side boxes were soon painted and later panelled over, while on saloons the box became a small extra window. With so many routes spread over a large operating area, the transfer of buses between depots sometimes produced a vehicle with the wrong blind. It was therefore necessary to provide boards, which fitted into brackets at the top of the radiator and could be used if the correct blind display could not be found. In Cambridge the boards, which showed only SERVICE followed by the appropriate number, were kept in a shed in Christ's Lane. All subsequent buses had blinds, although drivers and conductors continued to refer to destination indicators as 'boards' for many years afterwards.

Above: The shape of things to come. As the availability of new vehicles improved, coach operators began to regard the half-cab layout as old-fashioned. Lightweight, full-front coaches became increasingly common, and one of the first to appear was the Commer Avenger. Progressive purchased this example (**HVE 841**) in 1950. It carried 33-seat Allweather coachwork. *(Author's Collection)*

Below: Not to be outdone by Burwell & District, Premier Travel also purchased a pair of Daimler CVD6 coaches, one of which is seen at Oxford showing off its impressive array of destination indicators. In common with several of Premier's earlypost-war coaches, **GCE 654** had a body built by Wilks & Meade of Leeds. *(J F Parke)*

NEW BUSES, RESTORATION OF
EXPRESS SERVICES

The first Eastern Counties vehicles with the new-style bodies were delivered in March 1946 and over the next few months another ten K5Gs were received. They were LK13-9 (FNG 810-6) and LKH7-9 (FNG 819-21). The missing registration numbers were not allocated until the following year. Six new L5G saloons delivered from September were LL130-5 (FPW 501-6). Many more buses of all three types were to follow over the next few years. The double-deckers had lowbridge (LK) or highbridge (LKH) bodies, while the single-deckers all had standard 35-seat bodies with rear entrances incorporating sliding doors. Many older vehicles were withdrawn over the next few years, including all the former Ortona single-deckers. The Leyland TS1s VE 2142-4) had been withdrawn in 1945 and were now followed by all the LT2s, TS2s and TS3s (VE 2874-6, VE 3783, VE 4802-7).

Another 1946 development was the restoration of express coach services, starting on 1st March with service E (Norwich - Cambridge - London). The first journey was worked by L5G coach LS1 (DAH 161), which dated from 1939 but was still one of the newest coaches in the fleet. Some of the other express routes also reappeared in the timetables, including the summer services D, N, W, X and Y. A new bus service was the 113A from Cambridge to Shelford Station via Babraham Road and the previously unserved Hinton Way.

The trickle of new buses became a flood in 1947. In January the first of 21 more standard L5Gs were delivered. They were to have been numbered LL136-56 (FPW 507-27) but a decision had been made in December 1946 to renumber the fleet, retaining the letter prefixes but with a single series of numbers from 1 to 999. Many older vehicles accordingly received new identities, and most of the year's new deliveries entered service with their new fleet numbers, the new saloons becoming LL636-56. Two further batches of L-types were numbered LM481-90 (GNG 511-20), followed by LM471-80 (GVF 471-80). Their chassis were new but the bodies had been built by ECW nine years earlier to rebody a batch of former United ADC (Associated Daimler) 415A buses, which dated from 1927. The hybrids produced from this operation had pre-war styling (complete with 'bible' indicators) but with the lower, post-war radiator, behind which lurked a noisy, four-cylinder Gardner engine, making the chassis type L4G. The first of these unusual machines was completed at the turn of the year, while the last did not enter service until early in 1948. One other odd single-decker entered service in 1947. Fleet numbers 901 to 999 had been reserved for non-standard vehicles and the new bus became D999, perhaps to emphasise just how non-standard it was. Registered FNG 818, it had a Beadle body and was powered by the Gardner 4LK engine removed from a United Counties Dennis Ace. It was actually the last of four prototype 'chassisless' buses built by Beadle for Tilling group companies, for it was clear that Bristol and ECW were unable to keep up with the demand for new stock, and most of the Tilling fleets received vehicles built by other manufacturers. Eastern Counties also received vehicles fitted with Bristol's own engine rather than the favoured Gardner unit. Early in the year the first of four Bristol K6B double-deckers were received (LKH60-2, FNG 822-4 and LK30, HAH 230). Further standard K5Gs were LK50 (FNG 817), LKH63-7 (FNG 825/6 and GVF 65-7). Eastern Counties was also one of several Tilling companies to receive Leyland PD1A double-deckers, which had standard ECW lowbridge bodies but were instantly recognisable by their wider radiators, many of which later had the shell painted red. Numbered AP346-65 (GPW 346-65) the Leylands worked mainly in the company's Eastern area but occasionally appeared closer to Cambridge on routes operated by Bury St Edmunds garage, which reached as far as Haverhill and Newmarket.

MORE NEW VEHICLES AND
NATIONALISATION

During the year the politicians continued with their nationalisation plans, and the Transport Bill of 1947 finally received Royal Assent. The Act came into force from the first day of 1948 and the British Transport Commission was set up, with several Executives to control particular sectors of the transport industry. The

Above: In another of the late John Parke's photographs of the Wilkes & Mead-bodied Daimler **GCE 654** the Premier Travel depot building is visible. *(J F Parke)*

Below: The boom in travel in the late 1940s led many operators to purchase larger vehicles. Premier's first double-decker was **BU 7601**, a formidable Leyland TD1. It had been new to Oldham Corporation and is seen at Chrishall depot. The bodywork was by English Electric with seating for 54. The staff regarded it as being particularly challenging to drive. *(J F Parke)*

nationalisation of the railways gave the BTC substantial holdings in several large road haulage companies (which were amalgamated as British Road Services) and many bus companies. Under the terms of the Act the BTC was required to investigate the setting up of Area Transport Boards to take over existing bus operators. Plans were actually released for the Northern Passenger Road Transport Board (covering Northumberland and Durham) and similar schemes were also proposed for other areas, including East Anglia, and the possibility of compulsory nationalisation now hung over the region's Tilling, municipal and independent operators. While business continued as usual, discussions began between the BTC and Sir Frederick Heaton, the Tilling Group Chairman, regarding a possible sale of the group if a favourable price could be agreed.

In the years up to 1947 the Eastern National fleet also received a substantial intake of new vehicles. Standard Tilling types were 26 K5Gs (including the 1944 ECW prototype mentioned earlier), 27 L5G buses and seven dual-purpose L5Gs. Non-standard vehicles were eighteen Leyland PD1s, eight Bedford OB buses with Beadle bodies and two prototype Beadle chassisless saloons. Seven Bedford OB coaches were also delivered, with Duple bodies. A further twelve K5Gs, four K6Bs and three dual-purpose L5Gs were delayed until 1948. As was usual for Eastern National, all the double-deckers had lowbridge bodies.

The first Eastern Counties buses of the 1948 order were actually delivered in November 1947, and a total of 52 new Bristol/ECW buses entered service over the following year. There were another 40 L5G saloons (LL657-96, GPW 657-96), seven K6Bs (LKH68-74, GVF 68-74) and eighteen of the more favoured K5Gs (LKH75-93, HPW 75-93). Most of the K6Bs, including the previous batch, later received Gardner engines. Notable withdrawals included the first of the

former Ortona TD1s to go (ER 8806, VE 2040, VE 3198), together with PLSC Lions ER 8802, ER 8886/7 and VE306. These vehicles had all been rebodied by ECW and the Lions were sold for further service elsewhere.

In September 1948 Sir Frederick Heaton announced that Tilling's bus interests were to be sold to the British Transport Commission, along with Bristol's bus manufacturing works and the ECW factory at Lowestoft. The takeover duly took place from 5th November (backdated to 1st January) and the BTC's Road Transport took over the control of Eastern Counties, Eastern National and the other former Tilling companies. From that date Bristol and ECW products would only be supplied to BTC companies, although existing orders took a while to complete and the nationalised companies still occasionally purchased vehicles from other manufacturers.

Although the Eastern Counties fleet had changed rapidly, the route network remained largely unaltered. The Sunday extension of service 107 to Somersham became a daily operation, with new Monday to Friday journeys to Over. Some of the services suspended during the war were restored, including Cambridge local 129 from 5th December 1948, which was extended at both ends. The route (usually worked by single-deckers) now meandered from the new houses at St Thomas's Road to Newnham, by way of Coldham's Lane, Mill Road and the Railway Station, avoiding the town centre altogether.

A few days later Eastern National restored the Royston to Cambridge section of service 41 from Hitchin. This continued to terminate in Gonville Place, although two schoolday journeys were extended to Mackenzie Road to serve the College of Arts and Technology. Eastern National also continued to receive new vehicles, its 1948 order comprising another fifteen lowbridge K5Gs and three L5G saloons.

Above: Four Leyland Tiger PS1/1 coaches were among Premier Travel's early postwar intake. New in January 1949, **GER 835** had Wilks & Meade 35-seat bodywork and is seen here in the rather bleak surroundings of Godmanchester depot, which was opened following Premier's takeover of Gill's Bus Service. *(Author's Collection)*

Below: The transfer by Premier of the former Long's routes to Haverhill required the use of lowbridge double-deckers because of a low railway bridge there. The highbridge buses acquired from Long's were moved to other depots and **JO 8663**, an AEC Regent I which had been new to City of Oxford Motor Services, is seen in Drummer Street working on a former Harston & District service to Royston. *(Alan B Cross)*

15. Independent Recovery and New Operators 1945 to 1950

By the end of the war most of the small operators in the area were running a motley assortment of largely life-expired vehicles, many of which had been obtained second hand. Only Burwell & District, Premier Travel and Weeden had received new vehicles since 1939, while the others had to make do and mend with whatever they could lay their hands on. With record passenger loadings and the slow delivery of new vehicles, many operators had to modify older machines to obtain a few more years service from them. In the immediate post-war period many elderly buses and coaches were rebuilt, rebodied or re-engined. Some also received new registration numbers, disguising the fact that they were not as new as they looked.

BURWELL & DISTRICT MOTOR SERVICE

In 1945 the Burwell & District fleet consisted of thirteen vehicles of five different makes. Only four had chassis built by Daimler, the company's preferred manufacturer, but this was to change steadily over the next ten years. The troublesome AEC 'Q' (KY 5141) was withdrawn in August, followed in May 1946 by the venerable Leyland TD1 (KJ 1912) and the Albion Valkyrie (CS 1998), both double-deckers seeing further service with operators in Suffolk. No new vehicles were delivered until the following spring. The first (FVE 220) was an AEC Regal with a Duple body, but the other two marked the company's return to Daimler coaches and had CVD6 chassis. One of these (FVE 559) had similar coachwork to that on the Regal, while the other (FVE 526) received the 1935 Duple body from Daimler CF6 MT 3957, the chassis of which was scrapped. For the next few years Burwell & District purchased only Daimlers. Two pre-war COG5 double-deckers were acquired from Birmingham Corporation in December 1948, but only one (AOG 669) went straight into service. The chassis of the second (AOG 647)

was involved in yet another body-swap, and received the 1940 Thurgood body from the Leyland TS2 (BU 6465) which had originally been built to rebody another Daimler CF6 (VE 1050), as already described. The chassis of the Leyland was withdrawn and the resulting vehicle entered service alongside another new CVD6 coach (GVE 781), this one carrying a Harrington body. A further Duple-bodied Daimler CVD6 coach (BCF 59) was obtained from Morley's Grey Coaches of West Row in the spring of 1949. Two more Daimler CVD6 joined the fleet in 1950. The first, delivered in January, was a double-decker (HER 784) with a very handsome Massey body. The Plaxton coach body on the second (HVE 426) added further variety to the fleet. The company's front line coach fleet thus consisted of an AEC Regal and six "luxurious Daimler saloon coaches" (as they were referred to in publicity material). They entered service on private hires, excursions and the revived summer expresses to Great Yarmouth and Felixstowe, while the coaches sometimes assisted the five double-deckers on the bus routes. Of these, service 1 to Cambridge remained the most important, along with its northward extension (4) to Soham. Service 11 was reintroduced on Saturdays and Sundays only, although the Mildenhall - Isleham section was not restored. Neither were the market day buses to Ely, but those to Bury St Edmunds and Newmarket continued. The route network then remained unaltered for many years.

WHIPPET COACHES

Having received no new vehicles during the war, Whippet had a rather elderly fleet when hostilities ended, the newest vehicle being a secondhand Dennis Lancet (DOP 511), which dated from 1938. After a gap of nearly three years two more secondhand Lancet coaches were acquired in 1946, BRW 372 with a Willowbrook body and APG 308 with a Duple

Above: The Burgoin fleet included this utility Bedford OWB with Mulliner bodywork, which joined several similar buses already in the Premier Travel fleet. The stark lines of the **GV 8751**'s Ministry of Supply-specification bodywork are apparent in this view, taken after repainting in Premier livery. The label in the foremost nearside window reads "Support Independent Enterprise". *(J F Higham)*

Below: Some of the vehicles taken over by Premier Travel could soon be found operating away from their original homes. This Bedford OB (**AGV 194**) with a standard Duple 29-seat body, was new to Burgoin but is seen here in Drummer Street on the ex-Drayton service 27 to Nuthampstead. *(J F Parke)*

body. The first new post war addition was a Duple-bodied Bedford OB (FEW 55), delivered in September 1947. It joined an older WTB, new to an operator in Wiltshire as BMR 124 but reregistered by Whippet as EEW 756. Another secondhand purchase to gain a new identity was EEL 571, a Harrington-bodied Albion PK115 new to Pounds ('Charlie's Cars') of Bournemouth, which became FEW626. This was added to stock in 1948 along with a secondhand Leyland TS7 (GXN755) and another new OB (FEW800). Most of these coaches, including the new Bedfords, had short lives with Whippet.

The London express service was restored in 1946 and extended in November across the River Ouse to start from Huntingdon. When service numbers came into use in 1947 it was numbered 4, while a new 4a was introduced from Wyton Aerodrome, restricted to RAF personnel. The 4b, which started in 1948, ran southwards from Huntingdon via the Old North Road and Royston.

Improvements were also made to the bus routes, including the introduction of through journeys from St Ives to Cambridge, although these initially ran on Wednesdays, Saturdays and Sundays only. The St Ives to Cambridge route became service 1 and from November 1950 it offered peak hour buses on weekdays between Bourn Turn and Cambridge, so that this part of the route now ran daily. The Caldecote and Hardwick circular was numbered 2, still running on Wednesdays and Saturdays. Adjustments and improvements were also made to the services from Hilton to Huntingdon (3/3a) and St Ives (5), with the Woodhurst and St Neots routes numbered 5a and 6. Service numbers appeared in timetables but were not shown on vehicles.

The need for larger, more robust vehicles soon became clear, and the first of four new Crossley SD42/7 coaches (GEW 100) was delivered in December 1947, with a 33-seat Whitson body. Three more (GEW 223/224/272, with Strachan bodies) joined the fleet early in 1948, along with another Duple-bodied Bedford OB (GEW300). Crossley products were rare in East Anglia but the Whippet examples had long lives, lasting until the late 1950s. A further Crossley (FFU391)

was purchased secondhand in 1950, together with three more new coaches. Two (HEW 357/8) had chassis built by Austin, much better known for cars and vans than for coaches. The chassis were model K4CWA and were bodied (as were a number of Austin coaches) by Kenex. A further Duple-bodied OB followed (HEW 500) but the trend towards bigger coaches was shown by the disposal of the two earlier OBs (FEW 800 and GEW 300). The new coaches also replaced all the pre-war vehicles, including the last Dennis Lancets, and in less than five years the average age of the fleet had been greatly reduced. The company now had eight coaches, not one of which was more than three years old.

LONG'S COACHES LTD

Shortly after the end of the war Mr and Mrs Long began to update their fleet, and a 24-seat Commer (WS 3407) replaced the last Reo in September 1945. The AECs had obviously made a good impression and another two Regals were added to stock. The first (VD 1289) had a Cowieson body and began its career in Scotland in the Western SMT fleet. A new 32-seat coach (FCE 290) followed in April 1946, fitted with a stylish Harrington body.

It was at about this time that Mr & Mrs Long retired, following the sale of their business to Mr and Mrs L Towse, whose interests already included Buckmaster Coaches of Leighton Buzzard. A change in vehicle policy saw the first Leyland join the fleet at the end of the year, in the shape of a Lion LT7 (TJ 9275) with a Duple body. A new limited company, Long's Coaches Ltd, was established and applied to operate two new market-day routes, both of which were in operation by March 1947. The first ran from West Wratting via West Wickham, Horseheath and Shudy Camps to Saffron Walden, extending Long's route network into Essex for the first time. The other new service offered additional buses to Newmarket, this time via The Thurlows, Great Bradley and Burrough Green. Long's existing services were all transferred to the new limited company in 1948, by which time the use of service numbers in timetables appears to have ceased. A further sign of change in September of that year was the purchase of a double-

Above: Another ex-Burgoin Bedford OB (**BGV 261**), with standard Duple Vista 29-seat coachwork, is seen here on express service 29 from London to Kedington. This followed many of the same roads as the former Burgoin service to Thurlow, which was numbered 38 by Premier. In the background are two London Transport country area buses. *(Alan B Cross)*

Below: The last of the three new Dennis Lancet coaches purchased new by Premier Travel in the years up to 1950, **HVE 707**, had 35-seat Duple coachwork and is seen outside Harston depot. It would be nine years before the company purchased any more new vehicles. *(Author's Collection)*

decker, a former Birmingham Corporation Daimler COG5 (AOP 777) with a BRCW 54-seat body. It carried an eye-catching yellow and black livery, complete with streamlined flashes and ornate LC ("Long's Coaches") monograms on each side. Two former City of Oxford AEC Regents (JO 8456 and JO 8663) were purchased two months later and carried the same livery style.

COACHING PROGRESS - PERCIVAL'S MOTORS (CAMBRIDGE) LTD

Two new coach operators also appeared soon after the war ended, although one of them had already been in business for some time. In May 1946 the Cambridge outpost of Percival's of Oxford became a separate company, Percival's Motors (Cambridge) Ltd, with Ralph Moore as Managing Director. The business continued to operate from King Street and the first vehicle permanently allocated there was of a type already familiar in the area. It was yet another former Alexander Gilford 168OT coach (WG 1272), with a Wycombe body. It was transferred to Cambridge from the Oxford fleet, which in 1947 also supplied a new Duple-bodied Bedford OB (MFC 340). A 1932 Commer Centaur (TL 2086) was also acquired but was kept for less than a year before being sold for further service. The Cambridge company received its first new OB (GER 72) in March 1948, while another Scottish Gilford was acquired in November (CS 115, new to Western SMT). The spring of 1949 saw the purchase of an AEC Regent, which started life as a double-decker in the City of Oxford fleet (registered WL 9356) but it received a new Whitson coach body and a new identity (EDG 422) in 1948. The fleet continued to grow and a second new OB (HVE 980) arrived in May 1950, followed by an elderly AEC Regal (KF 8681). The original Gilford was withdrawn and by the end of the year the fleet stood at six coaches, painted in a cream and light blue livery. As well as the private hire and contract work which provided much of the business, Percival's also regularly hired coaches at busy times to other local operators, including Burwell & District, Premier Travel, Progressive and Whippet. It was in conjunction with Premier that the

Oxford journeys developed into a regular coach service. The 'Inter Varsity Express' originally ran on Sundays only and was restricted to members of both Universities. The service was later available to the general public, although for many years railway objections prevented travel to or from any intermediate points.

KENZIE'S COACHES

Originally from Fowlmere, Bernard Kenzie worked as a baker's roundsman. He moved to nearby Shepreth before the war to work for Waller & Woodham's Nursery, delivering produce to Cambridge and London, until the war put an end to this. Mr Kenzie then bought a van, followed by a lorry. Next came a 7-seat taxi, followed by another, and he diversified into the hire car business. With petrol still on ration, one of his regular early jobs was to transport the Cambridge Hockey Club to away matches. Mr Kenzie's accountant was one of the hockey players, and he suggested that the purchase of a small bus or coach would make it possible for the team to travel together. Mr Kenzie agreed and, in August 1947, purchased a Bedford WLB with a Willmott 20-seat coach body for £475. Registered CBH 422, it had been new to The Lee & District of Chesham, whose maroon and cream livery it retained. A thriving private hire business was soon built up, providing transport for local sports teams and clubs, including theatre trips to Cambridge. The little Bedford lasted until December 1948, when a larger coach replaced it. At that time it was not easy for small operators to obtain new vehicles, but a salesman for Murkett Brothers (the Vauxhall-Bedford dealer in Cambridge) lived locally and he managed to obtain a new Bedford OLBD lorry chassis. Mr Kenzie's son Cyril had already trained as a mechanic and he upgraded the chassis for coach use, including the fitting of improved suspension. It received a new, 29-seat coach body built by Thurgood of Ware and was registered GVE 586. It was taken to the ECW factory at Lowestoft to be tilt-tested before it entered service.

A very different vehicle had joined the fleet six months earlier. This was an elderly Leyland Lion LT2 (VT 6537) with a rear-

148

Above: The most eye-catching vehicles ever operated by Premier Travel were the three 'County' class Daimler CVD6 double-deckers. Intended for long-distance express routes, they were in theory allowed to work only on the London services, but also appeared on local bus routes and, as seen here, private hire work. **HVE 403** ('County of Essex') was photographed appropriately at Harlow, before the new town transformed the appearance of the area. *(Author's Collection)*

Right: The cover of Premier Travel's June 1950 timetable. *(Author's Collection)*

entrance, 30-seat bus body also built by Leyland. It came to Mr Kenzie from Tye of Mendlesham and was purchased for a workers contract service from the camp near Trumpington, which housed war refugees (referred to as 'displaced persons'). Cyril Kenzie recalls that he and his father had to be up at 5.30 every morning to swing the handle and start the old bus, which then did three return trips to local farms and cement factories. Inevitably the interior soon acquired a thick coating of cement dust, which also found its way into the various bits of carpet installed in the cab to prevent draughts. By December 1949 its appearance was quite unlike that of any Kenzie's coach before or since, and it was taken to Thurgood's premises at Wadesmill for scrapping. Kenzie's operation of the contract service then ceased.

In the meantime, the Bedford OLBD had not proved entirely satisfactory and in December 1948 it was sold to pay for the first new, purpose-built coach. This was a Bedford OB with a Duple 29-seat body, registered HCE 426, finished in blue and grey. Many years later Cyril Kenzie described it as "the one we should have kept" after he started his well-known collection of preserved coaches.

The business continued to grow and further secondhand Bedfords were obtained in the shape of a 25-seat WTB (BKU 925) in November 1949 and another Duple-bodied OB (MMT 864) in May 1950. Although an all-Bedford fleet would have been preferred, it was necessary to purchase other makes to cover all the work and to provide larger coaches, starting in December 1950 with a 35-seat Maudslay ML5 (CLA 933). The car-hire business continued and by this stage several lorries were also owned, including an ex-Army Bedford.

PROGRESSIVE COACHES

As traffic built up, 'Paddy' Harris's Progressive Coaches were also being kept very busy. Mr Harris acquired several small

vehicles obtained from the War Department, comprising a Dennis Dart (EV 4011), together with a Bedford WTB and an Albion, both of which received new registrations (FCE 535 and FER 872). Several pre-war vehicles had their petrol engines replaced by AEC or Leyland diesel units, and AEC Regal coach NG 4828 also received a new Burlingham coach body. The first completely new post-war coaches were three of the almost inevitable Bedford OBs, delivered in 1947 with bodywork by Duple (GCE 69) and the less-familiar Thurgood (GER 413, 842). More AECs followed, starting in 1948 with three more old Regal coaches (VT 9405, VH 6530 and HX 4358), which were also rebodied by Burlingham. The last one (which came from Eastern National) was also reregistered as HCE 441. A former Sheffield AEC Regent double-decker (EWJ 459) also received a new coach body (by Whitson) and a new registration (HCE 667), while four more pre-war Regents went into service as the company's first double-deckers. Two came from Halifax (JX 1789 and JX 5264) while the others had been new to Leeds (AUM 405/8). Loadings on some contracts were now sufficient to justify the use of double-deckers, which from then on were always a feature of the fleet.

A significant new coach delivered in 1950 was a Commer Avenger (HVE 841) fitted with a 33-seat Allweather body. This was an early example of the larger, full-front design, which would soon appear in many other fleets and would render the half-cab and normal control coaches obsolete. The new and rebodied vehicles allowed a clear out of much of Progressive's prewar collection, including all the Dennis, Leyland and Tilling-Stevens machines, together with the remaining AEC Regal and Reliance coaches, which were not rebodied. By the end of 1950 Mr Harris had an impressive, modern-looking coach fleet, the latest style of bodywork giving no clues as to the origins of his four remaining pre-war coaches.

Above: In 1950 tourists rarely visited the Mill Road area of Cambridge, but its many side streets of terraced houses once provided plenty of custom for the local bus routes. About to cross the railway bridge to Romsey Town, **LKH135** (**HPW 135**) is on the busy service 102, which ran every 10 minutes from Meadowlands to Perne Road. Behind The Ark Yeast Company was Dale's brewery, while the building in the background was one of Mill Road's two cinemas. The bus was one of those loaned to London Transport when new and remained in service at Cambridge until 1970. *(Alan B Cross)*

Below: Derek Carter, standing on the left, is seen during his brief career with Premier Travel. Unfortunately, no photos could be found of him working for Eastern Counties, with whom he spent most of his time as a busman. *(Author's Collection)*

16. Premier's Postwar Expansion Completed

The updating of the Premier Travel fleet continued during January 1948. Following the lead set by Burwell & District, the company took delivery of a pair of new Daimler CVD6 coaches (GCE 654/5). These had 33-seat bodies built by Wilks & Meade, a Leeds based firm associated with the coach operator Wallace Arnold. In line with Mr Lainson's policy of providing as much information as possible, they featured no fewer than ten destination boxes. In addition to the one each at the front and (unusually) the rear, there were also four along each side, so that the full extent of the express routes was clear for all to see. Another new Bedford OB bus (GCE 422) also joined the fleet, and the two former Gill Bedford WLBs were withdrawn. The heavy loadings on the bus routes prompted the purchase of Premier's first three double-deckers, none of which was in its first flush of youth. A ponderous Leyland TD2 (BU 7601) was acquired in April, fitted with a highbridge English Electric body. It had been new in 1932 to Oldham Corporation and was joined in August by a pair of even older all-Leyland lowbridge TD1s (DW 6942/4) from Red & White of Chepstow. These had short careers with Premier. DW 6942 lasted for just a year before it was destroyed by fire while working on service 9, while its twin survived until only 1950.

The summer saw the purchase of a Dennis Lancet J3 (GER 217) with a Duple coach body, followed in October by the first of four Leyland Tiger PS1/1 coaches, also with Wilks & Meade bodies similar to those on the Daimlers. The Leylands were registered GER 140/1 and GER 834/5, the last one arriving in April 1949 along with another double-decker, a former Plymouth Leyland TD4c (JY 6739) with a lowbridge body. By this time Premier's vehicles carried fleet numbers in almost chronological order, although the staff still tended to use registration numbers to identify their steeds. The new Leyland coaches were numbered 32-5, although the Dennis Lancet delivered earlier was allocated number 40 and DW 6942 and

JY 6739 were both numbered 37. The new arrivals replaced an assortment of generally older coaches, including vehicles inherited from Weeden, Gill and Drayton. Ex Gill Gilford Hera MJ 2154 moved onto its tenth owner for conversion to a caravan, leaving only one Gilford in the fleet (WG 329, also ex-Gill). Another three summer express routes were also introduced, these being:

34 Bedford - Skegness
36 Ramsey - Huntingdon - Godmanchester - Great Yarmouth
37 Berden - Saffron Walden - Haverhill - Lowestoft - Great Yarmouth

Many small villages were also served, while service 37 connected with service 6 (Great Chishill - Clacton) at Saffron Walden, giving the citizens of the Cambs/Essex/Herts borders a wide choice of holiday destinations. For passengers not tempted by their own service 4 to Yarmouth, Premier also included details of the York Brothers operation in their timetables. The Clacton to London service purchased in 1946 from W H Thorne was numbered 35. Several other new express routes also appeared in the public timetables, although they were restricted to RAF personnel for weekend leaves. They were services 30 (RAF Upwood - London), 31 (RAF Upwood - Leicester - Coventry - Birmingham) and 32 (RAF Stradishall - London), all of which departed from the aerodromes at noon on Fridays, with service 32 operating additionally on Saturdays. The airmen returned very early on Monday mornings. Those based at RAF Oakington also had the opportunity to travel on service 33, another one-way operation. It departed from Cambridge railway station at 1am, although it would wait if the trains were delayed. The war may have been over but the aerodromes were still busy, and National Service continued to provide valuable business for many of the region's bus and coach operators.

Above: The first new coaches to join the Eastern Counties fleet after the war were three Bristol L6Bs with luxurious Beadle bodies, seating only 28. Fleet number **LS495** (**GPW 495**) shows off its handsome lines when new. It later received red bus livery and ended its days as the Cambridge tree-cutting vehicle, painted green. *(John Banks Collection)*

Below: Eastern Counties received a number of Duple-bodied Bedford OB coaches, a type more usually associated with independent operators. Although based at Eastern area garages, they sometimes appeared in Cambridge on express services, as shown by **BS957** (**KAH 957**) entering Drummer Street. *(W J Haynes)*

fulfilled their intended role, for the Traffic Commissioners would not authorise their use on routes over 60 miles in length. Despite this setback they were allowed to operate on the London routes, and they were initially used on service 32 from RAF Stradishall to London, later becoming a familiar sight on service 38 from Thurlow. They were also used on private hire work, and for many years they offered a very luxurious ride into Cambridge or to weekly markets on the company's bus routes. Sadly they never appeared on services 3, 4 or 5, although for a while they retained the glass panels above their lower saloon windows. These proclaimed (for example) "Yarmouth-Clacton-Cambridge-Leicester-Birmingham-Skegness", another instance of making the public aware of what was on offer.

THE 'WINDMILL' TIMETABLE

The 'County' Daimlers entered service just as Premier's Directors were putting the finishing touches to a major reorganisation of their bus network, which started on 10th June 1950. An impressive, 80-page booklet was published, always referred to as 'The Windmill Timetable' because of the design on the front cover. It included details of all the company's bus, coach and leave services, together with a route map, lists of booking agents, advertisements and a full page illustration of 'County' Daimler HVE 401. Services were now numbered between 1 and 60 and incorporated several completely new travel opportunities, among them another express (29) from Kedington to London via Haverhill and Saffron Walden. The linking of existing routes resulted in an impressive-looking network, which included services 12 and 39 (Saffron Walden to Royston, with 12 continuing all the way to Hitchin), 46 and 51 (Saffron Walden to Newmarket), 56 (Haverhill to Newmarket). A closer examination of the timetables revealed that some of these only ran on certain days of the week, but a number of sections of route now had daily buses, including services 1, 2, 8, 9 and 45 into Cambridge. Villagers along the former Drayton route to Bishop's Stortford (26) were amazed at the number of buses now passing their doors. The depot at Chrishall became the

focus of several connecting services, and the whole package was designed to offer as many connections with as little 'dead' mileage as possible. While such a lavish network would be welcomed today, it was difficult in 1950 to persuade country folk to change their long-established travelling habits, while some of the new services passed through very thinly populated areas. Adjustments continued for the rest of the year to try to attract new business. In August service 53 (Haverhill to Halstead, which ran only on Sundays when there were no trains between the two towns) was given a Tuesday bus, which diverted via Birdbrook. In November service 27 (Nuthampstead to Cambridge) was extended to start from Little Hadham, where a bus and a driver were outstationed. The timetable gave a detailed description of the location of the bus stop, which was also served by London Transport's Hertford to Bishop's Stortford routes 350/350A. At the same time the almost passengerless service 41 (Baldock to Buntingford) was retimed to connect with the London train at Buntingford. Changes in the Haverhill area saw the former Long services 44 and 45 improved and amended to run from Great Wratting to Cambridge either via Withersfield and West Wickham (44) or via Great Bradley and Burrough Green (45). Traffic on these routes was steadily building up at the Cambridge end, particularly between Fulbourn and Cambridge, and service 44 also now ran daily. The villages between Haverhill and Saffron Walden were given an increased service to London on service 38.

WORKING IN THE POSTWAR BOOM (1) - REG ROOPE

A good idea of country bus travel in the early post-war period can be gained from the reminiscences of two long-serving Premier Travel employees. Reg Roope was a driver, starting with Long's Coaches in 1947 and transferring to Premier when they took over.

"Just after the war I was working in West Wratting at the Vicarage. Mr Long taught me to drive but I didn't start working for Long's Coaches until just after Mr Towse took over. I took three PSV tests altogether, in a 20-seater, a 32-seater and a double-decker. The depot

Above: This Bristol L4G was one of ten buses delivered in 1949 which were officially "rebuilds" of earlier Bristol B-type saloons, although it would have been difficult to say exactly how much of the old bus remained. Well away from home, **LL404** (**KAH 404**) is seen at Peterborough on the long service 151 to Cambridge, a route normally worked by the newest double-deckers. The 4-cylinder Gardner engine would have given a rather noisy ride on the 1 hour 52 minute journey. *(M G Doggett)*

Below: ECW adapted its standard single-deck body to produce the dual-purpose version shown here, with 31 seats and subtle 'streamlined' styling, although the large destination box was retained. This was being put to good use on LE700 (**KNG 700**), on service E at Victoria Coach Station in London. These vehicles were later repainted in standard bus livery, although surprisingly some received cream and maroon coach colours shortly before they were withdrawn in the mid-1960s. *(Author's Collection)*

was in the centre of the village. The cottage in front is still there, but there used to be a petrol pump on the front lawn. There was no electricity until Den Goodacre [one of the other drivers] rigged up some batteries. He moved to Premier along with me, Charlie Jaggard and Percy Radford. Most of the buses were blue. As well as the services we did excursions, and school buses to Linton Village College. After Premier took over they ran a contract from West Wratting to Gurteen's factory at Haverhill. The buses were often very crowded. My conductor and I were once fined 5 shillings each [25 pence] for being overloaded. One day we had so many passengers in a Bedford (GV 9860) that the conductor had to go out of the rear emergency door to get back to the front of the bus. Then on Sundays we sometimes did service 53 to Halstead, with the Leyland double-decker (JY 6739). There were so many wanting to get to the aerodrome at Ridgewell that we had to provide our own relief bus. We'd take half the load on the first trip and then come all the way back for the rest. It wasn't easy getting up that hill in Halstead with a full load."

Reg spent most of his time with Premier working from the Haverhill depot and for many years was one of the regular drivers on the former Long's routes into Cambridge. He was the last crew driver at Haverhill (with Conductor Jim Lamb) before he transferred to one-man bus work. He remained with the company until the late 1980s, latterly on school contract work.

WORKING IN THE POST-WAR BOOM (2) - DEN GREENHILL

Den was a conductor, who joined Premier Travel in 1950.

"I started on Premier Travel on 6th June 1950. Before that I'd worked on the land. My first journey was on service 26 from Nuthampstead into Royston, with ECE 948, one of the 'utility' Bedfords. We used Bell Punch tickets, and I had to carry a huge rack of them, with values from one penny up to half a crown [12½ pence]. The buses were so busy then, especially from Barkway. The Sandon road was another busy one. On one journey we must have had 60 passengers on a Bedford. I

couldn't shut the door and I had to hang on the bottom step. A passing hedge took my PSV badge (number FF12954) with it, but I got it back a few weeks later after a roadman handed it in. Later on I lost it again down a drain in Royston, but a council workman found it. I've still got it.

"One journey I didn't like was the 10.30 service 2 from Cambridge to Royston on a Sunday night, which was often packed with people from the displaced persons' camp at Trumpington. We pulled up one night with a double-decker and they all piled on, taking up all the seats and standing downstairs, upstairs and on the stairs. The bus was so full it wouldn't move. Nobody would get off so we called the police, who said 'Don't go until we get there.' Well, we couldn't! Eventually they turned up and made a load of people get off, and we left with eight standing. The police car followed us to Trumpington, and when we got there one very small chap came out from under the stairs to pay his fare. I hadn't seen him under there.

"Another decker job was service 33 to Oakington aerodrome from Cambridge station. It waited for three trains to come in before leaving at 1.30 in the morning, the last trip on a shift that started at 12.30 the previous day. One night we must have had about 80 on board and a lot of them were paying with notes. We were very surprised when we picked up Jack Stratton, the Inspector, who checked the tickets and then rang the bell to get off. The driver took him much further than he really wanted to go. He said he thought it was one of the airmen who kept ringing the bell! We finished at about 3 o'clock in the morning and when I counted the day's money I discovered that I had a hole in my pocket and was eight pounds ten shillings short [£8.50]. I telephoned the guard room at the aerodrome straight away and was told that someone had handed the money in. The next day I had another midday start, so in the morning I rode all the way from my house at Elmdon to Oakington on my moped to get the money back. I offered to reward the honest airman, but the sentry said that wasn't allowed. The money I'd lost was more than a week's wages, so I was very relieved to have it back.

"It wasn't an easy job, but I enjoyed it. The most comfortable bus we had then was

In 1949 Eastern Counties resumed the programme of rebodying prewar Leyland TD2s. As well as new standard Eastern Coach Works bodies, these elderly but still reliable buses also were fitted with new Cov-Rad radiators and Bristol front mudguards, as shown by **AH202** (**NG 3863**) at the Railway Station *(above)*, and **AH212** (**NG 5403**) *(below)* at King's Parade, a road now served only by City Centre Shuttle minibuses. Some of the rebodied TD2s lasted until 1960 in this form, and were particularly associated with services 101 and 115. *(Author's Collection; M G Doggett)*

Weeden's old Dennis (CVE 12). We called it 'The Old Thumper.' Another nice little bus was a Bedford, CVE 424, but the Leyland 'decker (BU 7601) was very rough and it swayed about all over the place."

Den stayed with Premier for over 24 years and was the last full-time conductor at Chrishall depot. The idea of being a bus driver did not appeal to him, although the management begged him on more than one occasion to take a PSV driving test. With the final conversion of Premier's Cambridge routes to one-man operation he was made redundant in 1974. He quickly found other work but stayed in touch with Premier Travel to the end. He passed away in September 2003 at the age of 83.

Still anxious to improve loadings on its large rural network, Premier made further adjustments in November 1950, when attention was drawn to the connections available from local bus routes, notably service 13, whereon the connecting journeys were coordinated with service 46 and extended from Linton to Balsham. Improvements to market day services in the area included a Saturday bus on the 55 (Haverhill to Bury St Edmunds), which previously ran only on Wednesdays. A new, unnumbered service was introduced on Wednesdays from Balsham via Great Bradley to Cowlinge, where it connected with service 55. Finally, improvements were made for cinema patrons travelling into Haverhill on services 56 (from Great Bradley) and 60 (from Kedington via Calford Green). Notable

vehicles withdrawn in 1950 were the last Gilfords (WG 329, also the last ex-Gill vehicle and GV 2405 ex-Burgoin), together with the Dennis F (MO 8513), the former Drayton Leyland Cub (FD 9601) and two double-deckers, ex-Long Daimler COG5 (AOP 777) and the surviving Leyland TD1 (DW 6944).

In less than five years Premier Travel had grown into a sizeable business. Mr Lainson's vision of a network of express coaches had become a reality, even though he was unable to make full use of the new double-deck coaches. Premier's country bus routes served many villages not reached by Eastern Counties or Eastern National, and some were now frequent enough to be useful to workers travelling daily into Cambridge, Haverhill, Royston and Saffron Walden. Contracts, excursions, private hire and weekend leave services also provided valuable revenue. Clouds were gathering, however, for a large increase in the Fuel Tax in April 1950 had added £6,000 to the annual bill. This, together with Premier's rapid expansion using largely borrowed funds, had left the company in a precarious financial position. Discussions regarding a possible takeover of Wiffen's Coaches of Finchingfield had come to nothing and there would now be no more takeovers (or new vehicles) for many years, although the express coach network would continue to grow. Hard times lay ahead, but Mr Lainson and his fellow Directors remained as optimistic as ever about the future of their independent enterprise.

Showing vehicles of the two operators taken over by Premier Travel in 1949, **GV 9861** was a Bedford OB new in 1946 with a 32-seat Duple bus body. In this Drummer Street view it is followed by former Long's Coaches AEC Regent **JO 8663**. *(Alan B Cross)*

Above: The Beadle-Bedfords were followed by sixteen more lightweights. These had new Eastern Coach Works bodies and Gardner 4LK engines removed from withdrawn Dennis Ace saloons. They too worked from Fenland garages and remained unique to Eastern Counties. Photographed at Newmarket, **CD813** (**HPW 818**) shows the deeper style of destination blind fitted when new, which was later reduced to a single-line display. *(W J Haynes)*

Below: Eastern National also continued to rebody prewar double-deckers, including No. **3707** (**FEV 176**), a Leyland Titan TD5. New in 1937 with a Brush body, it received a new lowbridge Eastern Coach Works body in 1949. It is seen on service 41, which at the start of 1950 had four weekday journeys from Hitchin to Cambridge. The section north of Royston was withdrawn in September of that year but was later restored, the school journeys surviving until the mid-1960s. *(Alan B Cross)*

17. Major Operators 1949 to 1950

THE BUSES THAT WENT TO LONDON

No fewer than 100 new vehicles were allocated to the Eastern Counties fleet in 1949, and in January the first of a batch of 49 highbridge Bristol K5Gs (LKH94-142, HPW 94-142) began to enter service, but not all in East Anglia. The newly formed London Transport Executive was desperately short of serviceable buses and appealed to the British Transport Commission for help. Many London buses had been destroyed or badly damaged during the war, while the survivors were becoming increasingly difficult to maintain. New ones were being delivered very slowly because of shortages of materials and skilled labour. The capital's needs were deemed to be so serious that the BTC agreed to hire 200 new Bristol double-deckers to London Transport, although in the event only 190 went. They came from twelve Tilling companies, some of whom were less than enthusiastic about being deprived of their newest vehicles. The loans included 38 from Eastern Counties buses, comprising LKH94-99 and LKH107-138. The first ones to arrive in London were LKH94/6/7, which were sent direct from the ECW factory to LT's Chiswick Works. They were then dispatched to Tottenham garage, where they worked alongside standard London buses on busy routes 73 and 76. In May they moved to Palmers Green for route 102, by which time the others were all at work in the capital. These were allocated to six other garages and could be seen on several major central London routes. London Transport also borrowed thirteen new Eastern National buses, three of which (4000-2, NNO 100-2 from the company's 1948 intake) were among the first Bristols to enter service in the capital.

MORE MEMORIES - DEREK CARTER

"My father left Eastern Counties in 1943 and went to work as a driver for the Army, based at Lords Bridge. After the war he went back to Eastern Counties for a while. They gave him his old road back until he left. After that he drove for MacIntoshes the ironmongers until he retired. The last bus he drove regularly was LL690 (GPW 690).

"I started on the buses with Premier Travel in July 1947 and took my single-deck PSV test in a Bedford, FER 241. My badge number was FF 9604 and I worked as a D/C [one-man driver] from Harston depot. I can remember driving Bedfords BVE 668 and CVE 424, and their first double-decker, BU 7601, after I took an upgrade test in 1948. I moved to Eastern Counties on 31st July 1949 as a driver, starting at the Royston outstation. We worked the 108 and 119 to Cambridge and I stayed there for two years. Then I transferred to Cambridge, where I worked on all the routes. There were so many duties that it took two years to do them all or, as we used to say, "to go round the tote". The best buses I drove were the ones with AEC, Bristol or Leyland engines. The Gardner engines weren't so good - they were what I'd call 'sloggers' and working on a rebodied Leyland 'decker were like trying to drive a ton of bricks along the road. [These were fitted with Gardner 5LW engines.] Some of the older buses still had indicator boards, lettered in black for the town routes and red for the country ones. Some buses had side blinds but they were hardly used at all and they soon painted them over. It was in the 1950s that they started to bring the one-man buses in. They converted one duty at a time, not whole routes. I never worked on them and there was a lot of opposition from the older crews, but the management saw them as inevitable.

"I left Eastern Counties for a while from March 1967 to November 1968 and worked at the New Addenbrooke's Hospital. I missed the buses so I came back as a crew driver. In 1969 I was made up to Inspector and then I stayed until I retired in April 1978."

Derek sadly passed away in June 2002 at the age of 81, shortly after recounting his life as a busman. A regular bus traveller to the end, he never lost his enthusiasm for traditional buses or his remarkable memory for numbers.

The green livery and lowbridge layout of the Eastern National vehicles made them stand

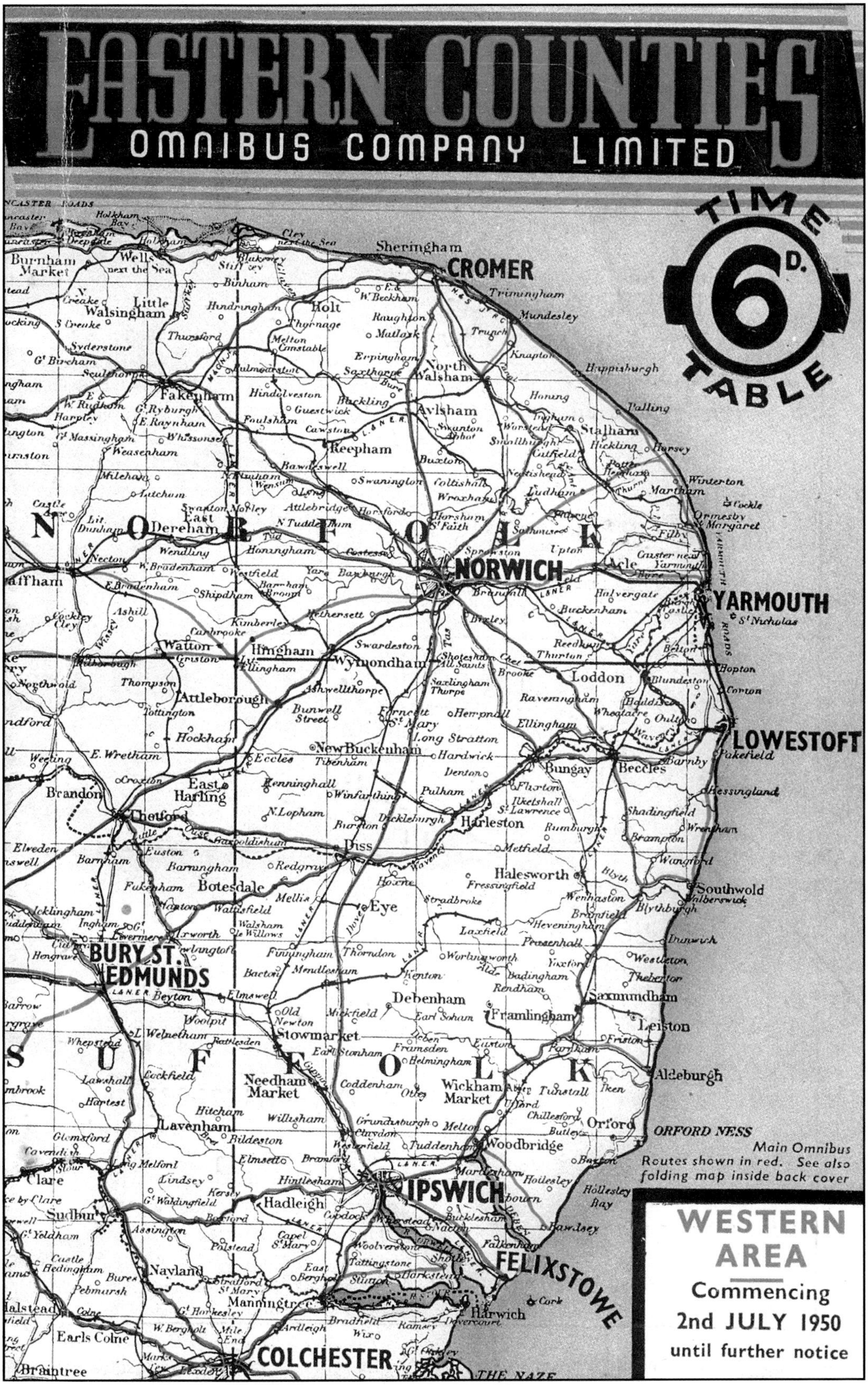

EASTERN COUNTIES
OMNIBUS COMPANY LIMITED
TIME 6D. TABLE
Main Omnibus Routes shown in red. See also folding map inside back cover
WESTERN AREA
Commencing
2nd JULY 1950
until further notice
NORFOLK
SUFFOLK
CROMER
Sheringham
NORWICH
YARMOUTH
LOWESTOFT
IPSWICH
FELIXSTOWE
COLCHESTER
BURY ST. EDMUNDS
Thetford
Dereham
Fakenham
Wells next the Sea
Holt
North Walsham
Aylsham
Reepham
Wymondham
Attleborough
Diss
Eye
Bungay
Beccles
Halesworth
Southwold
Stowmarket
Needham Market
Debenham
Framlingham
Saxmundham
Leiston
Aldeburgh
Woodbridge
Wickham Market
Orford
ORFORD NESS
Hadleigh
Sudbury
Lavenham
Clare
Braintree
Earls Colne
Manningtree
Harwich
Nayland
Brandon
Watton
Hingham
Loddon
Acle
Harleston
East Harling
Botesdale
THE NAZE

out even more than the Eastern Counties ones. The loaned buses were not popular with crews or passengers in London. Despite this they all remained there for over a year and the last did not enter service with their intended owners until June 1950. By then Eastern Counties had received fourteen more lowbridge K5Gs (LK366-79, KNG 366-79) and another five highbridge examples (LKH152-6, KNG 152-6). The last of these were delivered in December 1949 but none were sent to London.

SINGLE-DECK VARIETY AND FURTHER REBODYING

Eastern Counties also purchased a very interesting selection of single-deckers in 1949. Following the successful operation of the Beadle chassisless prototypes, several Tilling operators received batches of these useful lightweight machines. In March the first of sixteen Bedford-engined 35-seaters came, with the last delivered in the autumn. They entered service as CB816-31 (HPW 801-16), although the original intention was to classify them BC. They were nicknamed 'bread vans' (a name revived in the 1980s for van-derived minibuses) and they worked mainly in the company's Eastern area, although a few were allocated to Ely and Newmarket. In June the company received its first postwar coaches, three of which (LS493-5, GPW 493-5) had Bristol L6B chassis and luxurious 28-seat bodies by Beadle. The same month saw the arrival of seven standard Duple-bodied Bedford OB coaches (BS949-55, KAH 949-55), once again showing that the BTC was prepared to authorise other makes if Bristol and ECW could not supply all its needs. Also used on coach duties were the first of a batch of dual-purpose L5Gs (LE697/8, KNG 697/8). These were diverted from the Caledonian Omnibus Company of Dumfries and delivered in August. Their bus-style bodies were painted in a cream and red livery, with extra embellishments. They had 31 coach-type seats but the same plodding 5-cylinder engine of the standard bus version. At about the same time, ten more examples of what appeared to be the standard bus version also entered service, but they had 4-cylinder engines and were not quite what they seemed. The batch was numbered

LL401-10 (KAH 401-10) and while their bodies were certainly new the chassis, officially at least, were much older. They were classified for accounting purposes as rebuilds of Bristol B-type buses which started life with the Norwich Omnibus Company. Exactly how many of these were recycled is uncertain, although some of the engines may have come from the older vehicles. The last new single-deckers to arrive in 1949 were six more Bedford OBs, this time with Duple bus bodies (B938-43, KAH 938-43).

In October 1949 the rebodying of Leyland TD2s (which had been interrupted by the war) was resumed. Although their chassis dated from as long ago as 1932, another twelve of these reliable machines received the latest style of ECW bodywork during the course of the year. New, deeper radiators were supplied by the Coventry Radiator Company and these, (together with the Bristol front mudguards also fitted) gave the buses a "sit up and beg" appearance at the front, although from the rear they were indistinguishable from the standard Bristol/ECW products.

This large intake of new and rebodied vehicles allowed the withdrawal of many older machines, but only two former Ortona buses reached the end of the road, these being rebodied Leyland TD1s AH326 (ER 8805) and A290 (VE 3199). The last vehicles taken over from Varsity Express Motors were also withdrawn, these being the AEC Regals (VE 4853/4, now numbered KA768/9), which had been rebuilt as buses in 1942. One former Varsity Coaches TS2 survived until 1951 - this had been rebodied as a double-decker in 1934, as described earlier.

Further dual-purpose L5Gs were purchased in 1950, with fleet numbers which followed on from the 1949 batch and continued to LE703 (KNG 703). Further Bedford OBs took the buses to B948 (KAH 948) and the coaches to BS958 (KAH 958) and all had entered service by August. The Bedfords were the last petrol-engined vehicles purchased and were allocated mainly to Eastern area garages, although the coaches sometimes appeared in the Western area on express routes passing through. Further K5Gs delivered at the same time were LKH157-65 and LKH250-60 with highbridge bodies, and lowbridge LK380-95, all with matching KNG-registrations. LK390 suffered the indignity of being blown over in a freak gale at Sutton after only a few weeks in service, although no serious damage was done. In August four more lowbridge K5Gs (LK276-9, LNG 276-9) began a new series of fleet numbers. They were the last double-deckers to be built to the old length of 26 feet and were immediately followed by LK280-91 (LNG 280-91) with the new, 27ft KS5G, although the seating capacity of the buses was still only 55. The maximum length for single-deckers was also increased, from 27 feet 6 inches to 30 feet, and after the final four 35-seat L5Gs (LL709-12, KNG 709-12), twelve of the longer LL5G saloons entered service from August onwards (LL713-24, KNG 713-23 and LNG 724), with seating for 39 passengers. Another change very soon afterwards increased the maximum width of new PSVs to 8 feet, although all the 1950 deliveries were 7 feet 6 inches wide. This was quite wide enough for some of the narrow streets in the centre of Cambridge.

Undoubtedly the most interesting new buses to appear in 1950 were another batch of chassisless single-deckers, built to the old dimensions. Their 32-seat ECW bodies bore an obvious family resemblance to those on the L5Gs, but had smaller, one-piece destination displays and the emergency exit in the rear wall. The gearboxes and Gardner 4LK engines of these appealing little buses had been salvaged from withdrawn Dennis Ace buses, while their distinctive radiators proudly proclaimed ECW as the manufacturer. The first one entered service in May and eventually sixteen were built, numbered CD832-47 (HPW 817-32). Unlike the Beadle-bodied buses, the ECW/Dennises had half cabs and the type remained unique to Eastern Counties. They operated mainly in the flatter parts of the Western area, and the reliability of their 4LK engines persuaded the company to fit similar units to the Beadle-Bedford buses in place of their original Bedford units, starting in 1950.

The entry into service of so many new vehicles together with the return of the Bristol double-deckers from London Transport allowed a large clear out of older stock, including many Leyland TD1s. These included 15 former Ortona buses, along with those that had started with Eastern Counties Road Car, Peterborough Electric Traction and United. Also withdrawn were six of the first batch of TD1s supplied new to Eastern Counties in 1931, including the last unrebodied examples. The first four TD2s were also withdrawn, although another fourteen of the same type went to ECW for rebodying.

Eastern National received 86 new vehicles during 1949 and 1950. Thirty were lowbridge K5Gs (five of which began their careers in London). There were also ten standard L5Gs with bus bodies and ten L6Bs with full-front coach bodies. Nine Beadle-Bedford saloons similar to the Eastern Counties vehicles were also supplied, together with ten Duple-bodied Bedford OB coaches. From 1949 several pre-war Bristol and Leyland double-deckers received new ECW bodies. Longer Bristol vehicles were supplied from 1950, starting with seven KS5G double-deckers and ten LL5G saloons. Eastern National also took over the large and varied fleet of Hicks Brothers of Braintree. The Royston to Cambridge section of service 41 was again discontinued in September 1950, but subsequently reappeared.

Eastern Counties made few route changes during this period. In Cambridge a new local 133 was introduced from Trumpington to Newmarket Road. The terminus was Barnwell Road (Peverel Close), referred to in timetables as 'Ring Road' (planned as such in the 1930s but not completed until many years later). Some of the Histon journeys on the 139 were extended to Impington. On the country routes the 113A was extended to Stapleford (Pump) while the 150 now continued from Horningsea via Clayhithe to Waterbeach (Bannold Road). Further improvements in the Newmarket area saw the introduction of a new service 114D (later renumbered 117B) and a proposed new 162A, although the latter materialised as an extra journey on 114C. Further to the north a new service 125C offered yet another way of travelling from St Ives to Ely on market days, this time by way of Willingham.

MORE MEMORIES - GLAD HUGHES

"I stayed on after the war. The jobs were still there and the men didn't want us to go. The

101 was still my favourite route because I knew so many of the passengers. There were seven buses on it and it was often very busy, especially when the college terms started. Students often brought trunks to the bus stop at the station and then expected us to lift them onto the buses. One afternoon an old couple came along with a big nanny goat. They'd bought it at the cattle market and walked over the bridge with it to the station. Now they wanted to get it home to Chesterton. None of the taxi drivers would take them, but we said we would if they sat upstairs at the front. We spread lots of newspaper out first. That goat gave all the other passengers quite a surprise when they went upstairs.

"Bill and I sometimes worked together but because he was the Driving Instructor I had to pair up with every Tom, Dick and Harry. I often went out with new drivers to show them the way. It was a great job, even though the pay and conditions were poor and there was no pension when I started. It was dreadful under Tillings but things were much better after the National Bus Company started. There were lots of moans when they brought in the one-man buses, and about women drivers, but they were always short of staff. I received a certificate for 40 years service in 1981, and I retired in December 1983. I never regretted going on the buses. I love people and I'd do it all again."

Bus travel was always a pleasure when Glad was in charge. She seemed to have a friendly word for everyone on board and, as well as being helpful and kind to young and old alike, she would always call out the name of every single bus stop.

<<< Page 163: The 1950 Eastern Counties Western Area timetable had 200 pages with full details of the company's services (but no others) in the Cambridge, Ely, King's Lynn, March, Newmarket and Peterborough areas. It also included a fold-out map, lists of market and early closing days and various stern warnings about forming queues, avoiding the last bus, saving money and teaching children about road safety. Priced at 6 old pence (2½p), it featured the Eastern Area on the front cover, with the Western Area relegated to the back. *(Author's Collection)*

Below: Bill & Glad Hughes often worked together as a crew and remained on the buses until they retired. They are seen here with a Bristol JO5G saloon. *(Courtesy G Hughes)*

18. Postscript

THE LOCAL SCENE IN 1950 - SIGNS OF THINGS TO COME

By the end of 1950, much of the pre-war route network had been restored and further improvements would follow. There were daily buses on most of the Cambridge locals, the only exceptions being the 133 and the section of the 139 beyond Roseford Road to Histon and Impington. These did not run on Sundays but were largely covered by other services on that day. Buses also ran every day on many country roads and there were few villages without a bus service of some sort. An important part of the routine in many rural communities was the arrival on one or two days each week of the bus to a nearby market. The market buses sometimes gave villagers a choice of destinations on different days and before the age of mass motoring they provided vital lifelines for many country people.

An all-time peak of 10,139 new buses and coaches entered service nationwide during 1949 and most of the local fleets had been updated with modern vehicles, although there were still plenty of pre-war machines giving good service. Business was booming and passenger numbers were still increasing. However, this would not continue for much longer, for the effects of the increased Fuel Tax and rising staff costs were already increasing the amount of unprofitable mileage being operated. Across Eastern Counties' large operating area this amounted to 53% of the total, while Premier Travel's 'windmill' scheme, launched in a blaze of publicity in June 1950, was still not producing the expected numbers of passengers. Country bus operators now faced a problem: they had persuaded the Traffic Commissioners that there was a demand for their services, but it was much harder to convince them that the demand was falling and that the services were losing money and should be reduced or withdrawn. Council subsidies were unknown in 1950, and Eastern Counties was forced to submit its first application to raise fares. Such increases then became an almost annual event. Despite their lower operating costs the smaller operators followed suit, especially on common sections of route.

From then on there would be a steady decline in bus travel. The advent of television would have a major effect of cinema and theatre audiences. Cambridge then had eight cinemas, three theatres and several dance halls, but some of these would not last for much longer. There would also be an increase in car ownership, while staff shortages would eventually make some services less reliable. All of this would dramatically change the nation's travelling habits, especially in the evenings and at weekends, and operators began to search for ways of cutting costs. New single-deckers were about to appear in the major fleets, with underfloor engines, larger seating capacities and front entrances. These required fewer staff and would eventually lead to the large-scale adoption of one-person operation, although in 1950 this was only allowed on small single deckers. Rear-engined double-deck buses were many years away, and the removal of conductors from double-deckers would not in any event have been considered at the time.

The boom was nearly over, but the years after 1950 would provide plenty of interest, which we hope will be described in a future volume.

APPENDIX A - ORTONA MOTOR CO LTD FLEETLIST

(Subsequent rebodyings by Eastern Counties are not shown here but are detailed in the main text)

Fleet No	Reg No	Chassis	Body	In	Out	New	Previous Owner	Note
	BN159	Scott-Stirling 14 hp	B--R	/07	By -/14	1906	Lancashire United	a
	BN276	Scott-Stirling 14 hp	B--R	/07	-/15	1906	Lancashire United	a
	M1558	Scott-Stirling 14 hp	B--R	8/07	By -/14	1907	Hallsworth, Hyde	a
	DU524	Maudslay 14 hp	B14F	8/07	By -/14	1905	Winchester Omnibus Co.	b
	XS93	Arrol-Johnston	O--/--RO	8/07	-/07	1905	Cambridge Motor Omnibus Co.	
	CE691	Scott-Stirling 14 hp	B--R	12/07	By -/14		New	a
	?	?	?	12/07	By -/14		New	
	CE894	Maudslay 25 hp	B--R	1/08	By -/19		New	a
	CE977	Maudslay 25 hp	B--R	1/08	By -/19		New	a
	CE1088	Commer	O--/--RO	1/08	By -/19		New	
	?	?	O--/--RO	1/08	By -/19		New	
	DU1752	Maudslay 40 hp	O--/RO	1/12	By /19		New	b, c
	DU176-	Maudslay 40 hp	O--/RO	1/12	By -/19		New	b
	CE1996	Straker-Squire	O18/16RO	11/12	By -/25		New	
	CE1997	Straker-Squire	O18/16RO	11/12	By /25		New	
	CE1998	Straker-Squire	O18/16RO	11/12	By /25		New	
	CE2153	Straker-Squire U	O18/16RO	11/12	-/22		New	
	CE480	Straker-Squire	O18/16RO	12/12	By /25		New	d
	?	Straker-Squire	O18/16RO	12/12	By /25		New	
	CE2552	Straker-Squire 36 hp	Ch28	-/14	By -/25		New	
	CE2894	Straker-Squire 36 hp	B--R	By 4/14	By -/25		New	
	CE3001	Straker-Squire 36 hp	O18/16RO	-/14	By -/25		New	
	CE3773	Austin	O-/-RO	-/15	By -/25		New	
	CE3886	Straker-Squire COT5	O18/16RO	-/15	By -/25		New	
	CE3976	Straker-Squire U	B--R	-/15	By -/25		New	
	CE4031	Straker-Squire 36 hp	O18/16RO	-/15	By -/25		New	
	CE4725	Straker-Squire 36 hp	O18/16RO	-/18	By -/25		New	
	CE4730	Straker-Squire 36 hp	O18/16RO	-/18	By -/25		New	
	CE4739	Straker-Squire 36 hp	O18/16RO	-/18	By -/25		New	
	CE4771	Austin 25 hp	O18/16RO	-/18	-/21		New	
	?	Austin 25 hp	O18/16RO	-/18	-/21		New	
	?	McCurd	O--/--RO	-/18	-/20		New	e
	AN1058	Straker-Squire 24 hp	O18/16RO	9/18	By -/19	1911	London General Omnibus Co	f
	AN1083	Straker-Squire 24 hp	O18/16RO	10/18	By -/19	1911	London General Omnibus Co	f
	AN1088	Straker-Squire 24 hp	O18/16RO	10/18	By -/19	1911	London General Omnibus Co	f
	AN1090	Straker-Squire 24 hp	O18/16RO	10/18	By -/19	1911	London General Omnibus Co	f
11	CE5098	AEC YC	O18/16RO	-/19	By -/25		New	g
10	CE5099	AEC YC	O18/16RO	-/19	By -/25		New	g
	CE5157	Leyland S5	O18/16RO	-/19	By-/30		New	h i
	CE5180	Straker-Squire 36 hp	B32-	-/19	By -/25		New	h
	CE5213	Leyland S5	O18/16RO	-/19	By -/30		New	h i
	CE5421	Leyland H	O18/16RO	-/19	By -/30		New	h i
12	CE5583	Leyland H	O18/16RO	-/19	By -/23		New	h i
	CE5962	Leyland H	O18/16RO	-/19	By -/30		New	h i
	CE6011	Leyland H	O18/16RO	-/19	By -/30		New	h i
	CE6399	Straker-Squire COT3	O18/16RO	-/19	By -/25		New	h
	CE6400	Straker-Squire COT3	O18/16RO	-/19	By -/25		New	h
20	CE6806	Leyland RAF	O18/16RO	-/20	-/31		New	j
24	CE6807	Leyland RAF	O45RO	-/20	-/29		New	i
21	CE7023	Straker-Squire A	Ch33	-/20	-/28		New	
22	CE7024	Straker-Squire A	Ch33	-/20	-/28		New	
23	CE7025	Straker-Squire A	Ch33	-/20	-/28		New	
25	CE8364	Straker-Squire A	B30-	4/21	-/25		New	
26	CE9178	Straker-Squire A	O56RO	11/21	-/28		New	
27	CE9179	Straker-Squire A	O56RO	11/21	-/29		New	
28	CE9180	Straker-Squire A	O56RO	11/21	-/28		New	
3	CE9786	Straker-Squire A	O56RO	6/22	-/29		New	
7	CE9829	Vulcan VSD	B20F	6/22	-/27		New	
6	CE9830	Vulcan VSD	B20F	6/22	-/27		New	
	LH8606	Tilling-Stevens TTA1	Tilling O18/16RO	7/22	-/23	1914	Thomas Tilling, London SE6	
	LH8616	Tilling-Stevens TTA1	Tilling O18/16RO	6/22	-/23	1914	Thomas Tilling, London SE6	
	LH8617	Tilling-Stevens TTA1	Tilling O18/16RO	6/22	-/23	1914	Thomas Tilling, London SE6	
	LH8672	Tilling-Stevens TTA1	Tilling O18/16RO	7/22	-/23	1914	Thomas Tilling, London SE6	
12	ER418	Leyland G7	O48RO	1/23	-/30		New	i
2	ER419	Leyland G7	O48RO	1/23	-/28		New	i
29	ER420	Leyland G7	O48RO	1/23	-/29		New	l

Fleet No	Reg No	Chassis	Body	In	Out	New	Previous Owner	Note
31	ER1022	Vulcan VSD	B20F	5/23	-/29		New	
30	ER1024	Vulcan VSD	B20F	5/23	-/29		New	
32	ER1134	Straker-Squire A	Ransomes B35R	8/23	-/29		New	k
10	ER1812	Leyland G7 Special	Dodson O48RO	1/24	ECOC		New	i
33	ER1813	Leyland G7 Special	Dodson O48RO	1/24	-/30		New	i
34	ER1814	Leyland SG7	Dodson B36F	5/24	ECOC		New	
?	?	?	?	-/24	-/24	?	Butler (Pioneer Bus)	
35	ER3137	Leyland GH7	Dodson O53RO	12/24	-/30		New	
25	ER3138	Leyland GH7	Dodson O53RO	1/25	-/30		New	
8	ER3139	Leyland GH7	Dodson O53RO	1/25	ECOC		New	
5	ER3140	Leyland GH7	Dodson O53RO	1/25	ECOC		New	
1	ER3141	Leyland GH7	Dodson O53RO	2/25	ECOC		New	
37	ER3142	SOS S	Brush B31F	2/25	ECOC		New	l
36	ER3143	SOS S	Brush B31F	3/25	ECOC		New	l
38	ER3144	SOS S'	Brush B31F	3/25	ECOC		New	l
41	ER4918	Leyland GH7	Dodson O53RO	11/25	ECOC		New	
42	ER4919	Leyland GH7	Dodson O53RO	11/25	ECOC		New	
15	ER4920	Leyland GH7	Dodson O53RO	12/25	ECOC		New	
4	ER4921	Leyland GH7	Dodson O53RO	12/25	ECOC		New	
40	ER4922	Leyland GH7	Dodson O53RO	1/26	ECOC		New	
39	?	?	?	-/25	By 2/26	?	?, Newmarket area (?)	
39	ER5038	SOS S	Brush B31F	2/26	ECOC		New	l
43	ER5039	SOS S	Brush B31F	2/26	ECOC		New	l
45	ER5302	SOS S	Ransomes B32F	3/26	ECOC		New	l
46	ER5303	SOS S	Ransomes B32F	3/26	ECOC		New	l
44	ER5304	Leyland SG11	Dodson B32F	3/26	ECOC		New	
47	ER5305	Leyland GH7	Dodson O53RO	3/26	ECOC		New	
48	ER5306	Leyland GH7	Dodson O53RO	3/26	ECOC		New	
49	ER5307	Leyland GH7	Dodson O53RO	3/26	ECOC		New	
52	ER6126	Ford T	Lambert B14F	6/26	-/28		New	
	EB3557	Tilling-Stevens TTA1	O37R	3/26	-/26	1912	Parnell, Stretham	
53	EB4319	Ford T	B14F	3/26	-/27	1923	Parnell, Stretham	
52	EB4703	Ford T	B14F	3/26	-/26	1924	Parnell, Stretham	
51	EB4858	Hawkeye	B20F	3/26	-/27	1924	Parnell, Stretham	
50	EB5893	Dennis 2½ ton	Dodson B32F	3/26	ECOC	1926	Parnell, Stretham	
?	?	?	?	4/26	?	?	Bedford, St Neots	
?	?	?	?	4/26	?	?	Bedford, St Neots	
54	CE6254	Daimler CD	B32R	4/26	-/27	1919	Piper, Longstowe	
55	NK4363	AEC Y	B24R	4/26	-/27	1922	Piper, Longstowe	
55	ER7105	SOS Q	Brush B37F	3/27	ECOC		New	
56	ER7106	SOS Q	Brush B37F	3/27	ECOC		New	
54	ER7107	SOS Q	Brush B37F	4/27	ECOC		New	
57	ER7108	SOS Q	Brush B37F	4/27	ECOC		New	
58	ER7107	SOS Q	Brush B37F	5/27	ECOC		New	
59	ER7110	SOS Q	Brush B37F	5/27	ECOC		New	
13	ER7111	Star VB3	Ransomes B20F	4/27	ECOC		New	
6	ER7112	Star VB3	Ransomes B20F	4/27	ECOC		New	
7	ER7113	Star VB3	Ransomes B20F	4/27	ECOC		New	
60	ER7114	Leyland PLC1	Dodson C28F	4/27	ECOC		New	
11	ER7115	Leyland GH7	Dodson O53RO	2/27	ECOC		New	
53	ER7838	Ford T	Lambert B14F	5/27	-/39		New	
51	ER8555	SOS Q	Brush B37F	12/27	ECOC		New	
21	ER8801	Leyland PLSC3	London Lorries C32D	3/28	ECOC		New	
22	ER8802	Leyland PLSC3	London Lorries C32D	3/28	ECOC		New	
23	ER8803	Leyland PLSC3	London Lorries C32D	3/28	ECOC		New	
2	ER8804	Leyland TD1	Leyland L27/24RO	4/28	ECOC		New	
26	ER8805	Leyland TD1	Leyland L27/24RO	4/28	ECOC		New	
28	ER8806	Leyland TD1	Leyland L27/24RO	5/28	ECOC		New	
63	ER8807	Leyland TD1	Leyland L27/24RO	3/28	ECOC		New	
61	ER8886	Leyland PLSC3	Leyland B36R	2/28	ECOC		New	
62	ER8887	Leyland PLSC3	Leyland B36R	2/28	ECOC		New	
	EB4858	Hawkeye	B20F	3/28	-/28	1924	Gammond, Chatteris	m
65	FE9094	Reo Sprinter	Applewood B20F	-/28	ECOC	1927	Bowyer & Topper, Ely	
67	?	Dennis	?	-/28			Harvey, Harston	
27	VE301	Leyland TD1	Hall-Lewis H28/24RO	1/29	ECOC		New	
68	VE302	Leyland TD1	Hall-Lewis H28/24RO	1/29	ECOC		New	
69	VE303	Leyland TD1	Hall-Lewis H28/24RO	1/29	ECOC		New	
70	VE304	Leyland TD1	Hall-Lewis H28/24RO	1/29	ECOC		New	
71	VE305	Leyland TD1	Hall-Lewis H28/24RO	1/29	ECOC		New	

Fleet No	Reg No	Chassis	Body	In	Out	New	Previous Owner	Note
66	VE306	Leyland PLSC3	Leyland B32F	1/29	ECOC		New	
53	VE307	Dennis G	Ransomes B20F	1/29	ECOC		New	
52	VE308	Dennis G	Ransomes B20F	11/28	ECOC		New	
76	VE309	Leyland TS2	Leyland B29R	6/29	ECOC		New	
77	VE310	Leyland TS2	Leyland B29R	6/29	ECOC		New	
32	VE501	SOS M	Brush B34F	3/29	ECOC		New	
72	VE502	SOS M	Brush B34F	4/29	ECOC		New	
64	VE503	SOS M	Ransomes B34F	3/29	ECOC		New	
73	VE504	SOS M	Ransomes B34F	4/29	ECOC		New	
24	VE1101	SOS M	Ransomes B34F	5/29	ECOC		New	
74	VE1102	Dennis GL	Strachan & Brown B20F	5/29	ECOC		New	
75	VE1103	Dennis GL	Strachan & Brown B20F	5/29	ECOC		New	
31	VE1952	Dennis GL	Strachan & Brown B20F	9/29	ECOC		New	
78	VE1965	Leyland TD1	Leyland L24/24R	10/29	ECOC		New	
79	VE1966	Leyland TD1	Leyland L24/24R	10/29	ECOC		New	
80	VE1967	Leyland TD1	Leyland L24/24R	10/29	ECOC		New	
81	VE1994	Leyland TD1	Leyland L24/24R	10/29	ECOC		New	
17	VE2039	Leyland TD1	Brush H28/24RO	11/29	ECOC		New	
29	VE2040	Leyland TD1	Brush H28/24RO	11/29	ECOC		New	
30	VE2041	Leyland TD1	Brush H28/24RO	11/29	ECOC		New	
2	VE2042	Leyland TD1	Brush H28/24RO	11/29	ECOC		New	
18	VE2043	Leyland TD1	Brush H28/24RO	11/29	ECOC		New	
83	VE2142	Leyland LT1	Dodson B32F	12/29	ECOC		New	
82	VE2143	Leyland LT1	Dodson B32F	11/29	ECOC		New	
67	VE2144	Leyland LT1	Dodson B32F	12/29	ECOC		New	
	?	Fiat	?	-/29	?		Meacham, Newmarket	
	?	?	?	-/29	?		Meacham, Newmarket	n
86	VE2874	Leyland TS2	Ransomes B26F	6/30	ECOC		New	
88	VE2875	Leyland TS2	Ransomes B26F	6/30	ECOC		New	
87	VE2876	Leyland TS2	Ransomes B26F	6/30	ECOC		New	
89	VE3198	Leyland TD1	Brush H28/24RO	6/30	ECOC		New	
90	VE3199	Leyland TD1	Brush H28/24RO	6/30	ECOC		New	
91	VE3783	Leyland LT2	Leyland B30F	8/30	ECOC		New	
14	VE4200	Leyland TD1	Brush H28/24RO	9/30	ECOC		New	
19	VE4201	Leyland TD1	Brush H28/24RO	9/30	ECOC		New	
9	VE4202	Leyland TD1	Brush H28/24RO	9/30	ECOC		New	
12	VE4203	Leyland TD1	Brush H28/24RO	9/30	ECOC		New	
33	VE4204	Leyland TD1	Brush H28/24RO	9/30	ECOC		New	
35	VE4205	Leyland TD1	Brush H28/24RO	9/30	ECOC		New	
25	VE4206	Leyland TD1	Brush H28/24RO	9/30	ECOC		New	
16	VE4207	Leyland TD1	Brush H28/24RO	9/30	ECOC		New	
92	VE4208	Leyland TD1	Brush H28/24RO	9/30	ECOC		New	
93	VE4209	Leyland TD1	Brush H28/24RO	9/30	ECOC		New	
	CF8117	Chevrolet LM	B14F	4/30	-/31	1928	Norman, Exning	
	UT2055	Chevrolet LM	B14F	4/30	-/31	1928	Norman, Exning	
94	UR6840	Dennis EV	Wilton FC32D	12/30	ECOC	1930	Leverett, Ashwell	
	CF6568(?)	Chevrolet	B14	-/30	ECOC	1926	Challice, Newmarket	n
95	VE4802	Leyland TS3	Leyland B30F	3/31	ECOC		New	
96	VE4803	Leyland TS3	Leyland B30F	3/31	ECOC		New	
97	VE4804	Leyland TS3	Leyland B30F	3/31	ECOC		New	
20	VE4805	Leyland LT2	Leyland B30F	3/31	ECOC		New	
84	VE4806	Leyland LT2	Leyland B30F	3/31	ECOC		New	
85	VE4807	Leyland LT2	Leyland B30F	3/31	ECOC		New	

Notes:

a	Later converted to double-decker (BN139, BN276 and M1558 to O10/--RO).
b	Originally registered by the Maudslay Motor Company. DU524 fitted with charabanc body by -/08.
c	Believed to have been a Maudslay demonstrator. Later received a different double-deck body, possibly second-hand.
d	Had a re-issued registration.
e	A second McCurd may have been operated.
f	New to Great Eastern London Motor Omnibus Company.
g	Seating increased later to 46.
h	Chassis ex-War Department. Double-deck bodies may have been second-hand. CE6400 possibly later received charabanc body.
i	Seating increased later to 53.
j	Rebodied 5/22 with Leyland B--R body.
k	Seating later reduced to 26.
l	Converted 1930-1 to SOS 'ODD' type and rebodied with United B26F bodies.
m	Originally acquired by Ortona from Parnell, Stretham. Gammond business acquired jointly with Peterborough Electric Traction Co.
n	CF6568 may have been purchased from Meacham, Newmarket in 1929, not Challice, Newmarket in 1930.

APPENDIX B - LIST OF BUS SERVICES FROM CAMBRIDGE IN 1950

D-Daily, M-Monday, Tu-Tuesday, W-Wednesday, Th-Thursday, F-Friday, Sa-Saturday, Su-Sunday, N-Not.
Except where noted, country services started from Drummer Street.

EASTERN COUNTIES OMNIBUS CO LTD

101   Town Service: Railway Station - Hills Road - Regent Street - Town Centre - Sidney Street (return Trinity Street) - Chesterton Road - Chesterton (Green End Road) (D).

102   Town Service: Perne Road (Brookfields) - Mill Road - Gonville Place - Regent Street - Town Centre - Hobson Street (return Jesus Lane & Trinity Street) - Newmarket Road - Meadowlands (D).

103   Cambridge - Trumpington - Great Shelford - Stapleford (P.O.) - Sawston (D).
Additional service as above to Stapleford (P.O.) then Stapleford (Pump). One journey extended to Duxford Aerodrome (Sa).

104   Cambridge - Histon - Cottenham (P.O.) - Cottenham Church (D). Additional service as above to Cottenham (P.O.) then Rampton - Willingham

105   Town Service: Drummer Street - Gonville Place - Hills Road - Cherry Hinton Road- Mowbray Road - Strangeways Road (D).

106   Town Service: Red Cross - Hills Road - Regent Street - Town Centre - Sidney Street (return Trinity Street) - Huntingdon Road - Girton Corner (D).

107   Cambridge - Girton Corner - Long Stanton (D). Some journeys extended to Willingham (Black Bull) - Earith - Bluntisham - Colne - Somersham. Additional service as above to Long Stanton, then Willingham (Church) - Over (NSaSu).

108   Cambridge - Trumpington - Hauxton Gap - Harston - Foxton Station - Barrington - Shepreth - Meldreth - Melbourn - Royston (D, coordinated with Premier Travel service 2). Some journeys via Shepreth Mill between Foxton and Melbourn.

109   Cambridge - Milton - Landbeach - Waterbeach - Chittering - Stretham - Ely (D).

110   Cambridge - Cherry Hinton(Robin Hood) - Fulbourn - Great & Little Wilbraham (D).

111   Cambridge - Bottisham - Swaffham Bulbeck - Swaffham Prior - Reach - Burwell (D).

112   Cambridge - Trumpington - Little Shelford - Whittlesford - Duxford - Ickleton - Littlebury - Saffron Walden (D). Two journeys as above to Whittlesford, then Duxford Aerodrome (Sa).

112A   Cambridge - Trumpington - Little Shelford - Whittlesford - Duxford - Ickleton - Hinxton (NSu).

113   Cambridge - Gogs Golf Links - Little & Great Abington - Linton - Horseheath - Haverhill (D).
Additional services as above to Linton, then either Balsham - West Wickham - Streetly End (MWSa) or Hadstock (F).

113A   Cambridge - Hinton Way - Great Shelford (Railway Station) - Stapleford (Pump) (NSaSu).

114   Cambridge - Cherry Hinton - Teversham (D). Extended to Fulbourn - Six Mile Bottom - Stetchworth - Newmarket (NTh).

115   Town service: Newnham - Fen Causeway - King's Parade (return Bene't Street) - Town Centre - Emmanuel Road - Victoria Avenue - Milton Road - King's Hedges Road (D).

115A   Town service: Trumpington (Bishop's Road) - Fen Causeway - King's Parade (return Bene't Street) - Town Centre - Emmanuel Road - Victoria Avenue - Milton Road - King's Hedges Road (D).

118   Cambridge - Barton - Comberton - Toft - Bourn - Longstowe - Caxton (D).
Extended to Great Gransden - Waresley (MWSa) or Papworth (TuFSu).

118A   Cambridge - Grantchester - Barton - Comberton - Toft - Kingston - Great & Little Eversden (WSa).

119   Cambridge - Grantchester - Barton - Haslingfield - Harlton - Orwell - Wimpole - Arrington - Kneesworth - Bassingbourn - Royston (D).

122   Cambridge - Quy - Swaffham Bulbeck - Swaffham Prior - Reach (Su) - Burwell - Fordham - Soham (NTh). One journey via Bottisham instead of Quy (Su). Additional service Upware - Wicken - Soham - Soham Cotes - Stuntney - Ely (ThSu).

123   Cambridge - Histon - Cottenham - Rampton - Willingham - Over - Swavesey - Fen Drayton - Fenstanton - St Ives (M).

123A   Cambridge - Long Stanton - Over - Swavesey - Fen Drayton - Fenstanton - St Ives - Needingworth - Bluntisham - Colne - Somersham (NTuTh). Extended Su to Ferry Hill - Chatteris. Additional service St Ives - Chatteris (D).

129   Town service: St Thomas's Road - Perne Road - Coldhams Lane - Vinery Road - Mill Road - Tenison Road - Railway Station - Fen Causeway - Newnham (D).

130   Town service: Trumpington (Bishop's Road) - King's Parade (return Bene't Street) - Town Centre - Regent Street - Gonville Place - East Road - Newmarket Road - Coldhams Lane (D).

131   Town service: Drummer Street - Mill Road - Coleridge Road - Cherry Hinton (Fisher's Lane) (D).

133   Town service: Trumpington (Bishop's Road) - Lensfield Road (return King's Parade) - Town Centre - Hobson Street (return Jesus Lane & Trinity Street) - Newmarket Road (Ring Road) (NSu).

136   Cambridge - Gogs Golf Links - Little & Great Abington - Linton - Bartlow - Shudy & Castle Camps - Helions & Steeple Bumpstead - Haverhill (NTuTh).

136A   Cambridge - Gogs Golf Links - Little & Great Abington - Linton - Bartlow - Shudy & Castle Camps - Haverhill (D).

137   Cambridge - Histon - Cottenham - Wilburton - Haddenham - Sutton - Witcham - Mepal - Chatteris - Doddington - Wimblington - March (D).

137A   Cambridge - Histon - Cottenham - Wilburton - Stretham - Ely (Th).

139	Town service: Mowbray Road (Glebe Road) - Perne Road - Mill Road - Burleigh Street - Fitzroy Street - Victoria Avenue - Victoria Road - Histon Road (Roseford Road) (D). Extended to Histon (Railway Station) - Impington (NSu). In two sections M-Sa: Mowbray Road - Roseford Road and Perne Road (Brookfields) - Histon Station - Impington.
150	Cambridge - Fen Ditton - Horningsea - Clayhithe Bridge - Waterbeach (D).
151	Cambridge - Fenstanton - Godmanchester - Huntingdon - Great Stukeley - Sawtry - Stilton - Yaxley - Peterborough (D).
151A	Cambridge (Merton Arms) - Fen Drayton - Fenstanton - St Ives (WFSa). Additional service Fen Drayton - St Ives (M).
152	Town service: Peas Hill - Bene't Street (return King's Parade) - Fen Causeway - Grange Road - Wilberforce Road - Madingley Road - Storey's Way - Huntingdon Road - Girton - Oakington (D).
153	Cambridge (Merton Arms) - Madingley - Dry Drayton - Cambridge (WSa).
154	Cambridge (Merton Arms) - Madingley Road - Coton (Sa).
162	Cambridge - Fulbourn - Balsham - West Wratting - Weston Colville - Carlton - Brinkley - Dullingham - Stetchworth - Woodditton - Cheveley - Newmarket (WSaSu). Additional service Stetchworth - Newmarket (Tu).
166	Cambridge - Newmarket Road - Newmarket (NSu).

EASTERN NATIONAL OMNIBUS CO LTD.
29	Cambridge (Railway Station) - Eltisley - St Neots - Eaton Socon - Wyboston - Roxton - Great Barford - Bedford (D).
29A	Cambridge - Barton - Haslingfield - Harlton - Orwell - Wimpole - Arrington - Wrestlingworth - Eyeworth - Dunton - Biggleswade - Sandy - Moggerhanger - Willington - Cople - Cardington - Bedford (D).
41	Cambridge (Gonville Place) - Trumpington - Harston - Foxton Station - Melbourn - Royston - Kneesworth - Bassingbourn - Litlington - Steeple & Guilden Morden - Ashwell - Baldock - Letchworth - Hitchin (D). One journey from and to Collier Road (NSu).

PREMIER TRAVEL LTD
1	Cambridge - Barton - Haslingfield - Harston - Newton - Thriplow - Fowlmere - Royston (D). Some journeys via Trumpington instead of Barton and Haslingfield (M-Sa).
2	Cambridge - Trumpington - Hauxton Gap - Harston - Foxton Station - Barrington - Shepreth - Meldreth - Melbourn - Royston (D, coordinated with Eastern Counties service 108).
8	Cambridge - Duxford Aerodrome (D).
9	Cambridge - Trumpington - Great Shelford - Stapleford (P.O.) - Sawston - Hinxton - Ickleton - Elmdon - Chrishall (D). Extended to Heydon - Great Chishill (W).
27	Cambridge - Trumpington - Hauxton - Newton - Fowlmere - Heydon - Great Chishill - Barley - Barkway - Nuthampstead (D).
33	Cambridge (Railway Station) - Oakington Aerodrome (M). Single early journey in this direction only, for RAF personnel.
44	Cambridge - Cherry Hinton (Robin Hood) - Fulbourn - Balsham - West Wratting - Weston Colville - Weston Green - Withersfield - Great Thurlow - Great Wratting (D).
45	Cambridge - Cherry Hinton (Robin Hood) - Fulbourn - Balsham - West Wratting - Weston Green - Weston Colville - Brinkley - Burrough Green - Great Bradley - Thurlow - Great Wratting (NSu).

BURWELL & DISTRICT MOTOR SERVICE
1	Cambridge - Quy - Longmeadow - Swaffham Bulbeck - Commercial End - Swaffham Prior - Reach - Burwell (D). Some journeys via Lode Church (NThSu).
3	Cambridge - Barton - Comberton - Toft - Kingston - Great & Little Eversden (Sa).
4	As service 1 to Burwell, then Fordham - Soham (D).
11	As service 1 to Burwell, then Fordham - Isleham (SaSu).

WHIPPET COACHES, HILTON
1	Cambridge (Merton Arms) - Madingley Road - Papworth - Hilton - Fenstanton - St Ives (WThSaSu).
2	Cambridge (Merton Arms) - Madingley Road - Hardwick - Toft - Caldecote - Cambridge (WSa).

F W BRAND, ELSWORTH
-	Cambridge (Merton Arms) - Madingley Road - Childerley Gate - Knapwell - Elsworth (WSa).
-	Cambridge (Merton Arms) - Huntingdon Road - Boxworth - Elsworth (WSa).

PAPWORTH VILLAGE SETLEMENT, PAPWORTH
-	Cambridge - Papworth Hospital

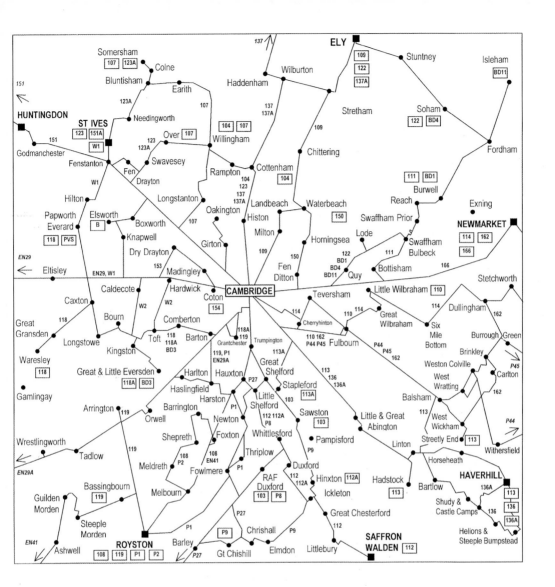

A Peep into Volume Two...

Upper: The early 1950s saw the introduction of underfloor-engined single-deckers, which ultimately led to the disappearance of half-cab saloons. They also allowed the introduction of one man operation, and the motorised Setright machine is clearly visible in this view of Eastern Counties **LE745** (**MAH 745**) leaving Drummer Street for Newmarket. This was one of five dual purpose saloons with LS4G chassis, which often appeared on express services when new, despite only having 4-cylinder engines. *(C W Routh)*

Centre: In 1963 Premier Travel purchased a batch of Leyland PD2/3 double-deckers from Ribble, who had used them on their longer limited stop routes. They had well-appointed lowbridge bodies built by East Lancs and they served their new owners well, lasting until the early 1970s. **DCK 206** stands in Drummer Street between trips to Fulbourn and the villages beyond. In the background is a former West Yorkshire Bristol K5G (BWY986), one of a batch very similar in appearance to contemporary Eastern Counties vehicles. *(A B Cross)*

Lower: The final (and in the author's view the best looking) version of the Bristol K-type was the KSW, of which Eastern Counties took 52, most with 60-seat highbridge bodies.

LKH168 (**OVF 168**), seen here at Great St Mary's Church, had a KSW5G chassis and was the newest example delivered to Cambridge. The white steering wheel reminds the driver that his bus is eight feet wide. *(M G Doggett)*

Upper: Purchased specifically for one-man operation, the Bristol SC4LK became a familiar sight on the less-busy country routes in the 1950s. Eastern Counties purchased 78 of these noisy but appealing little buses, together with a further ten optimistically described as coaches. Showing a familiar destination, **LC567** (**6567 NG**) has arrived in Drummer Street on service 150 from Waterbeach via Horningsea, a route on which the author made some of his earliest bus journeys. *(Author's Collection)*

Centre: From the mid-1950s Premier Travel regularly purchased batches of similar double-deckers, starting with a batch of ex-London Transport STLs. With its classic LPTB body clearly showing its ancestry, the former STL1746 (**DGX 285**) is seen at New Square Car Park in Cambridge, which was regularly used for parking buses between journeys in an effort to reduce congestion in Drummer Street. *(Author's Collection)*

Lower: The KSW was followed by the Lodekka. The first examples joined the Eastern Counties fleet in 1954, but the type appeared regularly on local services in Cambridge only after the first flat floor versions arrived in 1961. **LFS53** (**53 CPW**), a 60-seat FS5G, pulls into the lay-by at Bradwell's Court, which replaced the awkward Christs's College stops in 1960. *(Author's Collection)*

Upper: From 1966 Eastern Counties favoured the forward entrance FLF version of the Lodekka, with 70 seats. They were regular performers on the busy Arbury routes, which were numbered 185 and 186 in 1973. By then Eastern Counties had become part of the National Bus Company, whose corporate livery and fleetname are displayed in this view. **FLF427** (**LWC 665C**) was one of a pair transferred from the Eastern National fleet. *(Author's Collection)*

Centre: Although Premier Travel's country bus network declined in the 1960s, its express services became increasingly important, with many new coaches joining the fleet. Most distinctive were the AEC Reliances with Alexander bodywork, of which 20 were eventually owned. **GER 501E** was a regular performer on the busy Clacton to Birmingham service 5. Its regular driver Harold Lee kept it in excellent condition and did a great deal to build up traffic on the route. *(Author's Collection)*

Lower: The final Bristol/ECW double-decker was the VRT, with 70 seats, a rear engine and a front entrance. They entered service as crew buses but new regulations soon allowed driver-only operation. **VR400** (**JAH 400L**) is seen at Caxton on service 118. *(C W Routh)*